GREAT ARTISTS OF AMERICA

BY LILLIAN FREEDGOOD

Great Artists of America

THOMAS Y. CROWELL COMPANY

NEW YORK

TO MY MOTHER AND FATHER
for their patience with
and their belief in me

Author's Note

Behind every work of art there stands a being of flesh and blood. If the proper study of mankind is man, surely the proper study of art is the artist. This book presents in compact form the lives of great American painters from the beginnings to the present time. It is a record of their early days of struggle and their later days of acceptance; of their frustrations, strivings, and accomplishments; of their yearnings and hardships and adventures; of their defeats and their triumphs.

Owing to limitations of space, many fine American artists have been omitted who fully deserve to be included. The author, confronted with an embarrassment of riches, has been forced to make a number of decisions in choosing between artists of almost identical stature. In some cases, the balance has been tipped in favor of the artist who was most representative of his period; in others, of the artist who exerted the greatest influence on the development of American painting.

Acknowledgments

I should like to express my appreciation to Mr. Ben Shahn and Mr. Stuart Davis; to Mr. John D. Hoag and the staff of the Yale University Art Library; to Miss Mary Cole of the Baltimore Museum of Art; to the Sidney Janis Gallery; and to the many other persons who were kind enough to put at my disposal much of the valuable source material used in the writing of this book.

I owe special thanks to Mr. Henry Geldzahler and Mr. Alexander Leiber of the Metropolitan Museum of Art for permitting me to examine that portion of the American Art collection not on public display; to Mr. Bill Harris and his assistants, Doris Clarke and Pamela Cartmel, for making available the resources of the library of the Famous Artists School; to Miss Ruth Adams of the Westport Library, who responded with considerable patience and kindness to the constant demands upon her services; to my daughter for being my daughter; and to my husband for his most helpful suggestions and his own particular brand of patience.

Contents

List of Color Reproductions

Introduction

In 1492, the year in which Columbus stumbled on the New World, the Italian Renaissance was in full swing. Da Vinci, Michelangelo, Botticelli, Bellini, Mantegna, and literally dozens more who might be mentioned were producing a flood of masterpieces in a period of artistic genius unparalleled in history.

In stark contrast, America was a wild, rugged country inhabited by savages who lived in tents, hunted animals for their food, and fought each other with weapons little advanced beyond the weapons of primitive man. Their art, such as it was, reflected the crudeness of their culture.

It was more than a hundred years before settlers from Europe came to the new land in any significant numbers; more than two hundred years before the emergence of the first American artist of genuine, recognized talent.

How remarkable it is that, from this belated start, American art has managed to catch up to the rest of the world; if, indeed, it has not, in the present day, actually assumed the leadership.

There was no time for art in the early days of the new land. The existence of the colonists was hard, bitter, fraught with danger in the bountiful but strange country half a world away from home. Every effort, every sinew was exerted to provide food and shelter and warmth. But the Dutch, the French, and the English settlers had brought with them a heritage of European culture, and the urge to enrich the rigors of everyday existence with beauty started as soon as a foothold on the new land was secured.

The instinct to create first began to manifest itself in the shape of hand-painted illustrated signs hung outside of inns and shops, and in the decoration of furniture and even coffins. But it was the painted portrait that marked the fumbling beginning of formal art in America.

It was the practical aspect of the portrait, rather than the artistic, that first recommended itself to the American colonists. The portrait, in that day long before the invention of the camera, was the sole means of preserving a visual record of the members of a family. Not everyone could afford it, to be sure, so it was additionally a mark of financial and social prestige to have the portrait of one's wife, or an ancestor, hanging in the sitting room.

The first portrait painters in the colonies were known as "limners" or "journeyman painters." For the most part they were self-taught men of little talent and even less learning in the craft of painting. The original trade of many of them had been that of sign painter, or even house painter. Brushes and paints were scarce and of poor quality. With very few exceptions, therefore, these early portraits are of value to us mainly for their historical interest rather than as works of art.

Some limners worked in an interesting fashion. All through the cold winter months he busied himself at home, painting numerous portraits of men, women, and children, dressed in costumes ranging from the very elegant to the modest; from a gown cut low to reveal the shoulders and arms to one with long sleeves and high neckline; from the handsome garb of a squire to the sober, God-fearing black of an ordinary citizen.

These portraits were completely finished except for one detail—they all lacked a head.

With the coming of warm weather, the limner would pack his headless portraits and roam the countryside, seeking commissions. When he found a customer, and after a preference in costume had been expressed, it remained only for the head and features of the sitter to be filled in.

As time went on and the colonies prospered, the limners were succeeded—though not entirely supplanted—by a group of painters who were greatly their superior in craftsmanship, though not themselves first rate. It was not until the second half of the eighteenth century, with the appearance of John Singleton Copley and Benjamin West, that the American colonies produced their first artists of genuine stature.

Although both Copley and West were born in the colonies and came of age at a time when the revolutionary spirit was like wine on the American air, neither one was greatly infected by patriotism. Their overriding interest in life was their painting, and both left the colonies, without a qualm, for England where the arts were flourishing. Both became influential and successful painters there, and neither ever returned to America. For this reason, the dynasty of American painters can most properly be said to have begun with Gilbert Stuart. West, however, had many American pupils, who, on their return to America, imported their master's style and technique. Thus, through this influence, the English style predominated in this country for many years.

Despite sporadic attempts through the years to create an "indigenous" school of painting beholden to no Old World influences, American artists, for the most part, continued to face toward Europe, with its centuries-old traditions and its storehouses of great art masterpieces, for their schooling and direction.

But some of these efforts are worthy of note. The first mild rebellion against the English influence came in the early decades of the nineteenth century, with the emergence of the Hudson River School, a group of painters who "discovered" the beauties of the American landscape. Although none of them was a painter of the first rank, nevertheless each was, in his modest way, creating an American vision.

At approximately the same time, in the West George Caleb Bingham and George Catlin were creating a genuine American art almost entirely free of any outside influence. Bingham brought a down-to-earth lustiness to his portrayal of the American scene, capturing on canvas the day-to-day life and the regional accents of a still half-wild country. Catlin was fascinated by the American Indian, whose activities he painted in an endless series of variations on a theme.

For a brief while, the classicism of Italy and the German "schools" of Munich and Düsseldorf attracted a number of American artists. Bingham was one of those who studied in Düsseldorf, but, interestingly enough, the paintings that resulted were vastly inferior to the great work of his "untutored" period.

The American painter was seriously hampered by indifference in his efforts to establish a native art. Schools and museums were pitifully few in number and so poor that the aspiring painter had no choice but to turn to Europe for his study. Art and the artist were held in low esteem by most strata of American society; and the small segment which did buy pictures was governed by a form of snobbery under whose rules only the work of European painters was considered worthy of gracing a wall.

Beginning with the last third of the nineteenth century, the French school established a dominance that it maintained without challenge right up to the Second World War. Yet Winslow Homer and Thomas Eakins, two of the great painters of the latter half of the century, successfully resisted, even ignored, French influence and went their individual ways.

At the dawn of the twentieth century the so-called "Ashcan School" strove mightily to create a wholly native form of painting and came close to succeeding. But, even then, only one member of the group did not have European training, and he too eventually succumbed to the ideas of French modernism.

The revolutionary concepts that emerged from Paris in the nineteenth and twentieth centuries deservedly crowned the French capital as the ruling power of artistic creativity. But with the resurgence of painting at the end of World War II for the first time the arena of artistic activity shifted to the New World. Increasingly, American artists ventured onto bold experimental paths of their own. Today the United States is the undeniable leader in the creation of new concepts in modern painting. Tradition has been reversed. For the first time, the ideas of the New World are influencing those of the old.

American art has made astonishing strides since its birth a scant two hundred years ago. It is an accomplishment we may well be proud of.

1

The Genius of the Snuff Mill

GILBERT STUART

1755–1828

Gilbert Stuart was born on a cold, bleak, inauspicious day in December, in a back bedroom situated above his father's snuff mill, in North Kingston, Rhode Island. The year was 1755. The colonies were still under English rule, the American Revolution was twenty years in the future, but here was the child who would one day win enduring fame as America's first great artist.

Young Gilbert spent the early years of his life with the smell of ground tobacco ever-present in his nostrils. Apparently he found it a congenial aroma, for he developed a fondness for snuff that was to last his entire life. When he was six, the snuff mill failed, and the Stuart family moved to what Gilbert was later to describe as "a hovel on Bannister's wharf" in Newport, Rhode Island.

The Stuart family was poor, but Gilbert was its pampered darling, willful, mischievous, and bright. His mother and older sister adored him; his father denied him nothing. He was schooled in reading, writing, sums, and even a bit of Latin by his mother, who also taught him to play the organ. Although he was fond of music, and became a competent organist, Gilbert's consuming passion was drawing. In every spare moment, and with whatever crude materials he could lay his eager hands on, he was constantly making likenesses of people.

One day when Gilbert was ill, Dr. William Hunter called on the Stuarts to attend the sick lad. The doctor, who was greatly interested in art, became excited by the unusual talent displayed in the boy's drawings, which lay everywhere about the house. Hunter was so impressed that he gave Gilbert his first set of paints and brushes, and his first commission: he was asked to paint a picture of the doctor's two spaniels.

Dr. Hunter was so pleased with the resulting canine portrait that he invited Gilbert to his house to see the pictures he owned. These were the first real paintings Gilbert had ever seen. The doctor also persuaded Cosmo Alexander, a Scotsman and a dilettante painter, to accept Gilbert as an apprentice.

Alexander gave Gilbert his first lessons in drawing. The boy was such a remarkably apt and talented pupil that, when Alexander decided several years later to return to his native Scotland, he invited Gilbert to accompany him. For a boy interested in becoming an artist, it was an unbelievably exciting opportunity to be able to go to London. Here one could see the recent portraits of such famous artists as Reynolds, Romney, and Gainsborough. Perhaps Gilbert even dreamed that he might himself someday join their august company.

With the high hope and enthusiasm of a sixteen-year-old, he set sail with Alexander. But misfortune overtook him almost at once. Soon after their arrival in Edinburgh, Cosmo Alexander died. Gilbert was stranded, penniless and friendless, three thousand miles from home.

For many months, this pampered young man hunted for work. A series of odd jobs brought him barely enough to keep his stomach full; and worse, no one seemed the slightest bit interested in his paintings. So, his hopes dashed, homesick and unhappy, he signed on as a seaman on a coal vessel bound for Nova Scotia. More than a year later, he arrived back in America, physically ill, despondent and discouraged. He had endured hardships so harrowing that he never afterward talked about them.

But, with the resilience and confidence of youth, he soon recovered both his health and his spirits, and began painting again with renewed vigor. With the aid of his uncle, Joseph Anthony, he was able to secure several portrait commissions. If the pictures were crude efforts, still they showed a keen insight into character and pleased his sitters. Before long, Stuart was besieged by a flurry of requests for his work. "Our aspiring young artist," a friend related, "had as much business as he could turn his hand to. . . ." But his thoughts kept returning to London, the center of the artistic world, and away from the colonies, which were on the verge of war with England. While other young men were fired by a patriotic desire to fight for the New World's freedom, Stuart's only ambition was for the furtherance of his art. On June 16, 1775, on the eve of the Battle of Bunker Hill, he set sail for England.

Once again, he sought without success to establish himself

as a painter, and once again he was forced to live in squalor and poverty. He was saved by the timely intervention of Benjamin Waterhouse, a boyhood friend who had become a doctor and was practicing in England. Waterhouse introduced him to a number of wealthy people who wanted their portraits painted. But, instead of applying himself wholeheartedly to his work, Stuart spent much of his time pursuing a life of gaiety and squandering his money with reckless abandon. Dr. Waterhouse rescued Stuart from his folly many times over in the next few years, until even his patience wore out, and he finally refused to have anything more to do with the young American.

He was brought to his senses by Waterhouse's desertion. The realization that he was almost totally ignorant of his craft and was fast dissipating his youth and talent impelled Stuart to seek a new way of life. In desperation he wrote a humble letter to Benjamin West, the only person whom he thought he could turn to, pleading to be apprenticed. West, who had been born in the colonies but had come to England while still quite young, was one of the most prominent and successful painters in London. A generous and kindly man whose studio housed a number of other ambitious young American painters, West at once accepted Stuart as his assistant.

Upon his admittance to West's household, Stuart threw himself earnestly into the study of painting and drawing, not only with his own master but with Sir Joshua Reynolds, one of the greatest of English portraitists. In the next five years, Stuart learned not only the infinite complications of the craft of painting but also the social refinements necessary to the pursuit of a career as a portrait painter.

Finally, in 1781, Stuart sent a portrait he had painted of Benjamin West to an exhibition at the Royal Academy of

Art. It received much favorable comment, and, even more thrilling to Stuart, was hung in the company of pictures by Reynolds and Gainsborough. Stuart returned many times to the gallery to view his picture in its august surroundings. West discovered him there one day. "You have done well, Stuart, very well. Now you must go home and do better," West gently advised.

A short time afterward, West suggested that Stuart paint a whole figure. West obtained for him a commission to execute a full-length portrait of a prominent Londoner, William Grant. With some anxiety, Stuart went to see his client. After some talk, Grant suggested that, since it was a beautifully crisp cold day, they put off the painting and go ice-skating instead. At the rink, Stuart was struck by a brilliant idea. Why was it necessary to paint a portrait of a man sitting or standing? Why not skating? Grant enthusiastically agreed to the unusual suggestion.

All of London society was fascinated when this handsome picture was shown publicly. It had been executed with consummate skill, the figure beautifully drawn and balanced, the movement delicately capturing the grace of a skater gliding across the ice. The gallery was crowded with avid viewers, and Stuart was followed about by hordes of well-wishers. At last, after numerous false starts, he had achieved success.

He was invited to dine with dukes and princes. London society now came pounding at his door demanding that he paint their portraits. At the age of thirty he had become established as one of England's leading portrait painters. West, proud of his former pupil, said of him that he "nailed a face to the canvas." A critic called him "the Van Dyke of the time."

Years before, in youthful braggadocio, Stuart had said, "For my part, I will not follow any master. I wish to find out

what nature is for myself and see her with my own eyes."
Though he had somewhat tempered this extreme view, and
profited by his study of and with masters, it was the rare in-
cisiveness of his vision that made him great. He had a genius
for catching the true character of his sitters, and he was a
colorist with few equals. The inner reality of the man
emerged infallibly from the bold brush strokes and the rapid,
expert painting. The flesh tones of his portraits were not—
as Stuart said scornfully of one of his contemporaries—"like
tanned leather," but radiantly aglow with life. Nor was it
merely a superficial accomplishment. As West said of his star
pupil, "It is of no use to steal Stuart's colors; if you want to
paint as he does, you must steal his eyes."

Whether in reaction to the hardships of his early days, or
purely out of the exuberance and irresponsibility of his nature,
Stuart now began to indulge his every whim. He moved to a
large house in a fashionable quarter, he bought the most expensive clothes, his cooks were the finest and his meals the
most elaborate. He spent money lavishly and entertained ex-
travagantly. To help pay for these luxuries, he increased the
price for his work sixfold.

On May 10, 1786, he married eighteen-year-old Charlotte
Coates, a pretty girl endowed with a fine soprano voice, whom
he had won over the strenuous objections of her family. To
show off her unusual talent he gave a series of large, enor-
mously expensive parties, hiring the finest musicians of the
day to provide the accompaniment for his young wife's voice.

His despairing friends had hoped that marriage might help
him settle down. But instead of reforming, Stuart grew even
more extravagant. Despite a huge income, he was constantly
in debt and constantly pursued by his creditors and the threat
of jail. His need for more and more money frequently led
him into shady practices. He insisted on receiving payment of

half his fee at the first sitting, and then, money in hand, never completed the picture. Yet, in spite of this less-than-honorable behavior, he remained as popular and sought-after as ever. Nor was his attraction limited to his skill as a painter. He delighted his clients with his bluff charm, his wit, his gift for sparkling repartee.

In an attempt to escape his ever-increasing debts, Stuart fled to Dublin. But his creditors were hot on his heels, and, shortly after his arrival in 1787, he was thrown into debtors' jail. Here an extraordinary thing happened. The Irish gentry were so eager to be painted by him that they flocked to his cell for their sittings. It was not long before Stuart had accumulated enough money to pay his bills. However, his term in prison did not give him pause, nor inspire him to reform. No sooner was he freed than he at once returned to his usual reckless way of life.

He remained in Ireland several years, then, a jump ahead of the bailiff, departed for Paris, where he had received a commission to paint the portrait of Louis XVI, King of France. In Paris, he began to roll up debts anew. And once again, to rid himself of the persistence of his creditors, and possibly to avoid being jailed again, he decamped. This time he set sail for America, which he had not seen for almost fifteen years.

Toward the latter part of 1792 or early in 1793, Stuart arrived and settled himself and his family in New York. His reputation as a master portraitist had preceded him and he found commissions plentiful. The young nation had begun to forge ahead after the deprivations of the War for Independence, money was freer, and people were eager to display signs of their wealth. Stuart decided to remain for the rest of his life in the country of his birth, where, clearly, a lucrative future stretched before him. Perhaps as a symbol of his repatriation or perhaps because he knew it would add a priceless luster to his name, he made up his mind to paint George Washington.

In 1795 he moved to Philadelphia, then the capital of the United States, but it was not until autumn of that year that he was able to persuade President Washington to sit for his portrait. Stuart had already become the darling of Philadelphia's social set, besieged by rich and beautiful women who were clamoring for him to put their likenesses on canvas.

When Washington at last arrived to sit for Stuart, the artist did not have an easy time of it. Too many painters were claiming the President's time. He was a busy man and could ill afford the many hours required for the numerous sessions. By nature an active man, he was bored by the tedium and confinement of posing and sat, as he put it, "like Patience on a monument." Even Stuart, with his great experience and skill at putting his sitters at their ease, could not get the President to relax. However, he managed to complete the painting, which is known as the Vaughan type portrait. It is of the right side of Washington's head, and it shows the President in a stern, austere mood. People praised it as an excellent likeness, but Stuart was dissatisfied with it.

Instead of offering it to Washington, as custom would have dictated, Stuart kept it for himself. His motive was not that he wanted the President to have only a perfect picture, nor that he was reluctant to allow a "bad" portrait to go out into the world, but simply that he saw a way of turning a profit. He made fifteen copies of the Vaughan portrait and sold them for handsome fees to wealthy patriots eager to own a likeness of the first American President.

The following year he painted another picture of Washington, a full-length portrait. This likeness, known as the Lansdowne, fell far short of the standards of his finest work, betraying a weakness in the handling of the figure and a general uneasiness with his subject. Throughout his career, no matter how brilliantly he painted the faces of his sitters, Stuart failed to render their figures with equal brilliance, largely because of his lack of interest, for he maintained that the face was the man, not the clothes or the body. Yet, when his attention was roused, as in the case of the skater, he could handle the figure with great competence.

Largely through the good graces of Martha Washington, Stuart prevailed upon the President to sit for him once more. This time, painting the left side of the head, he caught all of the warmth and humanity of Washington, and the portrait, known as the Athenaeum, has become world-renowned. It is the picture by which Stuart—as well as Washington—has become best known throughout the years. Stuart also painted an admirable portrait of Martha Washington in this same period.

With the Athenaeum, as with the earlier portrait, Stuart was up to his old tricks again. When Mrs. Washington called for her husband's likeness, Stuart put her off, saying he had not yet completed the background. The President's wife never received the painting. Stuart gave her, instead, one of the many copies he made; the original remained in his own possession until his death. According to his daughter, Stuart was still making—and selling—copies almost up to his last days.

In 1803, three years after the seat of the U.S. Government moved from Philadelphia to Washington, D.C., Stuart moved with it, first settling his family on a farm in Bordentown, New Jersey. In the new capital, as in the old, he painted the portraits of many of the great military and political leaders of the time: John Adams, Thomas Jefferson, James Monroe, James Madison, John Quincy Adams, John Jay,

Generals Gates and Knox, Pennsylvania Chief Justice Shippen, and many others.

When he was fifty years old, Stuart moved for the last time in a life which had been full of wanderings. He went to Boston, and established his wife and children (there were twelve of them), and his omnipresent snuff box, in a studio-home on a fashionable street. Immediately after his arrival, the usual rush of wealthy clients began. At the same time, Stuart collected a small group of students eager to study with the man who had become an acknowledged master among the great portraitists of his time; who was regarded, in the idolatrous words of one of them, as greater than the combined genius of Rembrandt, Rubens, Van Dyck, and Titian.

As he aged, Stuart, whose character was never of the best, grew slovenly and vain. His snuff box was his constant companion. He believed himself (not entirely without justice) to be the greatest living artist of the day, and was convinced that all art elsewhere was in a state of serious decline.

He became increasingly irritable with his sitters, and would flare into a temper at the slightest criticism of his work. Frequently, he refused profitable commissions simply because he disdained answering letters or had taken a dislike to the client's looks. On one of these occasions, he complained, "What a business is that of a portrait painter. You bring him a potato and expect he will paint you a peach!" On another, feeling himself to have been slighted by his sitter, General Knox, he took the finished portrait and used it as the door to his pig pen.

As always, he showed his wide streak of irresponsibility. He would accept commissions, paint furiously, and then, becoming bored, skimp on the figure. Once, when a client complained that the clothing in his portrait was only barely sketched in, Stuart replied sarcastically, "I copy the works of God, and leave clothes to tailors. . . ."

In his last years, Stuart's arrogance and arbitrary behavior began to catch up with him. Prospective clients were increasingly alienated by his bad temper, his sharp tongue, his personal peculiarities, and his unsavory business habits. His reputation waned, and, despite the huge sums he had made, little or nothing remained.

"A noble type, robust, hearty and with large frame"—so one contemporary of Stuart's characterized him at the age of sixty-five. But another, less well disposed, described him as "bloated and red" and "noted for his eccentricity and love of good eating and drinking." He had been suffering considerably for a number of years from the gout, possibly as a result of his excesses. Yet, despite this infirmity and a pronounced tremor in the hands, Stuart continued painting until a short while before his death, without any noticeable decline in his powers. He died at the age of seventy-two, penniless, leaving his widow and surviving children impoverished. For lack of funds, his funeral was the cheapest that could be bought.

For many years, the site of Stuart's grave was unknown. But, in 1900, its whereabouts was finally discovered—a small mound in an old cemetery, marked only by the number 61, without even a simple headstone.

Today, rescued from obscurity, Gilbert Stuart's grave is marked by a bronze tablet in the shape of a palette, commemorating the talented, restless spirit who was America's first great artist.

2

The Man Who Had Everything

WASHINGTON ALLSTON

1779–1843

In a letter to his mother, written shortly after his graduation from Harvard, Washington Allston stated his determination "to be the first painter . . . from America."

In someone else this might have been indulgently regarded as the fine exuberance of youth. But to those who knew Washington Allston, his resolve to be "the first painter . . . from America," would have appeared a reasonable and modest goal. For a young man of Allston's amazing endowments, everything must have seemed possible.

Few men before or since have been so favored. As if it was not enough to be handsome, aristocratic, a brilliant intellect, an uncommonly gifted artist, a writer of talent, Allston also possessed such a bounty of warmth, modesty, wit, charm, and personal magnetism that men of all kinds—including the greatest minds of his age—were instantly and irresistibly attracted to him, and thereafter remained his lifelong friends and ardent partisans.

Yet this remarkable man, upon whom the gods lavished all of their most precious gifts, died believing that he had betrayed his own genius, and convinced that he was a failure. His contemporaries—however reluctantly—were in agreemen with this harsh verdict. For all the promise of his youth and the accomplishment of his middle years, his reputation scarcely survived his death.

But the final story was not yet written, and, in time, posterity reversed the decision. Today, Washington Allston is regarded as one of the great painters of America. In fact, fully bearing out the prophecy of his letter to his mother, he has been adjudged the "first painter . . . from America," at least, in his time.

Washington Allston was born on November 5, 1779, the second of the three children of Captain William Allston, an officer in the Revolutionary army, and Rachel Moore. The ancestral home was Brook Green Domain, a prosperous plantation in the Georgetown District of South Carolina. Here the Allston family lived in almost baronial splendor, on a narrow strip of land lying between the Waccamaw River and the Atlantic Ocean.

When Washington was two years old his father died, and, some time later, his mother remarried. Her new husband, Dr. Henry Collins Flagg, the son of a shipping merchant of Newport, Rhode Island, was a former chief of the medical staff of General Greene's army during the War for Independence. A quick and lasting bond of affection was soon established between the child and his new stepfather.

Washington's early years were happy, almost idyllic. His childish imagination fed delightedly on the ghost stories and tales of witchcraft spun for him by the Negro slaves. This glimpse into the world of the supernatural made a deep impression on him, and, possibly, was later reflected in the mysticism of his paintings. As he roamed through the southern countryside, he began to develop an appreciation of the beauty of nature. "I remember," he said in later years, "that I used to draw before I left Carolina, at six years of age . . . that my favorite amusement was making little landscapes. . . ."

The education of the young patrician was a serious matter requiring careful planning. He was first enrolled in Mrs. Calcott's School in Charleston, and later sent to Newport, where Robert Rogers conducted one of the finest academies in the new country. And in 1796, at the age of seventeen, he was admitted to Harvard College.

At Harvard, Washington distinguished himself as a brilliant and inquiring student, and won high academic honors. His wit, charm, and courtesy earned him many devoted friends. Among these was Edward Greene Malbone, later to win fame as the foremost painter of miniatures in America. The two young men had first met at Newport, where their mutual interest in art had forged the bonds of friendship.

During his four years at Harvard, young Allston applied himself to art with growing seriousness. Since there was no formal art education in the curriculum, he took private lessons in drawing and painting from Samuel King, a self-instructed portrait and house painter, who did some teaching. At the same time he worked on his own initiative. He made copies of what few engravings of pictures were then available; painted romantic fantasies peopled with idealized bandits; and executed a series of satirical drawings called "The Buck's Progress," full of a young man's vitality and high spirits.

Despite Allston's comparative ignorance of the fine points of the artist's craft, these youthful works gave evidence of a considerable talent. Indeed, one of the paintings of this early period was deemed worthy of exhibition at the British Institution a number of years later.

Allston graduated from Harvard in 1800 with honors. He was elected class poet, and read one of his own works at the commencement exercises. The future lay open before him, bright and beckoning.

After his graduation, Allston hurried to Newport to see Ann Channing, his future wife, sister of William Ellery Channing, who was later to become the leader of the Unitarian movement. He had first met them during his undergraduate days at Harvard. Although Ann Channing and Allston felt a deep affection for each other and considered marriage, they both acknowledged that Allston's studies as a painter had to come first.

Allston's decision to pursue a career as an artist was a grave disappointment to his family. Such a calling might be suitable enough for a person of lower degree, but hardly for a young man of Allston's social background. But to all the pressure exerted by his family Allston remained impervious. His mother and stepfather finally bowed to his unshakable resolve, and permitted him to sell his share of an inherited property. The proceeds of the sale afforded him complete financial independence for the long years of study ahead.

The seriously aspiring artist of those days had no choice but to seek out the teachers and art treasures of the Old World. America was still too raw, too untutored, too much occupied with the problems of subsistence to be greatly interested in cultural matters. So, in May of 1801, Allston, now twenty-one, accompanied by his friend Malbone, embarked for England, where the best training by the best teachers was to be found.

Allston took lodgings at upper Titchfield Street in Maryle-bone, London. When the Royal Academy of Art opened its doors in September, Allston was waiting on the steps. Granted admission, he began an intensive study of drawing from casts and from life. But the Academy did not teach painting, and so, like so many other American hopefuls, Allston applied for admission to the classes of Benjamin West, and was accepted by him as a student. Formerly somewhat scornful of West's work—with which he was acquainted only through inferior reproductions—Allston soon changed his opinion and termed his teacher "one of the greatest men in the world."

The city of London caught Allston's imagination and fired it with excitement. In contrast to America, artists were re-garded with respect, galleries held well-attended exhibitions of their work, the fields of arts and letters were pulsating with vitality. Allston eagerly absorbed everything the old city had to offer. At the end of his first year in London he was given an exhibition at the British Institution. For a young man, and an American at that, it was a rare compliment.

Allston might have remained comfortably on in London—where, inevitably, he had attracted the friendship of many of the famous and great men of the day—but his desire for broader knowledge and experience made him restless. In the summer of 1803, he met the talented young American painter, John Vanderlyn, and it seemed to him that fate had sent him the perfect companion with whom to explore the art treasures of the Continent. Like Allston, Vanderlyn was a passionate admirer of European life, traditions, culture, landscape, and painting in "the grand manner"—large can-vases of historical events or heroic feats of Greek or Roman antiquity.

The impending threat of the Napoleonic Wars held no terrors for the two young men. After traveling through Holland and Belgium, they arrived in Paris on a bleak November day. The Louvre had just been converted from a royal palace into a museum, and its maze of corridors and passages and salons were crammed with the art masterpieces of all nations, the spoils of Napoleon's victories. Allston lived most of the hours of each day in this incredible treasure house, studying, copying, straining to pierce the mystery of the technique of the great Italian masters. Feasting his eyes on the first Titian, Veronese, and Tintoretto he had ever seen, he marveled that they "absolutely enchanted me, for they took away all sense of subject. . . . I thought of nothing but the gorgeous concert of colors, or rather of the indefinite forms . . . of pleasure with which they filled the imagination. It was the poetry of color which I felt."

Inspired by the discoveries he made about the use of color as radiant light, Allston abandoned bandits and satire and now turned to romantic themes for the subjects of his paintings. In "The Deluge" and "Rising of a Thunderstorm at Sea" he depicted the ocean as an element of terrifying and awe-inspiring intensity. The paintings held a new luminosity and a dark, brooding quality of the mystery of nature.

In "Rising of a Thunderstorm at Sea" two ships fight the violent fury of a storm-tossed sea. Lowering clouds hang over them like the finger of impending doom. In contrast, a clearing portion of the sky is illuminated by an almost unearthly radiance, as if to symbolize man's hope. The painting was invested by Allston with an intense emotional response to the half-understood mystery of supernatural forces. It was this quality that was to occupy his talents and become a hallmark of his best and most mature work.

Having discovered the painting of Italy, Allston felt impelled to explore the country itself. In the late spring of 1804, he spent some time in Siena learning the language, and then, with breathless anticipation, left for Rome. From the moment he set foot in the ancient capital, he was enchanted. The landscape, the eloquent ruins of an ancient culture, the operatic intensity of the Italian people delighted his eye and enamored his soul. His romantic nature and imaginative mind burgeoned in the beauty and warmth of this land.

The four years Allston spent in Italy were the happiest of his life. He pored over the great Italian masterpieces, he slaved on his own paintings, and, characteristically, soon became a friend to the great and noble men in the area. With Samuel Taylor Coleridge, the English poet, he formed a lifelong friendship. Both men were unabashedly infatuated with Italy, and wandered together through the streets of the Eternal City and its environs feasting their eyes on the landscape.

When Vanderlyn arrived in Rome he was immediately drawn into the intimacy, as was, later, a budding lawyer from America named Washington Irving. It is to Irving, who later changed his career and became one of America's most famous writers, that we are indebted for a description of Allston at that time. Irving described his friend as "of a light and graceful form, with large blue eyes, and black, silken hair waving and curling around a pale, expressive countenance." So completely did Irving succumb to Allston's magnetism that he half seriously played with the notion of becoming a painter himself. Although he abandoned the notion, there is some evidence that the artistic and intellectual stimulus of his Italian interlude may have been instrumental in causing Irving to give up the law for a career as a writer.

The quartet of gifted young men lived, conversed, explored, and studied with youthful joy and enthusiasm in a golden world that seemed to promise all things. To each of them, immortality seemed within easy reach. Only the menacing shadow of Napoleon troubled their contentment. Cole-

ridge was the first to desert the Continent for the island safety
of home. But, before he left, Allston persuaded him to sit
for his portrait. The result was a romantic picture by a romantic painter of a romantic poet. A skillful and affectionate
work, the portrait showed the influence of Titian in the
brooding interplay of light and dark.

Shortly after Coleridge's departure, Allston, too, decided
to return home. In April, 1808, he traveled to Leghorn, and
sailed for America. He returned to Boston, where he was
warmly received by old friends. Reports of his work had preceded him, and his many admirers were quick to hail him as
the new great name in American art.

Allston renewed his acquaintance with Ann Channing
and, at length (after what his brother-in-law characterized
with considerable restraint as "a long and patient courtship"), they were married. The union, so long in coming to
pass, proved to be a happy and mutually devoted one. Allston
had meanwhile set up a studio in Boston, and plunged directly into work. He painted a number of landscapes, and a
few pictures which echoed his earlier flair for humor. But
the greatest proportion of his output was in the field of portraiture, paintings of members of his family and his newly
acquired relations. In addition, he wrote a volume of poetry
that was published in 1813 in London and Boston.

Allston's future in America looked promising. The country
had entered upon a period of prosperity, and it seemed as if
art might at last begin to flourish. But the atmosphere of
Boston was withering to the creative urge of a man of
Allston's temperament. Although his friends were the greatest literary and intellectual figures in America, he sorely
missed the warmth and pride of place accorded to the artist
in the Old World. He was convinced that, in order to paint
in the grand manner, he needed more conducive surround-

ings. So, in July, 1811, accompanied by his wife and a young pupil, Samuel F. B. Morse, he sailed for England. Young Morse, then a talented art student, would later become immortal as the inventor of the telegraph.

Allston and his party had scarcely set foot on English soil, following the docking of their ship at Liverpool, when the mayor of the city arrived in person and requested their immediate departure. Ill feeling between the governments of Great Britain and the United States, which was soon to bring on the War of 1812, had affected the manners even of local officials. Although Mrs. Allston was in poor health, and in need of rest, the Allston party had no choice but to leave at once. A week later, the Allstons and their young charge arrived in London, where they hoped a more hospitable outlook might be expected. Without incident, Allston rented lodgings for himself and Ann, and Morse found rooms nearby.

With Mrs. Allston's health improving, Allston once more entered into the artistic and literary life of the metropolis. He resumed his friendship with Coleridge, and, as always, attracted the leading figures of the day. Among his many friends were Robert Southey and William Wordsworth, who, with Coleridge, were the outstanding triumvirate of English poetry. He spent countless hours with these and other companions, in discussions that frequently lasted until dawn. A brilliant conversationalist, he was never so happy as when he was matching wits with his intellectual peers.

In his thirty-second year, happy in his marriage, bursting with ambitious plans, and confident that he was on the path leading to greatness, Allston began to paint the now famous "The Dead Man Revived in the Tomb by Touching the Bones of the Prophet Elisha." Based on a biblical incident, it counterpoised the real and the supernatural in the play of "mystery and fear in the human relationship"—a theme that had now become dominant in Allston's mind. Upon its completion, the picture was exhibited in the British Institution. Its enthusiastic reception filled Allston with pleasure and a rewarding sense of having at last been recognized. Despite the fact that England and America were now at war, the British Institution awarded "The Dead Man" its prize of two hundred guineas. The success of the picture had repercussions in America. At the conclusion of the war, the newly organized Pennsylvania Academy of Fine Arts raised thirty-five hundred dollars to purchase the painting for its permanent collection.

Allston's reaction to his triumph was to plunge even more feverishly into work. In his unabated desire to establish himself as an artist of first consequence, he drove himself without mercy. Finally, his health failed under the strain of his overzealous schedule, and he was forced to take a vacation from his easel. Returning to work before he was fully recovered, he suffered a serious relapse. His doctor ordered an immediate change of air. Allston's uncle, who was the American Consul at Bristol, came to the rescue. He insisted that his nephew come to his home, where he could recuperate in the invigorating sea air. Ann Allston and Morse undertook the difficult task of transporting the ailing painter. En route, Allston became so desperately ill that they were forced to halt. In a panic, Morse rushed back to London to summon Coleridge, who arrived with his personal physician. A few days later, Allston felt sufficiently strong to resume the journey.

Allston chafed under the slowness of his recovery, impatient to return to London and his work. He was finally allowed to do so, on the condition that he would husband his strength. Possibly as a concession to this dictum, he now applied himself to smaller paintings and a group of portraits, among them pictures of his friends Coleridge, Southey, and Benjamin West.

Eager to hold a large showing of his canvases, he arranged for an exhibition in Bristol. Anxiously he hung his paintings. But the exhibition was a complete failure. The sole purchaser was his uncle, the sole favorable criticism that of his friend Coleridge. This time the English were unwilling to grant the American a generous reception.

Allston refused to allow his disappointment to undermine his belief in himself. He returned to his easel with renewed determination. As a measure of his confidence in himself, he bought a house on Tinney Street, in London. Enthusiastically, he and his wife set about furnishing their first real home. Then disaster struck. Ann Allston became ill, and died on February 2, 1815, a few days after they had moved into the Tinney Street house. She was buried at St. Pancras Chapel. The mournful services were attended only by Allston, his devoted pupil, and an unknown man.

Allston abandoned his new home in an access of despair, and moved into rented rooms in Buckingham Place. Fresh surroundings did nothing to alleviate his sorrow. He was haunted by nightmares, plagued in his waking hours by horrible fantasies. He felt that his sanity was slipping away. On Coleridge's advice, he sought solace in the Church of England. But he found his greatest comfort by submerging himself in his work.

Early in the spring of 1817, his sorrow somewhat eased by the passage of time, Allston began work on a painting which he had contemplated for many years. He envisioned it as the most ambitious effort of his entire career, as a crowning achievement, a masterwork that would, he hoped, establish him unquestionably as a great artist, and secure for him the immortality he so longed for and so honestly believed he deserved. The idea for this magnum opus, titled "Belshazzar's Feast," while it might have been inspired by Rembrandt's treatment of the same subject, was also uniquely the embodiment of the mystical approach which Allston had been pursuing in other works. His conception of the painting, he wrote to his friend Washington Irving, was to embrace "a multitude of figures," uniting "the magnificent and the awful."

Quickly, he made his preliminary studies, and executed two finished, detailed drawings in which the color harmonies were worked out. Then he unrolled a huge sheet of canvas, twelve feet high by sixteen feet long, nailed it to a stretcher, and began to paint "Belshazzar's Feast."

Once again the future looked bright. In May, he had been elected to the American Academy of Fine Arts, and also to the British Royal Academy. His position in English art was solidly if not spectacularly established. The "masterwork" was well under way. Then, abruptly, although only "about six or eight months work" on the canvas remained, he decided to return to America. He was experiencing "a homesickness, which (in spite of the best and kindest friends and every encouragement as an artist)" pushed him in the direction of home.

A month before his thirty-ninth birthday, in October, 1818, Allston arrived in Boston. With little delay, he set up his studio in a large barn near the waterfront. The way seemed clear for him to assume the mantle as the leading painter in America. Stuart was an old man, the nation's economy was again stable, its wealth was increasing, and the outlook for American art to expand seemed promising. Ironically, it was Allston's very giftedness that now blocked his path.

Although he wished for nothing better than to immerse himself in his work, he was drawn inevitably into the vortex of Boston's brilliant intellectual and literary circles. Shortly after his return, he was visited by his old friend Richard Henry Dana, the poet. Dana was in the process of creating a new literary magazine, the *Idle Man,* and pleaded with Allston for contributions. Allston responded with two essays and a romantic novel of Italian life entitled *Monaldi.*

"Belshazzar's Feast," Allston's pledge to posterity, meanwhile remained untouched.

Soon he began to be plagued by financial troubles. He had no funds left to support him while he worked on his masterpiece. In an effort to earn his living, he now began to paint a number of small pictures which he put up for sale. But the income derived from this source was barely sufficient for the necessities, and the work occupied so much of his day that it left no time for "Belshazzar's Feast."

At this juncture, ten well-to-do Boston gentlemen came to the rescue. As a measure of their belief in his greatness they set up "The Allston Trust." Each of them subscribed one thousand dollars to a fund to purchase the finished "Belshazzar." The ten thousand dollars so raised was meanwhile to be used by Allston to support himself while he worked on the picture, thus freeing him from the drudgery of making a living.

Two years after his return to the United States, Allston at last unrolled the huge canvas, and made ready to resume his major work. But now, looking at it, he felt profoundly dissatisfied. The composition, and the play of light on the figures, were not to his liking. Worst of all, the vision that had originally inspired him seemed to have vanished. On the advice of Gilbert Stuart, he undertook to alter the perspective of the buildings in the background. This comparatively simple task stretched out to several months. He could not seem to recapture his inspiration. As a relief from his obsession with "Belshazzar," he painted several other pictures during this time, among them "Moonlit Landscape" and "The Flight of Florimell." Interestingly enough, these luminous, richly colored, evocative canvases are today numbered among the finest of his works.

Agonized, driven, Allston returned once more to "Belshazzar's Feast." If common sense told him that it was the better part of valor to abandon a project that had now become a millstone around his neck, his sense of obligation to his benefactors, as well as his own thirst for immortality, forced him to continue. He kept reworking the entire picture, taking out one figure, substituting another, and blocking out whole areas. None of it seemed satisfactory. The heroic canvas had by now grown famous. Newspapers published frequent reports on the state of its progress. The public followed its development with interest. This unwanted attention was a torture to the sensitive Allston. He began to be convinced of his ultimate failure. He confided some of his desperation to a friend: "I began to look upon my picture as something I must finish in order to get so much money . . . and the spirit of the artist died away within me . . . I was like a bee trying to make honey in a coal hole." By now, Allston was all but certain that he was attempting to achieve the unachievable.

In 1827, the Boston Athenaeum opened its galleries for the first time, and Allston was asked to submit some of his works to the inaugural exhibition. The show attracted an enormous public, but there was little enthusiasm for Allston's canvases. The proper Bostonian, whose tastes tended toward the exact, topographical reproduction of nature, found Allston's imaginative landscapes "too exotic and vague." Allston's reputation, which had begun to sag with his failure to complete "Belshazzar's Feast," now fell even lower.

Shortly thereafter, on a cold winter's day, Allston received the unsettling news that the barn he used as a studio had been sold, and was to be turned into a livery stable. He found new quarters, but once again was compelled to roll up "Belshazzar's Feast." His new studio was too small to house the enormous canvas.

On the first of June, 1830, fifteen years after the death of his first wife, Allston married Martha Remington Dana, sister of Richard Henry Dana and a cousin of Ann Channing Allston. Their first move, immediately after the ceremony, was to settle in a rented house in Cambridgeport, with a "painting room" at a small distance from the living quarters.

While "Belshazzar" remained rolled up in a corner, Allston worked on other paintings. For the Mayor of Boston he painted "Italian Landscape," a beautiful and tender evocation of his memories of the country he had loved so deeply. In a sense, the picture was both a tribute and a farewell to the joys and dreams of his youth.

Past fifty now, Allston "starved spiritually in Cambridgeport . . . stunted by the scant soil and cold winds," in the words of one of his pupils. "There was nothing congenial without, and he turned his powers inward and drained his memory dry." The yearnings and ideals of his youth were now irrevocably lost. His conscience was heavily burdened with the debt he owed to his ten patrons and to those faithful adherents who still believed in his genius. He found it increasingly difficult to paint at all, and instead turned his thoughts to the question of the relationship between the artist and his art. These reflections led to a treatise, "Lectures on Art," in which he drew on his experiences to formulate a philosophy. He stated his conviction that the "aim of the artist is . . . not to please, but to be true to that life within us." This latter statement, which is easily applicable to the theories of modern abstract art, was indeed a revolutionary thought in his day.

In his sixtieth year, still handsome, dignified, silver-haired, Allston was given a retrospective show in the Boston studios of Chester Harding, a painter and friend. Included were his portraits, his landscapes, his biblical and allegorical paintings. The show was a notable local triumph. A respected critic of the period wrote: "I have more and more appreciated the sober grandeur of his compositions." For the first time, New England's literary circle was prodded into an awareness of the importance of another art than their own in the nation's cultural development. Emerson was moved to write an essay on art. Oliver Wendell Holmes published a review of the exhibition. Poems about various of the pictures in the show, discussions of art, and an article on Allston himself all made their way into print.

Gratifying as this reception must have been to Allston, nevertheless it still fell far short of the recognition he sought for himself. Repercussions of the praise for his work scarcely penetrated beyond the outskirts of Boston; certainly they didn't reach New York, the center of activity in the field of art. But, more important than any of this in Allston's mind, was the fact that he still saw his final stature as an artist inextricably bound up with "Belshazzar's Feast." So long as it was incomplete, he regarded himself as an incomplete artist; to the extent that it would succeed or fail, he read his own eventual success or failure.

Once more he unrolled the giant canvas, and set to work to wrestle with his grand conception. New figures were painted in, and old figures painted out; whole areas were covered over; colors were changed and then changed again. Frantically, he pursued perfection, and perfection fled just beyond his grasp. He took to locking his studio door, so that no one might enter. He refused to tolerate any inquiry about the progress of the picture, or even any mention of it in his presence. In the words of a friend, "his sensitiveness on this one point did at last verge on insanity."

Overwork put a strain on his strength, and late in 1841 he became critically ill. His recovery took many months. His first act, on leaving his sickbed, was to move with his wife into their newly built home. "I have at last, in my old age," he wrote poignantly to a friend, "got into a house of my own. . . ." He had scarcely settled in before he turned feverishly once again to the task of finishing "Belshazzar."

On July 9, 1843, the final day of his life, Allston went to his studio, as usual, to work on his painting. With what a heavy heart he must have stared at what he now could no longer doubt was a monumental failure. Still, habit drove him. He picked up his brush and had just painted out the central figure of Belshazzar, all except the right hand, when death closed his eyes, and relieved him, at last, of his impossible burden. "By dying," his brother-in-law sadly commented, Allston had finally escaped from "that terrible vision, the nightmare . . . the tormentor of his life. . . ." Yet, even after his death, the travails of "Belshazzar's Feast" were not over. After long and serious consideration, his friends decided to restore the painting to what it was before Allston had begun his final revision of the figure of the king.

Washington Allston was buried in the Dana vault in the churchyard on the Common in Cambridge. Harvard students ceremoniously carried his coffin by torchlight to its final resting place.

When Vanderlyn, the companion of Allston's brightest years, heard of his death, he commented bitterly: "When I look back some five or six and thirty years since, when we were both in Rome together, and next-door neighbors on the Trinità dei Monte, and in the spring of life, full of enthusiasm for our art, and fancying fair prospects awaiting us in after years, it is painful to reflect how far these hopes have been from being realized."

Vanderlyn's view of Allston as a failure coincided with that of Allston himself, and with the majority verdict of his generation. But time has found this judgment erroneous. In the broad perspective of the years since his death, Allston has come into his own as—in the words of E. P. Richardson, an authority on American art—the first major American artist "to establish the art of painting on its full imaginative and figurative scale."

It is no exaggeration to state that, posthumously, Allston finally achieved his dream of becoming the "first painter" of his time, "from America."

3

Champion of the Common Man

GEORGE CALEB BINGHAM

1811–1879

For most of his adult life, George Caleb Bingham was pulled in one direction by his vocation as a painter, and in another by his urge to become a "man of action." His artistic impulse had to compete with a deep-rooted and burning hatred of injustice that impelled him into the arena of politics.

A man of less energy and moral fiber than Bingham might have been split hopelessly in two by this internal tug-of-war, and been a double failure. George Caleb Bingham was a double success.

The painter in Bingham predominated over the man of action until the latter period of his life, when his passion for

30

politics finally conquered. If it is regrettable that the last twenty years of his life produced few new paintings, and none of consequence, nevertheless the industry of his earlier days left a legacy of work that firmly fixes his place in the heritage of American art. Bingham is our first great painter of the West, and the first to depict the common man against the background of his daily pursuits.

The second son of a family of six children, George Caleb Bingham was born March 20, 1811, to Mary Amend and Henry Vest Bingham, in Augusta County, Virginia. His early years were spent in the healthy outdoor environment of his father's gristmill and 1,180-acre farm. A sturdy, handsome, blue-eyed and black-haired little boy, George Caleb learned to ride early, and spent much of his childhood on horseback, wandering over the Virginia countryside.

He first gave evidence of artistic leaning when, at the age of five, he decorated the walls of his father's farm buildings with drawings of animals. This display of precocious talent clashed with his father's passion for neatness. The boy was firmly lectured and commanded to wash the walls his drawings had defaced. However, the elder Bingham did encourage him to follow his artistic bent along more conventional lines. Later, in fact, he even tried to help his son cope with some of the intricacies of drawing.

The education of the Bingham children was administered by their mother. She taught them the three R's, history, and geography, and encouraged them to read at random in the family's good-sized library. The Bible, of course, was required reading. George Caleb's particular favorite was a book of Renaissance engravings. These were his first actual contact with art, and he pored over the pictures with endless delight.

The depression which had hit the country after the War of 1812 was indirectly responsible for the Bingham family's move to the West. Henry Bingham had generously put up his farm as security for a loan taken by one of his neighbors, who had been hard hit by the economic slump. When the neighbor was unable to redeem his loan, the Bingham farm and home were lost. Not a man to be downed by adversity, Henry Bingham took a trip to the West to investigate the opportunities that were said to abound there. He returned full of enthusiasm, and in the summer of 1819 moved his family to Franklin, Missouri.

The town of Franklin was a bustling, expanding, colorful community of one thousand inhabitants. It boasted a library, a busy main street, and the first newspaper to set up publication west of the Mississippi. It was also the hub for the rowdy, high-spirited men who piloted and manned the river boats that plied the great western waterways. The river men and their boats enchanted young George Caleb. He spent hour upon fascinated hour observing the men at work and at play, eagerly drinking in the details of an exciting life that would one day provide him with the material for his major subject.

The family's fortunes were again prospering. Henry Bingham bought a partnership in a tobacco factory, opened a tavern, won a county judgeship, and purchased a farm and homestead in Arrow Rock, a settlement a few miles removed from Franklin.

George Caleb's artistic bent received fresh impetus when a professional painter (it may have been Chester Harding, an eastern portrait painter of some note) passed through Franklin one day, pausing long enough to give a demonstration of his ability in the village square. George Caleb had never before seen a real painter. As if mesmerized, he followed each movement of the artist's hand, his brush strokes, the way in which he mixed colors—and tried to commit all of it to memory. Before the painter departed, he left several brushes with the eager boy who had plied him insistently with so many questions.

But George Caleb's dreams of becoming an artist suffered a serious setback with the death of his father on the day after Christmas in 1823. The settlement of the elder Bingham's estate revealed that he had once again allowed his generosity to prevail over his common sense, and had underwritten the loan of a considerable amount of money for his partner. His widow was left penniless, with only the farm at Arrow Rock remaining of all her husband's assets. She opened a school— the Franklin Female Academy—but the proceeds were insufficient for the support of her children, and her oldest boys were compelled to give up their own schooling. Fourteen-year-old Matthias was hired to work on a neighboring farm, and George, not quite thirteen, went to work in the tobacco factory which had formerly belonged to his father.

When he was sixteen, he found new employment in nearby Boonville as a cabinetmaker's apprentice in the shop of Justinian Williams. For the next three years, he spent his days learning the craft of cabinetmaking, and arguing the Bible with his devoutly religious employer. Soon he began accompanying Williams on his Sunday round of preaching at the local churches, and occasionally himself delivering a sermon —a young, earnest figure with a powerful command of rhetoric and knowledge of the Bible. He flirted briefly with the idea of entering the ministry, and gave some thought to the law as an eventual career. But he still felt that his true vocation was that of an artist.

When he was twenty, young Bingham set out on foot for St. Louis to begin his study of drawing and painting. He never arrived. En route, he was stricken with a severe case of measles. After recovering, he returned home, minus his curly black hair, which had fallen out as a result of his illness. He rapidly acquired a wig, which he wore for the rest of his life.

Young Bingham abandoned the idea of going to St. Louis, opened a studio in Franklin, and set himself up as a portrait painter. Although his early efforts were stiff and untutored, the drawing was vigorous and the likeness to the subject remarkably accurate. Before long he met a young woman whose delicate sweetness of face enchanted him. He fell in love with Elizabeth Hutchison, and now became fired with the ambition to prove himself capable of earning enough money to support a wife. While ardently courting Elizabeth, he toured the neighboring towns and cities seeking portrait commissions. He attracted some attention, and one local newspaper, more than a little prematurely, referred to him as a "western meteor of art." Eventually he made his way to St. Louis, where he opened a studio. The city afforded him an opportunity to see portraits by Stuart and others, as well as copies of the old masters. Writing to Elizabeth, perhaps fresh from a visit to a museum, he confessed that he often felt unsure of his talent. "Nearly three years have elapsed," he wrote, "and I have scarcely learned to paint the human face, after having accomplished which I shall have ascended one step towards that eminence to which the art of painting may be carried." But there was no thought of giving up.

The St. Louis *Commercial Bulletin* in commenting on his portraits, on the whole favorably, declared that "there is a want of skill in coloring evinced, which does not disclose a want of genius, but of instruction." Commissions were few and widely spaced, but Bingham remained resolute. If he could not paint portraits, he would find "subjects from among the cats and dogs, I can't endure the horrors of inaction."

In December of 1835 his fortunes took an upward turn. He was commissioned to paint ten portraits and two landscapes. As soon as he had completed his assignments, he hurried to Franklin, married Elizabeth, and brought her back with him to St. Louis. A year later, he became the father of a son, who was given the name of Isaac Newton. In all, in the course of his three marriages, Bingham was to father six children, only three of whom survived.

With the proceeds from an increasing number of portrait commissions, he bought land at Arrow Rock and built a home for his family. But neither a modicum of financial success nor personal happiness obscured his knowledge of his own imperfections as an artist. His portraits had lost some of their stiffness and his use of color had improved, but his work still suffered from a woeful lack of knowledge of the craft. Bingham, well aware of his shortcomings, decided to go to Philadelphia for "the facilities offered there."

He enrolled in the Pennsylvania Academy of Fine Arts, and for three months worked on drawing from casts. Hanging in the Academy's galleries were paintings by Stuart, Allston, West, and several Italian masters. He studied these avidly, and bought engravings of paintings and drawings so that he could study from them at home. In the brief time he spent in Philadelphia, Bingham utilized every available moment in study. Inspired by all the paintings he had seen, he set to work on a picture of Western life as he knew it at first hand. Drawing on his vividly remembered observations of the river boatmen of his boyhood, he painted "Western Boatmen Ashore." It was his first attempt at utilizing a Western setting, and his first "genre" painting—the depiction of the daily life of the common man.

On his return home, Bingham resumed the painting of portraits. Now the untutored efforts of his earlier years were replaced by a more knowledgeable hand, a greater refinement of color, and a skillful employment of light and shadow. In the spring of 1840, combining a growing absorption in politics with his talent as an artist, he painted a political banner for the Whig party of his home county.

A curiosity to observe—and possibly to participate in—the political scene in Washington, together with the hope of securing portrait commissions from important national figures, gave Bingham a reason for moving his family to the capital late in the year. He rented rooms in a boardinghouse on Pennsylvania Avenue, and established a studio nearby on the same street.

Work was slow in coming, and Bingham grew impatient. With characteristic determination, he decided that, if Mahomet would not come to the mountain, the mountain would come to Mahomet. Setting up a tent close to the Capitol, he fixed his alert blue eyes on potential customers. But his only visitor was a stately old gentleman who stopped not to have his portrait painted but to argue religion. Day after day the old man came back to resume the interminable debate. Bingham had by now learned that his adversary was John Quincy Adams, sixth President of the United States, and presently a member of the Congress. During a lull in the discussion, he would urge Adams to sit for his portrait. Finally, the old man conceded. "Sir," he said, "if you can paint as well as you can argue religion, you may do my portrait."

The successful completion of Adams' portrait led to other commissions, and soon "The Missouri Artist," as he was called, was painting the most important figures in Washington, among them Martin Van Buren, the eighth President of the United States, Daniel Webster, Henry Clay, John Calhoun, Andrew Jackson, James Buchanan, John Howard Payne, author of "Home, Sweet Home." Despite the money and modicum of fame he was now earning, Bingham grew restive. Money and fame were not to be despised, but they were merely way stations along the road to his artistic destiny. He sensed that he must push on in the direction pointed out by "Western Boatmen Ashore." Late in the summer of 1844, Bingham returned to his home town, after an absence of three and a half years.

He was thirty-three, and acknowledged to be the West's leading painter. Although he might have made an excellent living at portraiture, he plunged instead into a series of paintings depicting the river boatmen at work and at play. By 1845 he had completed a number of canvases, including the now famous "Fur Traders Descending the Missouri" and "The Jolly Flatboatmen." These serene, timeless evocations of the Western scene far surpassed his previous work, and are now classed among the finest examples of American genre painting.

Popular recognition for the river pictures was swift in coming. Bingham's pictures of Western life were bought by the Art Union, an organization that sold engravings of paintings by public subscription. Although the Art Union was dissolved a few years later, during its existence it did much to bring genuine works of art to the people. With the wide distribution of "The Jolly Flatboatmen," Bingham became an overnight success. Still, it rankled that the jealously guarded art circles of the East refused to grant him any real measure of acceptance. The critic of the New York *Literary World* found his color "disagreeable," his texture "monotonous" and his pyramidal composition "unsuited" to his subject. His work was too raw and uncouth for the civilized palate of "cultured" Easterners.

Meanwhile, local political issues had more and more begun to engage Bingham's energetic attention, and in 1846 he accepted nomination on the Whig ticket for the Missouri House of Representatives. He campaigned with typical vigor and actually won election—by a scant three votes. Through legal red tape and behind-the-scenes maneuvering, however, the results were overturned and Sappington, his opponent, was seated instead. Bingham returned to his home disheartened and disgusted. "I intend," he solemnly vowed, "to strip off my clothes and bury them, scour my body all over with sand and water . . . and keep out of the mire of politics FOREVER." It was a rash promise for a man of Bingham's temperament.

Whatever the experience might have cost him in heartache, his first political campaign resulted in his first political picture. Titled "Stump Orator," it depicted a politician haranguing a crowd. Before long, he was once more deeply involved in "the mire of politics," despite his fervent vow. In the summer of 1848 the Whigs again nominated him for the legislature, and he again opposed Sappington. This time he won easily.

Tragedy struck as he was preparing to move himself and his family to Jefferson City, the seat of the Missouri Legislature. Elizabeth, his wife, died of tuberculosis; and soon afterward, his new son, Joseph Hutchison, died at the age of seven months. Bingham was inconsolable. For a protracted period his paints and brushes stood idle, and he entertained the idea of resigning from the Legislature. But his was too fiery and buoyant a temperament to be permanently crushed by adversity. In time, he returned to the Legislature, where he became embroiled in the intensifying debate on slavery. He quickly made his position on the subject unequivocally clear: "Those who seek to make slavery a national practice," he thundered, "are not motivated by patriotism but by selfish feelings."

Bingham's interest in painting suddenly revived. He decided not to stand for re-election, but to move to New York and the great art markets of the East. He found quarters on Grand Street in lower Manhattan, where he attempted to work. Restlessness, and perhaps the conviction that it was wrong to separate himself from the source of his inspiration and material, soon had him hurrying home. Shortly after his return, he married Elizabeth Thomas, the daughter of a professor at the University of Missouri, and herself a woman of considerable education and culture.

Bingham's next years were highly productive. Aside from the portrait commissions with which he earned the better part of his living, he painted many genre pictures of the Western scene, among them such well-known works as "Shooting the Beef," "Watching the Cargo," "Fishing on the Mississippi," and "Daniel Boone Coming Through the Cumberland Gap."

Politics still exerted a strong pull on his imagination. He managed to resist becoming involved as a candidate, but not as a painter. He started work on a new painting, "County Election," his most ambitious picture to date. Encompassing some sixty figures, shown in painstaking detail in a remarkable variety of poses, "County Election" was a triumph.

Before long he was embarked on the even more ambitious "Verdict of the People," a robust and exciting panoramic view of a political contest at the instant when the final result of the ballot is proclaimed from the judges' stand. His crowning achievement, in the opinion of some critics, "Verdict of the People" was also his last picture of any serious artistic consequence.

Although he was now at the height of his fame as a painter, Bingham was still being ignored by the Eastern critics. Even at this point in his career, they contemptuously dismissed his canvases as "self-taught" and "untutored." Because he was absolutely determined to acquire the gloss and polish which impressed the East, Bingham decided to go to Europe for additional study. After a sojourn in Paris, where, like all visiting American artists, he spent countless hours in the Louvre, he went on to Düsseldorf, Germany, then the center of a thriving school of artists of many countries. He rented a house for himself and his family next door to the American painter Emanuel Leutze, the creator of "Washington Crossing the Delaware," and participated in the city's artistic life.

Bingham returned to the United States late in 1858, after an absence of three years, to find his native state and the nation in a turmoil. Abraham Lincoln was running against Stephen Douglas for the Presidency. The issue of slavery had boiled over into bitter dissension, the sovereignty of the Union was being forcefully challenged, neighbor was pitted against neighbor, and there was somber talk of war in the air.

In this atmosphere, Bingham again succumbed to the recurrent lure of politics. Although he still had twenty years to live, and those years were exciting and adventurous, they were almost meaningless so far as painting was concerned. The politician in Bingham had finally vanquished the artist.

He plunged headlong into the political whirlpool, announcing his position on the burning issue of the day in a ringing speech. "I am conditionally for man," he said, "though unconditionally for the Union!" Missouri voted overwhelmingly to remain in the Union. In 1862, Bingham was appointed State Treasurer.

The following year, he became embroiled in a famous cause célèbre that was to occupy him to his grave and—melodramatic though it may sound—beyond the grave.

On the 25th of August, 1863, the Union General Thomas Ewing, in an effort to end the raids along the Kansas-Missouri border by small bands loyal to both the Confederacy and the Union, issued Order Number 11. The order provided for the clearing out of various border communities. Regardless of whether their loyalties were to North or South, the residents of these communities were forcibly evicted, their homes burned and looted, and their livestock confiscated. If they resisted, they were shot down.

Bingham's always burning sense of justice was outraged. He confronted Ewing, and demanded the rescinding of Order Number 11. Ewing refused. "Then," said Bingham, breathing fire, "I shall make you infamous with my pen and brush!"

Riding out to the scene of the evacuations, he was horrified at the sight of men "shot down in the very act of obeying an order, and their wagons and effects seized by their murderers." Joining with other Missourians, Bingham succeeded in having Ewing removed by Lincoln to a command in St. Louis. But his private war against the general had barely begun.

After Lee's surrender at Appomattox, Bingham set out to make good his threat. He started a painting entitled "Order No. 11," in which he would expose the monstrous injustices perpetrated by General Ewing. Its completion was delayed while he painted a portrait in order to earn money; stood for nomination to Congress—and was defeated; and painted two pictures protesting what he felt was the unfair jailing of a Baptist clergyman who refused on religious grounds to take an oath of allegiance.

By the end of 1868, he had completed "Order No. 11." The picture was a crude and effective piece of propaganda, entirely lacking artistic merit. It depicts a family being forcibly evacuated, their home looted, the husband and father lying dead, the wife and mother prostrated with grief. A Negro slave and child, bowed with sorrow, are shown in the right foreground. In the background, other anguished victims are pictured against a horizon red with the flames of burning homes. Astride a horse sits General Thomas Ewing, stern and unyielding.

Bingham painted two identical pictures of "Order No. 11," one to be exhibited, the other to be used for an engraving for public distribution. He printed a circular to accompany the picture called "Address to the Public," in which he declared, "I could not find a nobler employment for my pencil than in giving . . . truthful representations . . . of the military rule which oppressed and impoverished large numbers of the best citizens of our state during the late sectional war."

Bingham now dedicated himself to traveling to various states, soliciting orders for his engravings, and rousing opinion against Ewing. His income had dwindled alarmingly, and he was compelled to fall back on such portrait work as he could find. His wife was seriously ill and his own health had become uncertain. In 1874, he accepted an appointment as Commissioner of the Kansas City police board for the income it provided. With his usual forthrightness, he promptly closed down the gambling houses, and forced the saloons to remain shut on the Sabbath. A short while later he was named Adjutant General of the State of Missouri. He was a good public servant: honest, fearless, tireless, a wrathful enemy of tyranny. One of his last acts as Adjutant General was to break up the Ku Klux Klan in Missouri, and imprison its leaders.

In the fall of 1876, Elizabeth Thomas Bingham died, leaving her husband alone and bereft at the age of sixty-five. He resigned from public office, and returned to his private war against General Ewing, who was now running for Congress. Although he received some support from Ewing's political opponents, the issue had grown stale, and the electorate uninterested. Ewing won the election easily. Bingham returned home dejected by his defeat, but a great honor awaited him;

he was named professor of the new Art School of the University of Missouri, the first school of its kind west of the Mississippi.

Earlier in the year, Bingham had met Mattie Lykins, the widow of a Kansas City doctor. They found solace in each other for their loneliness, and in June of 1878 they married. Bingham's contentment was short-lived. The name of his arch enemy, Ewing, now cropped up as presidential timber. Weakened though he was by a bout with pneumonia, Bingham renewed the attack. But the issue had been vitiated by the passage of time and by Ewing's prestige. Newspaper editorials inveighed against Bingham's stand, urging that the matter might best be forgotten. In a rage, Bingham began a vitriolic letter in reply, but collapsed before he was able to finish it. He had been stricken with cholera. Less than a week later, on July 7, 1879, George Caleb Bingham lay dead.

But the ghost of Bingham rose, and the ghost triumphed where the man had been unable to. In the midst of Ewing's campaign for Governor of the state of Ohio—which, it was understood, was to be a prelude to his seeking the Presidency—Bingham's son James released to the press his father's last, unfinished letter. Published under the ominous title of "A Voice from the Tomb," it disclosed hitherto unpublicized material. Ewing's political enemies were quick to make capital of the drama of the situation, and used it to defeat him. Bingham had won his final victory. Ewing's political career was brought to an abrupt end.

As, after his death, he triumphed over the forces of injustice, so, posthumously, did he gain the position that had been withheld from him in his lifetime. "The Fur Traders Descending the Missouri" today hangs prominently in the Metropolitan Museum of Art, a symbol of his acceptance—not alone by the West, but by all America—as a great American artist.

4

Missionary of the Modest Little Acre

GEORGE INNESS

1825–1894

Of the thirteen children of John William Inness and Clara Baldwin Inness, only the fifth, George, ever refused to follow in the footsteps of his father. Unlike the rest of the family, he had little esteem for the merchant. He was a dreamer. He wanted to be an artist.

In a last-ditch effort to divert George from a path that could only lead to a life of shiftless Bohemianism, his father bought him a grocery store. At the age of fourteen, George was installed as proprietor, with the anxious hope that blood would tell, that he would grow out of his distressing ambition and instead carve out a respectable future as a merchant.

But George had some ideas of his own. He smuggled in his brushes, canvas, paints, and an easel, and hid them away behind a counter. When customers ventured into the store, he hid himself behind the counter, and impatiently waited for them to go. One day, a little girl entered. More perceptive, and perhaps more patient than the adult customers, she sensed that the store was not empty. Jingling her pennies, she hopped as high as she could in an effort to see over the wooden counter. When it was certain that this small customer would not leave, George suddenly sprang up from behind the counter in a rage, and screamed at the startled child: "What in the name of all the devils do you want!"

"Candles! Candles! Candles!" shrieked the terrified child as she ran out the door.

With tight-lipped finality, George packed his painting materials, put up the wooden shutters, locked the door securely behind him and departed without a backward glance. His mercantile career was finished. Realizing the strength of his son's conviction, his father bowed to the inevitable. Nothing he could do or say would swerve George from his goal.

This resolution, this stubborn resistance were characteristic of George Inness. Throughout his life, he single-mindedly defied both tradition and contemporary trends. In a day when such artists as Albert Bierstadt and Frederick Church set the popular style with their huge panoramic landscapes, Inness tenaciously kept painting his modest little acre, his intimate vision of American soil. The unyielding Inness ultimately triumphed. He became America's finest landscape painter.

George Inness was born on May 1, 1825, on a farm two miles from the city of Newburgh, New York, where his father, John William Inness, had retired with his family to assure himself of a well-deserved rest from the labors of running a prosperous grocery business. During his infancy, the Inness family moved to New York City and four years later to the outskirts of Newark, New Jersey. George spent his childhood playing in the fields of what was then open, rolling country. He was a pale, none-too-robust, strong-willed child, nervous and "different" from the rest of his family. It is thought that he may have suffered from epilepsy in his boyhood, and this has been advanced as a possible reason for the emotional outbursts and periods of ill health that marked his adult years. His attendance at the local academies was short-lived. He was an incorrigibly poor student, refusing either to work or to conform. His teachers, exasperated by his behavior, declared he "would not take education." His parents recognized the futility of pushing him in a direction he refused to go, and withdrew him from school. Now young George was free to wander through the fields, in happy communion with nature.

Young George was fascinated by the occasional artist who came out to the country to paint the landscape, and presently himself came around to the view that painting the sky, the earth, the trees was a most suitable and congenial occupation. He didn't question his ability, only the impossibility of laying his hands on a sheet of paper large enough to contain the entire landscape, which spread so far and held so many objects! In later years, this same problem, translated from childish to adult terms, continued to plague him. It was many years before he found the solution, but when he did he gave to America a golden vision of her own land.

After the fiasco of the grocery store, George's father decided to follow the lines of least resistance and allow his son to take up the study of art. For a brief period George was apprenticed to a man named Barker, a teacher of painting and drawing in Newark. Before long, Barker admitted that George had absorbed all he had to give him. George's next apprenticeship, when he was sixteen, was to the firm of Sherman and Smith, map engravers in New York City. After a year, George's health suffered a serious decline, and he was forced to leave his position. Following a long period of enforced rest, he cast about for a master with whom to study, and decided upon a French painter named Régis Gignoux, who had settled in New York City.

At this time, the painting of the Hudson River School was in its ascendancy. Grand vistas of the American countryside, tightly painted and minutely detailed, were the prevalent concept of landscape art. Gignoux was a disciple of this school, and passed his methods on to his pupils. After a month of attempting to conform, Inness resigned, taking away with him what small knowledge he had gained about the handling of color and composition. Shortly afterward he married Delia Miller, a young girl whom he had known in Newark. She died six months later. Little is known of this brief affair. In his biography of his father, George Inness, Jr., merely remarks that the senior Inness was little affected.

There now ensued a curiously inconsistent relationship between what Inness felt he must do, and what he actually did. He recoiled from the tight, finicky landscapes of the Hudson River painters, yet he studied their work exhaustively. He wished to paint "nature . . . grand instead of being belittled by trifling detail and puny execution," yet he painted "trifling detail" with "puny execution." Perhaps he was not yet sure enough of his techniques to paint as he wanted to; perhaps the inconsistency was due to his somewhat erratic nature.

In 1845 he rented a studio in New York City. Ill health kept him from attending classes at the National Academy of Design, so he devoted himself to studying the engravings of the masters, and of such artists of the Hudson River School as Thomas Cole and Asher B. Durand. Mostly, though, he taught himself; he never ceased to observe nature, learning at first hand "the action of the clouds," responding to the emotions that the landscape awakened in him.

He exhibited some of his early landscapes at the National Academy Galleries. They were immature, tightly rendered pictures, crammed full of minute detail—precisely the formula his mind rejected. Only now and then did they show any hint of the later Inness in an elusive "tenderness" for the American landscape.

His canvases won little notice, nor brought any financial success. A friend declared that "to receive twenty-five dollars for a picture was a triumph for him." He paid for his board at the Astor House with his paintings, but it was the business-like generosity of his brothers that tided him over this lean period. They bought his paintings—and as soon as they could find a purchaser, they resold them.

It was Ogden Haggerty, a dry-goods auctioneer, who lent Inness the moral and financial support needed to reach his goal. One day, while Inness was painting out in the country, a small group of people gathered round to watch him. Presently, all but one man had drifted away. Approaching Inness, he said, "If you will bring the picture to my house when you finish it, I will give you a hundred dollars for it." So began the long friendship between the indigent artist and the perceptive merchant, who saw genius where others had thus far failed to do so.

In 1847, Ogden Haggerty generously offered to finance a trip to Europe to allow Inness to see and study the old masters. Inness spent more than a year abroad, mostly in Rome. After his return to the United States, his paintings began to show some of the impression the French and Italian masters had made on him. His brushwork had become freer, his composition simpler. Most important, he had learned to "see" landscape as a unified relationship of earth and sky.

For a number of years, Inness had joined a bewildering variety of religious denominations in a restless quest for spiritual fulfillment. The most recent of these affiliations was with the Baptist Church. Sitting at services one Sunday morning, his attention was attracted by a comely young woman. Smitten by her charm and beauty, he at once decided to marry her. After he had followed her home and learned her name, he set about with characteristic perseverance to woo her. His suit succeeded with the young lady. Although her family had objections to a son-in-law who was a ne'er-do-well artist, Elizabeth Hart married George Inness in 1850. Inness was twenty-five years old, his bride seventeen. Through the forty-odd years of their marriage, Elizabeth was a good wife, helpful, uncomplaining, modest in her demands. She guarded the purse strings against her husband's total inability to manage money; tempered his sometimes impulsive liberality; bought him new clothes before his old ones hung in tatters; and watched carefully over his delicate health. Through all her life, her faith in her husband's genius never wavered.

Shortly after the wedding, Ogden Haggerty proposed another trip to Europe, offering to assume the expenses for both the artist and his new bride. George and Elizabeth departed for the Continent, where they spent about fifteen months in Italy, and returned by way of Paris. In Europe the first of their children was born. There were subsequently five more children born to George and Elizabeth Inness, of whom all but one survived. They were Elizabeth, Rosa Bonheur (named after the French woman painter), George, Jr., who later became a painter, Louise, and Helen. Inness was a most devoted father. "His tenderness and love for the family," his son has recalled, "were beautiful. He sought to understand his children, and entered into their games and pleasures. . . ."

Inness and his family returned to the United States in
1852. He had begun to work out the ideas formulated during
his trip abroad. His canvases grew more assured technically,
his color warmer and more vibrant. However, he was still
painting pictures that were almost literal interpretations of
nature. He was exhibiting regularly at the National Academy
and had begun to build up a reputation as a fair landscape
painter. When he was twenty-eight years old, Inness was
voted an associate member of the Academy, but the coveted
full membership was denied him for another fifteen years.
Had he painted the grand, the gigantic, the theatrical
panorama, instead of the modest, intimately observed portion of the countryside, he would undoubtedly have been accorded this honor a great deal sooner.

Inness and his family sailed for Europe again in 1854. This
time they settled in the Latin Quarter of Paris, so that Inness
could conveniently study the great masters in the Louvre. A
group of French painters, known as the Barbizon School,
were currently attracting a great deal of attention. They had
abandoned the "false civilization of Paris," for the simplicity
of peasant life. Inness was immediately drawn by the spiritual
warmth of their paintings, although he found things to cavil
about in each individual artist. He also discovered the work
of the English landscape painter, John Constable, whose rich
tonalities impressed him and influenced his palette.

On their return to the United States in the same year, Inness established his family in living quarters in Brooklyn and
rented a studio in Manhattan. He worked tirelessly for the
next few years, struggling to achieve a personal style. His canvases were inconsistent and widely varied in their handling.
Breaking away from the tight mannerisms of the Hudson
River School proved difficult, despite the broader outlook he
had absorbed from the European painters. Even after his

eventual "breakthrough," his work occasionally reverted to the old mannerisms.

Inness could not find a ready market for his paintings. His work lacked the picturesque qualities that appealed to popular taste, and he was incapable of painting for mass appeal. With a wife and five children to support, he frequently found it hard to make ends meet. So, when he was offered the inadequate sum of seventy-five dollars by the president of the D. L. & W. Railroad to paint a picture of the line's roundhouse, he quickly accepted. He entrained for Scranton to make some on-the-scene sketches for the projected canvas. En route, he lost his baggage. Because of the delay involved until it was found, he ran out of money. He had been given just enough to get him to Scranton and back, since he was incapable of handling any sizable amount of cash. It was not until he had sent word to his wife about his predicament that he was able to continue the journey.

The completed painting was pronounced unsatisfactory by the purchaser, who insisted that all four of the road's trains be included as well as the letters D. L. & W. on the locomotive. Inness was outraged by this request, particularly since there had been only one train present when he had made his sketch. But Elizabeth Inness, practical in her outlook, persuaded him to comply with his client's demand. In "The Lackawanna Valley," as the picture is titled, Inness treated the rolling Pennsylvania countryside, as he said, in "the truest tone of nature . . . full of air." The picture was infused with a new depth of emotion and poetry of expression, marking the maturing of his love affair with the American soil. It was a major advance in the development of his work.

By a remarkable coincidence, "The Lackawanna Valley," which had been lost for many years, was found by Inness himself some thirty years after he had painted it. "When I was in Mexico City," he reported, "I picked it up in an old curiosity shop." Then, without any false modesty, he added, that "there is considerable power of painting in it, and the distance is excellent." Interestingly enough, the picture, which Inness painted for seventy-five dollars in 1855, sold for twenty-seven hundred dollars in 1927, and would bring many times that amount today.

In 1859, Ogden Haggerty urged Inness and his family to move to Boston. Here Haggerty believed Inness might find a more receptive market for his work, and he persuaded the firm of Williams and Everett, picture dealers, to become his agents.

Inness now entered the "middle period" of his career, a time in which he painted many of his finest works. In such canvases as "Delaware Water Gap," "Peace and Plenty," and "Hackensack Meadows," he imbued the familiar tranquillity of the landscape with a tender, poetic feeling. Under his brush, the prosaic fields were transformed into an emotional vision of the land, bathed in golden luminosity. He saw, as he said, "the mystery of nature with which wherever I went I was filled."

Inness had found a house for himself and his family in Medfield, a suburb of Boston. He worked in a barely furnished studio, located in an old barn on the property. His young son, even then aspiring to follow in his father's footsteps, helped wash the dirty paint brushes and in return was privileged to watch his father at work. Inness would attack a canvas with frenzied intensity, sometimes working as much as sixteen hours at a stretch. He became so absorbed in his work that he was oblivious of the passage of time and unaware of the pangs of hunger. His long hair flying wildly, his eyes burning behind steel-rimmed spectacles, he was a man possessed by the demon of artistic creation. The clothes he wore so carelessly would quickly become streaked with paint, bearing vivid witness to his color scheme of the moment. He rarely painted directly from nature, preferring to sit quietly for long periods absorbing the feeling of the countryside, observing the effect of the clouds, and the color of the landscape at different times of day. Then he made notes and sketches on the spot, and later developed his ideas in the studio. He painted rapidly, frequently finishing a canvas in a single day. But he found it impossible to refrain from reworking his pictures. A painting that he termed a masterpiece at completion was nothing but "dish water" or "twaddle" the next morning. Canvases that started out as evening scenes ended up as sunrise vistas; snow scenes changed to summer landscapes, marines to rolling countryside. It was not unusual for him to repaint his canvases as many as six times. This passion for revision, motivated by a desire to attain perfection, extended beyond his own studio; in his passion to see only a faultless canvas, he often repainted the work of his fellow artists. Because of this trait, he was expressly forbidden to enter the studio of the painter A. H. Wynant.

The famous picture called "Peace and Plenty" bears witness to Inness' insatiable urge to improve his own work. This large canvas, originally entitled "The Sign of Promise," had been a painting of a wheat field against a rainbowed sky. One day, it fell from the easel, the wet paint smearing over the canvas. This unhappy accident, which might have driven another painter to despair, merely provided Inness with an opportunity for improvement. He converted the original composition into a scene of the countryside, wheat fields now only in the foreground, lighted by the golden glow of the late-afternoon sun. Unlike most of his work, it was a huge canvas.

But, no less than his smaller landscapes, it is serene, peaceful, idyllic in mood—the exact opposite of the stormy nature of its creator.

When the Civil War began, Inness, an ardent Abolitionist, promptly volunteered for the army. Turned down for reasons of health, he worked hard for the Union cause by helping to raise money to feed, clothe, and arm the troops. He continued to paint, and was still producing many of his finest and most serene works during this time.

The years in Medfield were hardly prosperous. The paintings which would eventually be worth many thousands of dollars sold for a pittance. The problem of supporting his growing family continued to plague Inness. Yet, as always, he was completely without any sense of the value of money. Once, having just been paid for a painting, he dashed off to buy his wife a piece of expensive jewelry. Mrs. Inness, who loved her husband to a fault, expressed her pleasure at his thoughtfulness, and then proceeded to return the present to the jeweler and deposit the money in the bank. Had it not been for her level-headedness, the family might often have gone hungry.

Inness' individualism sometimes bordered on the eccentric. He had a passionate distaste for dentists, barbers, and new clothes. He dressed as he pleased, rather than as fashion dictated. Once, invited to dinner at the home of a very proper hostess, Inness chose to forgo the wearing of a tie. Mrs. Inness took him to task for this breach of etiquette and insisted he make amends the next day. Whereupon Inness enclosed a tie in a box and sent it to his hostess with a note saying that she was to keep the tie in her house for the same length of time he had spent there tieless the night before! On another occasion, when he was already a rich man, he went for a walk dressed in a disreputable old overcoat and an atrocity of a hat.

Mistaking him for a pauper, a photographer offered him a quarter to pose for a picture. Innes accepted. Asked to buy a pair of shoes for one of his children, he had a whole case of shoes sent home, paying for them with one of his paintings. If he was charged with the purchase of a pie plate, he bought, as his son relates, "a hogsheadful."

The recession that hit the nation at the close of the Civil War made the problem of feeding and clothing his family more acute than ever. Therefore, Inness was easily persuaded when Marcus Spring, a patron of the arts, suggested that he move from Massachusetts to Eagleswood, New Jersey. Spring, who became Inness' agent, knew a number of wealthy men in New Jersey who might be induced to buy paintings. He helped Inness build a house, for which he received "Peace and Plenty" as part payment. A few collectors did buy some of Inness' work, but not in sufficient quantity to make an appreciable improvement in the family's income. Inness also took some students in an effort to earn a little more money.

In the spring of 1867 the Innesses moved back to Brooklyn. The next few years were quiet and highly productive. Inness' reputation had been growing unspectacularly, but steadily, and in 1868 the National Academy finally granted him the status of full membership.

He might have bettered his financial position quickly, if he had not been, in the words of one critic, "capricious, headlong, impulsive." He believed that a client's reason for being began and ended with payment of the purchase price of a picture. He insisted that the artist did not relinquish ownership of his paintings even after they had been sold. If the artist wanted to take it back to work on, he had a sovereign right to do so.

He detested bargaining, feeling that to haggle degraded the artist. More than once he refused a sale, even though he needed money desperately, rather than "degrade" himself. On one occasion, a wealthy American financier came to his studio to look at two canvases, priced at five thousand dollars each. What price would Inness make him, he asked, if he took both pictures? "Ten thousand," Inness replied promptly. Another time, a client offered fifteen hundred dollars for a painting priced at two thousand dollars. Inness removed the picture, turned back to his easel, and said, "You will have to excuse me, I am not selling pictures today. I am very busy, and will bid you good day."

Criticism or suggestions from anyone but his very closest friends were intolerable to Inness. Comment from a mere client he regarded as the supreme insult. At a time when he was in serious financial straits, a wealthy lady client came to the studio, anxious to add to her collection of his work. Timidly, she advanced the hope that he might use the figure of a dog in one of the paintings. "Madame," Inness screamed, "you are a fool!" The woman was scandalized. Not only did she never again purchase an Inness painting, but she proceeded to sell those she owned.

In order to stimulate sales, Williams and Everett, Inness' dealers, suggested that he paint foreign subjects, offering to subsidize him if he went to Europe. Inness was outraged. "Nothing is good," he ranted, "without a foreign name on it. Why, when one of our biggest dealers on Fifth Avenue was asked to procure for a gentleman two American pictures for one thousand dollars each, he said he could not take the order because there was not a picture produced in America worth one thousand dollars. Why? Because they can go to Europe, buy a picture for twenty-five francs, with a foreign name on it, and sell it at a large profit!" But the urgency of Inness' need for money triumphed over his convictions, and once again, in the spring of 1870, he took his family to Europe.

After a brief sojourn in London and Paris, he went to Italy, where he remained for the next four years. A romantic at heart, Inness enjoyed visiting the birthplaces of the masters and imagining himself in their times. Study of their work helped to enrich his own paintings, which, increasingly, reflected the individuality of his vision. Unity, order, and realization were, he declared, the touchstones of a successful work of art. He tried to catch in his pictures the "solidity of objects and transparency of shadows in a breathable atmosphere through which we are conscious of spaces and distances."

A new crisis arose when a fire in Boston seriously damaged the firm of Williams and Everett, and they were forced to suspend payment to Inness for his pictures. He rushed back to the United States to see if he could make an arrangement with another dealer. The firm of Doll and Richards offered a contract in which they would handle his entire production, including his sketches, in return for advancing him a monthly stipend. Hard-pressed, Inness signed the contract, but within a few months the payments stopped, the firm insisting that they could not sell any of the paintings. After some litigation, as the result of which Doll and Richards were awarded "The Barberini Pines," Inness severed relations with them.

His family had followed Inness back to the United States. They lived in Boston briefly, then in New York, and finally rented a house in Montclair, New Jersey. During this rather unsettled period, Inness painted two landscapes that were a foreshadowing of his final concept of painting. "Autumn Oaks" and "Approaching Storm" were more fluid in form than his previous work, softer in brushwork and execution, showing a new concern with the play of light on landscape.

Inness was now fifty-three years old, respected in his field, but without any considerable earning power or reputation. His meeting with Thomas B. Clarke was to change all this. Clarke, a man of wealth, was the first to collect the works of Americans when all other collectors were buying only European art. He bought many of Inness' paintings, became his close friend and later his agent. Most important, he conveyed his belief in Inness' genius to wealthy and discerning clients. Among them was Roswell Smith, the founder of the *Century Magazine*, who bought a painting for five thousand dollars. Before long, Inness' income skyrocketed and he was able to afford a large home for his family and many of the luxuries that he had previously been forced to deny them. His days of struggle were over.

The final period of Inness' life was easy and affluent. But his passion for painting remained to the end as compulsive and intense as ever. For a brief time, he interested himself in painting the figure, but soon returned to his beloved landscapes. He began, knowingly or not, to work in the manner of the French Impressionists who were beginning to revolutionize the concepts of art. Like theirs, his paintings became less realistic, the objects in them vaguer in shape, almost misty. Nature's forms were diffused in a shimmering mist of light. Trees, sky, and earth merged into a radiant dream of the land.

Inness objected violently to being labeled an impressionist. In a letter to a newspaper, he wrote: ". . . when people tell me that the painter sees nature in the way the Impressionists paint it, I say, 'Humbug!' . . ." Despite this disavowal, he went on with typical contrariness to say he devoutly believed that the "purpose of the painter is simply to reproduce in other minds the impression which a scene has made upon him."

Inness' enjoyment of his new prosperity and fame was clouded by failing health. The years of deprivation and struggle had taken their toll of his always frail constitution. His doctor ordered him to take a sea voyage for the sake of his health. Accompanied by his loving and devoted Elizabeth, Inness sailed abroad on his last passage. From England they proceeded to Bridge-of-Allan, a tiny hamlet in Scotland. On the evening of August 3, 1894, while his wife was dressing for dinner, Inness decided to walk out to look at the sunset. A few minutes later, he collapsed. Shortly after Elizabeth reached him he was dead.

It was a somber voyage back to America for the grieving widow. Perhaps it was some consolation that the honors withheld so long while he lived were not denied to him in death. His funeral was held in the galleries of the National Academy, where his body lay in state. The casket was of silver and velvet covered with palm leaves, wreaths of white roses, ivy and lilies-of-the-valley. A bust of Inness stood at the foot of the bier. Black bunting draped the balustrade of the staircase. The Academy flew its flag at half mast. Friends, collectors, fellow artists came great distances to pay their last respects.

Newspaper obituaries followed suit in granting Inness the full measure of recognition he deserved. The *New York Times* said, "He had obtained glory more solid, more durable and more universal than many great men of his time." In the Boston *Transcript* the noted critic Walter Church paid tribute to ". . . America's greatest landscape painter." Another paper wrote that he was "the pioneer . . . of American landscape painting," still another that "he towered as a giant."

Inness probably would not have quarreled with these judgments.

5

The Yankee Individualist

WINSLOW HOMER

1836–1910

Early in his life, Winslow Homer declared: ". . . I have had no master; and never shall have any."

This credo lasted him a lifetime. He followed his own lead, seeking the truth not along the well-traveled roads of conformity, but through whatever byways his own honesty and keen observation led him. In an era when idealized beauty, noble sentiment, or the grandiose was the accepted standard of art, he painted his own brand of realism with an imperturbable disregard for what was fashionable. This "Yankee of Yankees," as he was once called, became the greatest marine painter America has ever known. And, almost singlehandedly,

60

he rescued the art of watercolor painting from its low status as "colored drawing," elevating it to the highest plane of artistic expression.

Winslow Homer's Yankee heritage traced back through a line of rugged, long-lived Boston merchants. Charles Savage Homer, his father, following a family tradition, was an importer of hardware. Henrietta Maria Benson Homer, his mother, was a Maine Yankee. She was a well-educated woman, a fairly gifted painter of floral watercolors. Her interest in art was not mere ladylike dalliance, but a genuine devotion that continued throughout her life. Relatives and friends of the family were inclined to give Mrs. Homer the credit for her son's talent. "He got it all from his mother," a cousin of Winslow's once said. "She was always painting pictures. I went to see her just before Winslow was born, and she had on a big pinafore and was standing before a large easel painting."

Shortly after this visit, on February 24, 1836, Winslow Homer made his appearance in the world. The second of three sons, Winslow got on extremely well with his brothers, Charles, Jr., and Arthur. Indeed, the whole of the family, including the future daughters-in-law, were an extraordinarily close-knit clan.

When Winslow was about six years old, his parents moved from Boston to nearby Cambridge, where Winslow attended the Washington Grammar School. He was "a nice boy—studious, quiet, sedate," said a schoolmate. His artistic bent first manifested itself in the form of drawings on the flyleaves of his textbooks. His mother, although she dutifully scolded him, was delighted by her son's display of talent. She persuaded her husband to buy a series of lithographs illustrating the various parts of the head, as well as trees, houses, and animals, which Winslow could copy. Young as he was, Winslow's drawings were unusually strong and full of character. Each finished picture was fully signed and dated, in serious childish imitation of his mother's practice.

As is usually the case with landscape painters, Winslow's love of nature was equal to his passion for drawing. Hiking, fishing, exploring the countryside were alluring diversions which attracted him all his days. Later, when he got a job that required him to report for work at eight o'clock, he would rise at three in the morning, and go fishing before breakfast. As he grew older, this love of the country kept him content to live alone in a Maine seacoast cottage, not only in fair weather, but through the long, freezing, desolate winters.

In 1849, Winslow's father, succumbing to the gold fever, left to join the rush to California. After two years he returned home, richer only in experience, and buckled down once again to being a hardware merchant. In his absence, Charles, Jr., had attended Harvard College, but Winslow was showing signs of balking at the prospect of further education. He cared only about drawing. When it was suggested that he attend Boston's only art school, the Lowell Institute, young Winslow declined. He preferred to work out his problems in his own way. The elder Homer knew that his son would not consider entering the family business, so he set about looking for a job congenial to Winslow's interests. One morning his eye was attracted by an advertisement seeking an apprentice for Bufford's lithographic plant—a boy with "a taste for drawing." Mr. Homer promptly dispatched Winslow to Bufford's for an interview. It was customary in those days for an apprentice to pay the firm three hundred dollars to learn the trade. After a year of service, the apprentice received a weekly stipend of five dollars. The people at Bufford's were so impressed with Winslow's ability that they consented to reduce the initial payment to one hundred dollars.

Winslow Homer was nineteen years old when he began his apprenticeship, a short, wiry young man with a remarkably erect posture. He was so proud of his bearing that he performed his work standing, for fear that sitting on a stool might cause him to become round-shouldered. His dark brown hair, mustache and beard framed a strong, handsome head from which hazel eyes looked squarely at the world.

Homer detested his job at Bufford's. He found the work—which consisted of drawing covers for popular sheet music, cards, posters, and advertisements—a boring and unrewarding grind. He was extremely quiet and reserved, and rarely spoke his mind. When he did, he came right to the point. A fellow employee, who knew of his ambition to become a painter, once asked him what sort of pictures he would like to paint. Homer looked at the second-rate landscape he was copying and, without a moment's hesitation, declared, "Something like that, only a damned sight better."

Homer waited until the day of his twenty-first birthday before he quit his job. He then rented a studio of his own, convinced that he could earn a living as a free-lance illustrator. His first assignment was a drawing for Ballou's, a firm which published a number of periodicals that were "beautiful specimens of art and pleasing and pure caskets of literature." When *Harper's Weekly* was launched, Homer sent the magazine some drawings depicting the life of an undergraduate at Harvard. They were accepted, and published in an August, 1857, issue. Thereafter, he flooded *Harper's* with drawings of various aspects of the urban and rural life of the time. All were accepted. Inside of two years, he had become one of the country's leading illustrators.

In the fall of 1859, he moved from Boston to New York, the hub of the publishing and art worlds. He rented a room in a boardinghouse on East Sixteenth Street, and a studio on

Nassau Street in lower Manhattan. With his living assured, he now began to prepare himself to become a painter. He attended classes at the National Academy of Design, but his individuality balked at following traditional teaching methods, and he soon quit. In any event, only drawing was taught at the Academy's school, and it was painting that he was interested in. Previously, he had turned down a lucrative offer of a full-time position with *Harper's* because he "had had a taste of freedom," and refused to be tied down to a daily routine. However, he still did free-lance work for the magazine.

In March, 1861, *Harper's* assigned Homer to cover Lincoln's Presidential Inauguration in Washington. His drawing of the event was given two pages in the magazine. With the outbreak of the Civil War, *Harper's* commissioned him as a war correspondent. Little interested by the great issues of the war, although his general sympathies lay with the North, Homer was fascinated by the daily routine of the soldier, the commonplace, unheroic existence of army life. By the time he returned from the battleground to New York he had amassed sufficient material for many years of work. Some of his sketches were later used as the basis for a series of paintings. He visited the front several times more and was present at Lee's exhausted defeat.

Homer's interest in illustration was fading. *Harper's* received fewer and fewer contributions from his pen. Increasingly, he was becoming preoccupied with painting. Several years later, he had taken a few lessons from Frédéric Rondel, an obscure French artist, persisting only long enough to learn the bare essentials of applying color and handling brushes. With this meager background, at the age of twenty-six he painted his first two serious canvases. Both were war scenes. One depicted a sharpshooter drawing a bead on a Rebel soldier, the other showed a soldier undergoing punishment for drunkenness. These two paintings were to be his acid test, he wrote his brother Charles. On their reception alone would depend his fate as an artist. If they sold he would continue to paint; if not, then he would accept the job as staff artist that *Harper's* had again offered, and forget all about art. On this slender thread hung the future of one of America's great painters.

Unlike most dedicated artists, Homer was not prepared to starve for his art. He believed, in true Yankee fashion, that art was a business, and that one must earn a living by it. As he grew older, this attitude became even more pronounced. He was constantly threatening to give up his "business," as he called it, whenever sales were slow. Whether he would actually have stopped painting if his first pictures had failed to sell there is no way of knowing. Fortunately, the issue was never put to a test. His brother Charles secretly bought both paintings, swearing the dealer to silence. It was only after many years that Homer discovered the truth, and, when he did, he flew into a rage, refusing to speak to Charles for some time. He saw the deception as a reflection on his Yankee independence.

With no reason to doubt the authenticity of the purchases at the time they occurred, Homer now plunged in. After painting several more war pictures, he turned to scenes of country life. Although his canvases were awkward compared to the work of his maturity, they were notable for an honesty and freshness of observation. Despite the untutored use of color and the faulty brushwork, his early work contained more than a hint of his eventual mastery. Nowhere did Homer seek to imitate any other artist. He painted what he saw as he saw it.

Recognition came quickly. By the time he was twenty-nine,

he had been voted a full member of the powerful National Academy, one of the youngest artists to have been granted this honor. When the spring exhibition of the Academy opened in 1866, Homer was represented by his largest and most ambitious canvas to date. Titled "Prisoners from the Front," it shows a well-dressed Union officer pensively regarding a group of shabby captured Confederate soldiers. Despite the pointed contrast between the victor and the defeated, the picture expressed understanding and sympathy for both. Completely absent were the posturing attitudes and heroic symbolism commonly found in scenes of victory. "Prisoners from the Front" created immediate and widespread interest. "No picture has been painted in America in our day," said one critic, "that made so deep an appeal to the feelings of the people." The painting was shortly purchased by John Taylor Johnston, an important collector, later the first president of the Metropolitan Museum. Homer's reputation was established overnight.

At the end of the year, Homer went abroad, having first held a sale of his paintings to raise money for passage. When he arrived in Paris he found a studio in the Montmartre section, an area famous for its artistic tradition. Typically, he did not enroll in an atelier to study, but wandered through the city sketching Parisian life. The ten months he spent in Paris, in the midst of artistic revolt, seems to have had little or no effect on his ruggedly individualistic viewpoint. Undoubtedly he visited the galleries of the Louvre, but if he was excited by the great masterpieces of the past he did not record the fact. He enjoyed the colorful daily life of Paris as a spectator, not a participant. When his money ran out, he returned to America.

Once again he turned to illustration to replenish his depleted funds. His work was in demand not only by magazines but by book publishers as well. Many of his illustrations and paintings during this period were of children and young women. For the first time the American girl was depicted neither as languorously swooning nor excessively prim. Homer portrayed her as she was—healthy, interested, and alive. He made a number of paintings of country and resort areas in which the landscape was subordinate to the figure. As his technique steadily improved, his colors became purer, his compositions more decorative.

Early in 1872 he moved to studios on Tenth Street. The building housed a number of artists, many of whom became his friends. One of them, John La Farge, has said of Homer, "He was a quiet man, not given to saying much. He had manners of telling things without words." Homer dressed in the fashion of the day, in a checked suit, high collar, and a bowler hat. He still wore a regimental mustache although the beard had disappeared. His characteristic close-mouthedness extended even to art. One of his friends declared that he had never "heard what he [Homer] thought or said of the great masters' work. He might have been as silent upon that subject as on most."

Homer was at the top of his profession as an illustrator, and might have become a rich man if he had continued in the field. But he begrudged the time it stole from his painting, and began to withdraw from it. He had been experimenting with watercolor for several years, and was eager to devote more effort to mastering this difficult medium. His first attempts were conventional except in their use of sparkling color. Homer had a natural feeling for this medium, and it was not long before he was using it with such boldness and directness that it revolutionized the entire approach to watercolor. Where previously it had been treated as an opaque medium which could be overpainted, he handled it with deft swiftness, laying down the clear, limpid color in brilliant transparencies. To the end of his life, he divided his time between painting in oil and in watercolor, producing some extraordinary work in each medium.

The watercolors were well received from the start. His oils, with the exception of "Prisoners from the Front," enjoyed less success. The critics were offended by his subjects, which they considered not "quite refined." Commonplace pursuits such as people bathing in the surf were considered not lofty or pretty enough for a painting. Nor did Homer's technique have the polish so necessary to a work of art. One critic complained that ". . . with a few dashes of the brush, he suggests a picture, but a mere suggestion only, and it is a mistaken eccentricity which prevents its finish." But Henry James, the great American novelist, who was then an art critic, wrote: "He is almost barbarously simple, and to our eye, he is horribly ugly; but there is nevertheless something one likes about him. . . . He has chosen the least pictorial features of the least pictorial range of scenery and civilization; he has resolutely treated them as if they *were* pictorial . . . and, to reward his audacity, he has incontestably succeeded."

Had he wanted to, Homer could have done a thriving business in the sale of his watercolors. But, despite his avowals to the contrary, he was much more interested in the pursuit of his vision than in money. He continued to paint as he pleased, always searching to express deeper meanings in both his watercolors and his oils. In the National Academy show of 1876 he exhibited "A Fair Wind," which was "settled upon as the author's greatest hit since 'Prisoners from the Front.'" His name was now frequently mentioned in art magazines, and a number of articles were devoted entirely to his work. Homer's reaction to these portents of budding fame was the vinegary comment, "For fifteen years the press has

called me 'a promising young artist,' and I am tired of it."
Although his pictures had always sold well, few brought in
any sizable amount of money. "There were times and seasons," a friend said, "when he announced to friends with
great bitterness and the utmost solemnity that he proposed to
abandon art for business." Of course he never did.

Never a particularly gregarious soul, Homer had for several years begun to withdraw from social contacts. Although
no details are known, it is thought that he had been deeply
wounded in an unhappy love affair, and as a consequence retired into himself. In any event, he never married. By the time
he reached his mid-forties, he was recognized as one of
America's leading painters. As his reputation grew, so did his
hermitlike behavior. According to one of his friends, "He
would hardly open his door in response to a knock, and when
he did, he would open it for a few inches . . . and the
chances were that he would make some excuse not to let you
in." On one occasion, Homer invited a fellow artist to drop
in at his studio. When the friend arrived Homer peered from
behind his canvas, identified the man, and then announced
that he was too busy to see him. But "his friends gradually
became reconciled," according to one of his colleagues, "instead of resenting, they accepted his moods and left him
alone."

In the spring of 1881, Homer sailed for England—a move
that was to prove vital to his development as an artist. He
went to a small fishing village near Tynemouth, on the North
Sea. Here he discovered a new kind of people—the rugged,
heroic fishermen who fought the unyielding sea for their
living. These people became the subject for some of his most
evocative pictures. He spent two seasons studying the sea and
the fisherfolk, making countless drawings, sketches and watercolors. Rigidly disciplining himself, he worked directly from

nature, drawing his subjects over and over again, laboring with infinite patience to perfect technique, color, and brushwork.

The English watercolors and drawings he brought back found immediate success. His oils, although they were larger and more mature, did not fare as well. But Homer was scarcely interested in his reception. He was too immersed in the new path he had discovered to care about such unimportant matters. In the summer of 1883, in Atlantic City, he painted the two best oils of his career to that point, "The Life Line" and "Undertow." Both were dramatic pictures of actual events: one a rescue of a woman by a seaman in a breeches buoy, the other of four people struggling desperately against the savage tug of the undertow. Using as a guide sketches he had made on the scene, he finished the pictures on the roof of his New York studio, posing models drenched with water to catch the true effect of light on wet skin. His handling of "The Life Line" marked a significant improvement in his artistry. The painting of the stormy ocean in muted tones of greens and grays, the rhythm and boldness of the design evoked cries of "masterpiece" when the picture was exhibited at the Academy in 1884.

Homer was fascinated by the sea. He gave up his New York studio and moved to Prouts Neck, Maine, where he could live with the water at his door. This gaunt, rocky, forbidding coast of the Atlantic Ocean was to be his permanent home for the rest of his life. He moved into the large house bought by his brother Charles for his mother and father. Brother Arthur and his family were also part-time residents at Prouts Neck. Shortly after his mother's death, in 1888, Homer moved into the stable, which he altered to serve as his living quarters. A huge porch on the second floor gave him a splendid view of the ocean, and he frequently painted there when the weather was good. He also had a portable "painting house" built on wheels for use in inclement weather. It was heated by a stove, and had a large glass window, and could be pushed to any site where he wished to paint.

Despite the nearness of his family, Homer preferred to live alone. His only companion was a little dog called Sam. When Sam died, Homer was heartbroken. He obstinately refused to buy another dog, insisting that he could not risk becoming so attached again. When his brother Charles suggested a new dog to ward off burglars, Homer replied crustily, "As for robbers I have no fear of them, sleeping or waking. I am a dead shot and should shoot, without asking any questions, if anyone was in my house after 12 night." Homer did his own cooking, and was something of an epicure. He raised vegetables and flowers, and even experimented one year with growing his own tobacco. His simply furnished studio was cluttered with painting gear and all manner of hunting and fishing equipment, even including a large canoe.

The harshness of the Maine winter—"night before last it was 12 below zero here"—did not seem to bother him. When his New York dealer sent him a telegram, Homer replied testily, "I do not keep a horse & my nearest neighbor is half a mile away—I am four miles from telegram & P.O. & under a snow bank most of the time, so I *cannot answer telegrams.*" He welcomed the onset of cold weather because it marked the departure of the summer residents. "I like my home more than ever as people thin out," he said. The fall and winter seasons brought him a stormy sea, the sea he loved best. A calm ocean he referred to as "that duck pond."

Before long, Homer had earned a reputation as a recluse. It was a label, however, that he found offensive. In a letter to a friend he wrote, "I deny that I am a recluse as is generally understood by that term. Neither am I an unsociable hog. I wrote you it's true that it was not convenient to receive a visitor, that was to save you as well as myself. Since you must know it I have never yet had a bed in my house. I do my own work. . . . This is the only life in which I am permitted to mind my own business. . . . I am perfectly happy & contented." Whatever aspect he presented to the outside world, his relations with his family and neighbors were warm and cordial. Homer was very fond of children. He occasionally permitted them to enter his studio while he worked, whereas he refused the same privilege to all adults. He was the soul of generosity and the anonymous donor of many gifts to his needy neighbors.

New vistas opened up to him when for the first time he spent part of a winter in Nassau and Bermuda. The brilliant tropical sunlight upon the clear blue waters and the lithe, brown, sun-drenched bodies of the Negroes fascinated him. The watercolors he made of this scene were the finest he had ever done—bold, vivid, and stirring. He himself was aware of the merit of these paintings. "You will see," he said to a friend, "in the future I will live by my watercolors." He was only half right. He lives by his watercolors *and* his oils.

As Homer's work in oil matured, his canvases depended less and less on dramatic or storytelling content for their effect. The dominant theme of his work settled on the basic relationship between man and his environment. He produced fewer pictures, but they were simpler, more thoughtfully composed, and handled with consummate skill. As always, after he had carefully selected his subject, he would "paint it exactly as it appears." The desire to catch the precise effects of light and weather sometimes led him to extreme measures. In "Early Morning After a Storm at Sea," one of his best works, he patiently waited for two years to catch the exact atmospheric conditions he wanted.

As Homer approached his sixtieth year, he found himself deluged with honors. The Pennsylvania Academy purchased his "Fox Hunt." The Boston Museum acquired "The Fog Warning." He received his first major award in 1895 when he won the Pennsylvania Academy's Gold Medal of Honor. A critic who reviewed the exhibition wrote, "No painter in America is superior to Mr. Winslow Homer, and in painting the sea it is doubtful if he has an equal here or elsewhere." *Scribner's* magazine called him "the Walt Whitman of our painters." The following year, his painting "The Wreck" was awarded the Carnegie Institute's first prize of five thousand dollars. Many more honors were heaped upon Homer, but he was not impressed by his success. Some of his medals were thrown carelessly among his paints and brushes in the studio. One he carried in his pocket, along with a buttonhook and his house key. The only one he seemed to hold in esteem was a medal from the Paris Exposition. This he carried in the breast pocket of his jacket; and it was reported to have been discovered in the pocket of his nightshirt as he lay dying.

In the fall of 1899, at the age of sixty-three, Homer began work on his most famous painting, "The Gulf Stream." It was composed from notes made on one of his periodic trips to the West Indies, and depicted a Negro sailor lying apathetically on the tilted deck of a disabled boat drifting on shark-infested waters. He sent the canvas to his dealer in New York, urging that it be sold quickly. The dealer replied, informing him that a group of women queried the picture's meaning. "You can tell these ladies," Homer responded dryly, "that the unfortunate negro who's now so dazed & parboiled, will be rescued & returned to his friends and home & ever after live happily." Oddly enough, "The Gulf Stream" was received unenthusiastically by both the critics and the public, and it remained unsold. But when Homer sent it to the

National Academy exhibition in 1906, the reaction of his fellow artists was overwhelming and instantaneous. ". . . there was a murmur of admiration, and then someone called out, 'Boys, that ought to be in the Metropolitan.' " A letter was immediately dispatched to the Metropolitan Museum urging the picture's purchase, and signed by all the members of the jury. A few days later, the Museum announced the purchase of "The Gulf Stream" for forty-five hundred dollars.

Homer remained spry and active for most of his life. When dressed for an occasion, he looked more than anything else like a prosperous businessman. Although he was considered America's most important painter, his best works were still attacked for their "ugliness." He became increasingly sensitive to criticism, and, more than ever, "cussed" when his privacy was invaded. Interviewers were turned away abruptly. Even prospective buyers of his pictures got a cold reception. "I don't want to see them at all," he complained. In response to a request asking him to receive several distinguished members of the Academy, he declined testily, saying that he had no time to meet "art students." When a writer proposed to do his biography, Homer was aghast. "I think it would probably kill me to have such a thing appear, and as the most interesting part of my life is of no concern to the public I must decline to give you any particulars in regard to it."

His health now began to fail. In the summer of 1908 he suffered a slight stroke. His brother Arthur had him moved into his home to nurse. One morning Homer was gone. On a small piece of paper pinned to the pillow, he had laconically noted that he felt well and "had quit." He had returned to his own house and resumed work. "I am making arrangements," he had once declared, "to live as long as my Father & both my grand Fathers—all of them over eighty-five." Despite the precarious state of his health, he insisted on living alone. His only concession was to hire a local man to look in on him every day to see if he was alive or dead. As an additional caution, the postman was asked to knock when he delivered the mail. If Homer did not shout an answer, the door was to be broken down, and Charles was to be informed.

At the easel his power remained undimmed, his hand steady. His last work, "Driftwood," was as strong and sure as any he had done before his illness. Indeed, the color was even subtler in harmony, the composition more delicately balanced.

In the late summer of his seventy-fourth year, Homer was suddenly stricken with a cerebral hemorrhage. For about a week he lay in a delirium. When his mind cleared, it was discovered that he had become blind. By September, he was confidently planning a fishing trip with Charles and talking about painting again as soon as he had recovered his sight, which he had no doubt would happen. He was bored by his invalidism, and impatiently pressed to be "allowed to have a drink and a smoke." He felt himself to be on the mend, but death claimed him at 1:30 P.M. on September 29, 1910. He had failed by ten years and five months to reach the age of his long-lived forebears.

Winslow Homer was cremated and a service was held on October 3 at Mount Auburn Cemetery in Cambridge, Massachusetts. Only twenty-five people attended. The ceremony was starkly simple, without music or eulogy. His ashes were put to rest alongside his mother's grave. The last words spoken, before the funeral party disbanded, were those of a Maine neighbor. He said:

"We shall miss him for a long time to come."

6

The Outcast

THOMAS EAKINS

1844–1916

If Thomas Eakins had ever learned to compromise with his principles, he might have spared himself much suffering and defeat. But he could neither paint nor live a lie. Honesty, integrity, and the unremitting search for truth were as vital to his existence as his heartbeat. He held himself responsible to the stiffest tests that could be devised by an unyielding conscience.

Yet neither his virtues nor his extraordinary talent won him any laurels. Except for a few belated crumbs of recognition, he was denied his proper place in the world of art throughout his lifetime. Only when he was past enjoying it—when he was already in his grave—was he finally to gain acceptance as one of the greatest painters of his century.

Thomas Cowperthwait Eakins, first child and only son of Benjamin and Caroline Cowperthwait Eakins, was born in Philadelphia on July 25, 1844. He was descended from a mixed strain of Scotch-Irish, English and Dutch forebears. His grandparents were minor artisans—one a cobbler, the other a weaver. His father earned his livelihood as a writing master, or teacher of penmanship.

Thomas was two years old when the family moved to the house on quiet, respectable Mount Vernon Street where he lived almost the whole of his life. Here his three sisters were born—Frances, Margaret, and Caroline. The family led a modest but comfortable existence, in an atmosphere that was warm, liberal, and obedient to high moral standards.

Early in his young life, Thomas showed signs of a marked aptitude not only for drawing, but for science and mechanics as well. He was a friendly, cheerful, and more than ordinarily intelligent child. He shared with his father an intense enjoyment of outdoor sports. Together, father and son would engage in such activities as hunting, sailing, fishing, and ice skating. Both were excellent skaters. His father prided himself on the fancy figures he could perform, while Thomas' specialty was skating backward as fast as most people did forward.

At thirteen, Thomas was admitted to Central High School, the oldest secondary school in the United States. He was two years younger than the average student in a school geared to provide, in four years, the equivalent of a college education. He studied mathematics, history, languages, science, and drawing. He was a serious, capable student, strong in all his subjects. In the drawing class he was clearly outstanding. On graduating at the age of seventeen, he was awarded a Bachelor of Arts degree. He modestly declined to deliver a speech at the commencement exercises, stating that he had nothing original to say. Whatever he had learned, he added with his inherent honesty, could easily be learned by anyone else from the same books.

For a short period after graduating, young Thomas helped his father with his penmanship classes. Often, he would go out sketching with his friends, one of whom was William Sartain, the son of John Sartain, the engraver of George Caleb Bingham's paintings. At other times, he would go hunting or fishing with his father. He was also fond of boating and swimming. At the same time, his eager mind was anything but idle. He read science periodicals with avid interest, and taught himself French and Italian well enough so that he could converse in both languages. He had become so proficient in Latin while at school that he could speak even in that difficult tongue.

Tall, powerfully built, and proud of his strong constitution, young Thomas had inherited his father's Irish looks and his mother's dark complexion, dark brown eyes, and black hair. His manner was serious and thoughtful; his bearing reflected the proud independence of his spirit and mind. In a conservative age, he was a freethinker and an agnostic.

In 1861, the same year in which he had received his degree, Thomas Eakins entered the Pennsylvania Academy of Fine Arts. Although it was the oldest institution of its kind in the United States, the Academy was a mediocre school. Instruction was unorganized and indifferent, consisting in the main of drawing from plaster casts. So rigidly was this routine applied that Eakins acquired a lifelong antipathy to copying from the antique. Occasionally the students themselves hired a live model to pose for them, under the strict regulations then in force: talking between model and students was prohibited; and female nude models were chaperoned and required to wear masks over their faces.

From the very beginning, Eakins was fascinated by the human being as a subject. With typical thoroughness, he enrolled in the anatomy courses given at Jefferson Medical College, in order to learn everything he could about the human figure. He labored as tirelessly as the medical students, attending lectures and operations, dissecting cadavers, mastering the intricacies of human anatomy as thoroughly as any surgeon. Meanwhile, he kept up his full-time studies at the Academy.

In his five years at art school, Eakins received no instruction in painting. So, however reluctant he was to part from the affection and understanding of his family, he knew that he had to go to Europe to complete his training. His father agreed, and generously offered to finance his study. In September, 1866, Eakins sailed for France. He was twenty-two years old and impatient to probe the mysteries that lay before him.

Arriving in Paris, he settled in a *pension*, and immediately applied for admission to the Ecole des Beaux-Arts. In October he was accepted, and chose as his master Jean Léon Gérôme, the school's foremost teacher, and himself a distinguished artist. Full of anticipation, Eakins entered his class on the first morning, only to find himself the butt of his fellow students. As a *nouveau* he was teased mercilessly, baited with insults and crude practical jokes. Eakins responded quietly and in well-spoken French to his tormentors, determined to keep a firm grip on his temper. At the end of the day, he thanked them for their "kind attention." The next morning, he cheerfully and uncomplainingly performed such menial chores as lighting the fire and running errands, which, he was informed, fell to the lot of the newcomer. He was the only

American in the school until the arrival of his friend, Henry Humphreys Moore, a former classmate at the Pennsylvania Academy. To shield Moore, who was a deaf mute, from the hazing of the French students, Eakins begged them "not to amuse themselves at his expense." Not only did he appoint himself Moore's protector, but he also taught himself the sign language in order to communicate with his friend. Some time later, the two Americans were joined by William Sartain, who had also come to Europe to study.

Having learned the elements of drawing from the ground up—from mechanical drawing and perspective to the anatomy of the human figure—Eakins now began his education as a painter. Gérôme adhered to the classical method of instruction. A careful drawing from the nude was first made with the brush, and then rendered in color. The tight academic approach of Gérôme appealed to Eakins' passion for thoroughness, but did not satisfy his unquenchable curiosity. He rented a studio where he could experiment with the complexities of color in his spare time. He continued his anatomical studies in the Beaux-Arts' dissecting room, and in the Paris hospitals. To round out what he considered to be the fundamentals of the study of art, he also attended a class in sculpture.

For the next two years, Eakins worked like a man possessed, although he did allow himself some freedom to participate in the lively student life of Paris. "I have tried to act in moderation," he assured his father, "without being liberal like a poor man or mean as a rich one." His conscience never felt entirely free of the obligation he owed to the elder Eakins. "I hope not to be a drag upon you a great while longer," he wrote earnestly to his parent.

Aided by his command of the French language, which he spoke fluently, Eakins made many friends among his fellow students. On the rare instances when he allowed himself some diversion, he accompanied them to the opera, the circus, or the races at Longchamps. To keep himself in good physical condition, he spent a few hours each week wrestling with his French friends. In the art exhibitions which he visited, he looked only at the academic paintings. He displayed no interest in the experiments of the Impressionist movement. The furor over the exclusion from the exhibition of the Universal Exposition of 1867 of two of France's future great painters, Manet and Courbet, meant nothing to him. The intensity of his concentration on his own development as a painter allowed little emotion to spare for the problems of others.

By the fall of 1869, Eakins felt that he had learned everything he could from his master. "I am as strong as any of Gérôme's pupils, and I have nothing now to gain by remaining," he wrote. Meanwhile, his self-doubt, his grimly hard work had begun to show their effects. "For a long time," he confessed, "I did not hardly sleep at nights, but dreamed all the time about color and forms. . . ." In his debilitated condition, he contracted a severe cold from which he could not recover. He fled to the warmth of Spain, hoping that a change of climate might revive him.

In Madrid, Eakins went to the galleries of the Prado Museum, where he found little to admire. With the exception of Rembrandt, he was indifferent to the painters of the Dutch school. Of one of Titian's canvases, he commented only on its badly cracked condition. Goya he found fault with, and Rubens he declared to be "the nastiest most vulgar noisy painter that ever lived." But the realism of the Spanish masters Velázquez and Ribera moved him profoundly; particularly the masterful control of Velázquez' technique and color, and above all his penetration of the depths of human character. For the first time, with a sense of revelation, he knew how he was going to paint. Although he retained a lifelong devotion to Gérôme, it was now clear that he must travel a different path. He transmitted some of his excitement in a letter to his father. "In a big picture," he wrote, "you can see what o'clock it is, afternoon or morning, if it's hot or cold, winter or summer, and what kind of people are there, and what they are doing and why they are doing it." This was the credo that would govern his painting from that time forward.

After he had moved on to Seville, he started his first creative painting, "A Street Scene in Seville," portraying a family of street entertainers. He made hundreds of drawings of the figures and of the other details in the painting. His models sat on a roof so that he could study the pattern of sunlight on the figure. He spent many months on the picture, using it as a laboratory to test and expand his knowledge. It would be, he said with candid judgment, "an ordinary sort of picture, with good things here and there . . ." and he was quite accurate in his estimation. When he finished the picture, he felt that his education was complete. It was now time to go home.

The America to which Eakins returned on July 4, 1870, was growing rapidly in power and material development. New millionaires, eager to display their culture, bought art not for quality but for size. The academicians who set the standards in the world of art were painting prettified, sentimental images containing no slightest hint of unpleasantness. In this unreal atmosphere, Eakins, at twenty-six, settled down to paint the life he knew. The dominant element in all his work was the human being. Many of his pictures were portraits of various members of his family, friends, and acquaintances. He also expressed his fondness for sports in a number of now famous pictures of men rowing and sailing. Even in these outdoor scenes, the figures were handled essentially as portraits.

Although his painting was done in the studio, he made innumerable sketches at the actual site, using his knowledge of mathematics, perspective, and anatomy with telling effect. If he was unable to get a model, he created little wax or clay figures to familiarize himself with the movements of the body. A sensitive colorist from the start, he used a rich, dark palette to build up his forms. His compositions were marked by strength and clarity. The grinding years of study and self-discipline had borne fruit. The canvases he was now painting would, in years to come, be hailed as mature and finished masterworks.

Among the most tender of Eakins' many portraits is one of a girl sitting in a chair playing with a cat. The girl in the picture is Katherine Crowell, to whom Eakins became engaged shortly after his return from Europe. But Katherine died of meningitis before her twentieth birthday. Not long afterward, Eakins' mother died. The double tragedy left a deep wound, from which he was slow to recover.

Eakins' interest in science was second only to his love of art. For relaxation, he often read learned treatises on higher mathematics. His intense curiosity about the anatomical process of movement in animals and human beings led him to collaborate with Eadweard Muybridge, a pioneer photographer, in a series of investigations of the subject for the University of Pennsylvania. Not content with Muybridge's method, Eakins succeeded in devising a camera that recorded the continuous movement of one single action. This work pioneered the eventual development of the motion picture camera. The results of one of his investigations into the interplay between bones and muscles were published by the Philadelphia Academy of Natural Sciences. Yet Eakins never allowed his scientific knowledge to dominate his painting. Science, for him, was a means to understanding the nature of things, and was not for a moment to be imposed upon art.

Eakins had resumed his study of anatomy at the Jefferson Medical College. He knew many of the leading medical men of the time, a number of whom sat for portraits. As a means of "advertising" his work, he presented his sitter with the canvas. Since there were few opportunities open to him, he made practically no effort to exhibit his work. The National Academy in New York, the most important instrument by which an unknown could build a reputation, did not welcome outsiders, particularly if they did not conform to the Academy's standards. The Pennsylvania Academy, important but slightly less so than its New York neighbor, had temporarily closed its galleries during the construction of its new building.

Eakins, however, was painting neither for the public nor for posterity but for himself. At the age of thirty-one, he completed the most ambitious picture he had ever attempted; a work destined to catapult him from obscurity into the limelight. It was a scene thoroughly familiar to Eakins, and one which he deemed worthy of putting on canvas. "The Gross Clinic" depicts Philadelphia's leading surgeon, Dr. Samuel Gross, performing an operation. He stands toward the center, the dominant figure, surrounded by his assistants bending over the body of the patient. To the left and slightly behind, the patient's mother sits, her hand shielding her eyes from the sight. In the upper half of the dark background, rows of medical students sit attending the doctor's lecture. The dramatic quality of the work is heightened by the play of a strong light on the head and bloodstained hands of the surgeon, that is picked up again on the figures of the assistants and part of the patient's body. The painting was complex in composition and structure, containing a multitude of figures, many of them life size.

Except for the theatrical pose of the mother, it was a remarkably faithful and realistic picture of an operation in progress. The individual portraits were striking in characterization and likeness. The figures of the doctors performing their task held a vitality and emotion that reached out of the canvas to envelope the spectator in the unfolding drama.

Eakins had labored long and hard on "The Gross Clinic." The various portraits were posed for by friends, doctors, medical or art students, and by Dr. Gross himself. With great optimism, he sent the painting to the Haseltine Galleries in Philadelphia for a public showing. The reaction was instantaneous and startling. The picture created a wild furor in the city of brotherly love. Sensation-hungry Philadelphians rushed to see a painting of an actual operation in which the artist had dared paint blood on the hands of the doctor. They did not come to admire but to be shocked. Almost without exception, the critics were unsparing in their condemnation. Eakins' realism was revolting to an age enamored of sentimental, sugar-coated generalities. One critic demanded removal of the figure of Dr. Gross and of all traces of blood in the picture. Others attacked the style, the handling of color, "the puzzle" of the patient's body.

Although Eakins was taken aback by the violent reception of "The Gross Clinic," he nevertheless submitted it to the Philadelphia Centennial Exhibition of 1876. The response here was even more damning—the picture was promptly rejected. After much wrangling and dispute, Eakins arranged to have his canvas shown among the medical displays, where it hung ignored and unseen.

Undaunted by the storm of abuse he had already aroused, Eakins sent the painting to the exhibition of the Society of

American Artists in New York. If he had hoped for a more favorable judgment, he suffered only disappointment. One critic declared indignantly that "one must condemn its admission to a gallery where men and women of weak nerves must be compelled to look at it"; another that "the scene is so real that they might as well go to a dissecting-room and have done with it . . . a morbid exhibition. . . ." Eakins was decried as a "brutal artist," the painting as "a degradation of Art."

Despite all this, and perhaps because of the wide interest aroused by the painting, the Pennsylvania Academy requested that it be submitted for their exhibition. Yet, when the picture came before the jury, it was refused there as it had been elsewhere. Outraged, Eakins finally raised his voice in protest. Strangely enough, the Society of American Artists, which had itself refused the painting, took his side, threatening to withdraw from the exhibition. Reluctantly, the Academy reversed itself, but hung the picture in a dimly lit corner of the gallery. Three years later, this masterpiece of Eakins' was bought by the Jefferson Medical College for a paltry two hundred dollars, and for many years hung where it was rarely seen.

The sole satisfaction that Eakins derived from this sorry affair was that he made the acquaintance of the woman who was to become his wife. An artist herself, Susan Hannah Macdowell had seen in "The Gross Clinic" the authentic qualities of genius. When Eakins later became an instructor at the Pennsylvania Academy, she enrolled in his class as a student. Eakins and Susan Macdowell were married in January, 1884, after a courtship of several years, and moved into the old house on Mount Vernon Street. Susan was an unflinching companion and comfort to her husband in the long troublous years ahead. Shortly after their marriage, Eakins painted a handsome and loving portrait of his wife called "Lady with a Setter Dog."

In the spring of 1876, the Pennsylvania Academy opened its new art school. The building was of the latest design, but the teaching methods remained dated and outworn. Christian Schussele, an old, infirm exponent of the antiquated academic approach, remained as the principal instructor. Eakins, who had known Schussele for several years, offered to relieve him of some of the burdens of his job. When the old man agreed, Eakins took over the life classes, and conducted them for two seasons without salary or official recognition as a member of the staff. If he hoped that his connection with the Academy would advance his career, there is no evidence that it did so.

With Schussele's death in 1879, Eakins was finally appointed a professor of drawing and painting. He promptly set about to reorganize and revitalize the teaching methods of the school, instituting a program that was completely radical in that day. Under his supervision, the student drew from the cast only until he showed the first sign of any ability, after which he was transferred to a life class. Here he began to "learn to draw with color." To help the student understand the solidity of form, Eakins added a course in modeling for painters as well as sculptors. The most advanced part of the curriculum was a course in anatomy taught by a noted surgeon, Dr. William W. Keen. Live models, cadavers, and skeletons were used. A former student recalled times "when a skeleton, a stiff, a model, and the negro janitor Henry all jerked and jumped when the battery was turned on" in a demonstration of the action of various muscles.

Eakins' growing reputation as an inspiring teacher attracted a great many new students to the school. Robert Henri, later to become a famous artist and teacher himself, said, "It was an excitement to hear his pupils talk of him. They believed in him as a great master, and there were stories of . . . his unwavering adherence to his ideals, his willingness to give, to help. . . ." Eakins taught from his own exhaustive knowledge. He was never harsh but rarely praising. He detested "average kind of work," and insisted that his pupils "get the character of things," adding, "Respectability in art is appalling."

In 1882 Eakins was made director of the art school, over the opposition of the conservative members of the board that governed the Academy. Their uneasiness at his "radicalism" was aggravated by his insistence on teaching the figure from the nude human body. They felt it was little less than scandalous of him to ask female students to pose in the nude, to pose male and female professional models at the same time, and to touch a model's body when demonstrating the action of a muscle. When, finally, Eakins removed the loincloth from a male model before a class of women, to illustrate the movement of the pelvis, it was the last straw. The governors demanded that he renounce all such procedures or resign. He chose to resign, and the governors of the Academy heaved a great sigh of relief.

The students were appalled by the forced eviction of their favorite instructor, and protested vociferously. They sent a letter, which all but twelve of the women students signed, demanding Eakins' immediate reinstatement. They organized a protest march to the school with each student displaying a large E on the front of his hat. But the authorities were adamant. They refused unconditionally to take Eakins back. "The idea of allowing a lot of students to run the Academy is ridiculous," they announced. The attitude of the general public was typified by an article in the Philadelphia *Bulletin* which said: "Mr. Eakins has for a long time entertained and strongly inculcated the most 'advanced' views. He holds that . . . Art knows no sex. He has pressed this always disputed doctrine with much zeal and with much success, until he has . . . pushed his views to their last logical illustration by compelling or seeking to compel the women entrusted to his direction to face the absolute nude."

The majority of the students resigned in defiance of the Academy's ultimatum and formed the Art Students League of Philadelphia, with Eakins as their master. Deeply moved by this devotion, he now dedicated a major portion of his time to his new teaching duties. He refused all payment, although he could ill afford to do so. In the ten years since he had been painting, his total income from the sale of his pictures was less than two thousand dollars. Had it not been for a modest sum left him by his family, neither Eakins nor the League could have survived for very long. As it was, it lasted a half-dozen years before expiring. When it did, the "boss"—as Eakins was affectionately known to his students —took sorrowful leave of his "boys." His long years of dedicated teaching were at an end.

He was now past forty, at a stage of artistic development that should have seen him solidly established as a major painter. Instead, he had been called a "butcher," his most important painting had been characterized as "degrading," and he had been ostracized by the "respectable" art world. No man could fail to be shaken by such a series of defeats, and perhaps Eakins was not an exception. But he found solace in the knowledge that he had never acted other than in high conscience and in adherence to the purest artistic ideals. With grim determination, he plunged back into painting.

Turning away from his previous variety of subjects, he now concentrated on portraits. Since no commissions were forthcoming, he asked friends and relatives to pose for him. One of his most striking portraits was of the poet Walt Whitman. The sitting resulted in a long friendship between these two artists. "Eakins," Whitman said enthusiastically, "is not a painter, he is a force."

Eakins painted many pictures of the doctors and men of science that he knew. His models came from all walks of life. Their importance to Eakins lay in their humanity. His portraits are unfailingly alive with the character of his subjects. Despising flattery as a lie, he searched always for the unadorned truth, the unveiled essence of a person. Occasionally this unswerving honesty was brutally frank. In some of his portraits, particularly those of men, there is a sense of eavesdropping before unpleasant truths. An artist friend of Eakins flatly refused to pose for him, "because," as he explained only half in jest, "he would bring out all the traits of my character that I have been trying to hide from the public for years!"

Samuel Moore, a former pupil, requested Eakins' assistance with a sculpture commission he had received. Eakins worked with Moore on the figures for a Philadelphia building, and later another friend was instrumental in helping him obtain a commission to model the horses for the equestrian statues of Lincoln and Grant on the Memorial Arch in Brooklyn. The relief figures on the Trenton Battle Monument were his last works in this medium.

Although he now existed virtually outside the established world of art, Eakins did not withdraw into himself. His friends were loyal, and he enjoyed their company. Though he loved hearty conversation, he was usually the listener rather than the speaker. When he did speak, he was lucid, forthright, and quite often humorous. Only rarely did he display anger, but once aroused he could be devastatingly frank. He disliked snobbery and pretentiousness, and was

himself singularly free of either. Although he spoke five languages fluently, he never employed foreign words in place of
their English counterparts. His clothes were ordinary and
comfortable in an era devoted to starched collars and heavy
suits. He shocked proper Philadelphians by working in an
undershirt and old trousers, no less than by swimming in the
nude. His home life was warm and affectionate. He and his
wife shared many common interests, including a deep love of
music. Their delight in animals made their house a veritable
menagerie with its collection of dogs, cats, tame mice, rabbits,
birds, and a monkey.

When Dr. D. Hayes Agnew was about to retire in 1880, his
students at the University of Pennsylvania medical school offered Eakins a commission to paint the portrait of their
revered teacher. It was agreed that he would receive a fee of
$750 for a conventional full-length. However, Eakins em-
barked on a more ambitious work—one remarkably similar to
"The Gross Clinic" in both subject matter and composition.
Again, it was set in the operating theatre, with the surgeon
(this time Dr. Agnew) lecturing his students as he performed
an operation. More painterly and less dramatic than its prede-
cessor of fourteen years ago, "The Agnew Clinic" was an
even more powerful picture. The rendition of the head and
figure of Dr. Agnew was one of Eakins' most brilliant efforts.

To finish it in the stipulated three months, Eakins drove
himself mercilessly. He was ill for part of this time, but refused to allow his indisposition to interfere with the completion of the work. When Dr. Agnew finally saw the completed
picture, he asked Eakins to remove the blood from his hands.
Eakins refused. He painted the truth and the truth was that
Dr. Agnew's hands were bloodied during the operation.

It was "The Gross Clinic" all over again. Old wounds
that had begun to heal were brutally reopened. Once again,

Philadelphians indignantly cried "butcher." The Pennsylvania Academy's directors refused the picture space in the exhibition of 1892. Even the more liberal Society of American Artists, the only group with which Eakins still had any connection, rejected it, citing the artist's "neglect of the beauties and graces of painting." This was too much for Eakins. He lost his temper. In a letter severing his association with the Society, he wrote bluntly that his painting was "more important than any I have ever seen upon your walls!"

Eakins did not withdraw from the world to lick his wounds, nor did he ever so much as contemplate a compromise with his principles. He simply went back to work, and now his output was twice as great as before. In the late 1890's he returned to painting pictures of sporting events, particularly of prize fights. That this was hardly considered a refined subject meant nothing to Eakins. The sports world was a vivid area of life, as real as any other, and he did not paint his pictures to please polite society. Some of his finest canvases emerged from his interest in this subject, including the memorable "Salutat" and "Between Rounds." To the masterful interpretation of the figure in motion—unequaled in the history of American art—he now brought a greater refinement of composition and tonal harmony.

Eakins continued to spare no effort in achieving realism in his pictures. In "The Concert Singer," his model was the singer Weda Cook. He insisted that she start each session with a song, so that he could observe the motion of the muscles in her throat. The hand of the conductor in the lower left of this painting was modeled by a professional musician. The action in the picture is so convincing that one can almost hear the voice of the singer. When he painted "The Crucifixion," Eakins asked a friend to pose for the figure of Christ. To be better able to visualize the downward pull of the body, he

actually strapped his friend to a cross. Yet all this dedication
to the truth of things gained Eakins little work. Only rarely
was he commissioned to do a portrait, and then, as likely as
not, it would be refused upon completion. As Eakins himself realized, it was the very honesty of his portraits that
made them unsalable; they "trespassed" on people's "com-
placency." But he could not paint any other way, would not
paint any other way.

The turn of the century saw a growing trend toward realism. Eakins finally began to receive a grudging measure of
recognition, mainly from organizations outside his own city.
The Carnegie Institute in Pittsburgh invited him to exhibit in
their international shows, and to sit on their jury of awards.
In March, 1902, the National Academy in New York belatedly gave him an associate membership, and several months
afterward granted him full membership. Then, in his sixtieth
year, the Pennsylvania Academy awarded him the Temple
Gold Medal for a portrait, "Archbishop Elder." On the night
of the presentation, Eakins dressed in old clothes, mounted
his bicycle, and pedaled through the streets of Philadelphia
to attend the ceremonies. Next morning, to complete his
gesture of bitterness and scorn, he turned in the medal for its
cash equivalent of seventy-five dollars.

It was not until 1912, at a minor exhibition in Lancaster,
Pennsylvania, that "The Agnew Clinic" was belatedly hung
in the place of honor. Although he was ill at the time, Eakins
insisted on attending the ceremonies. When his presence in
the gallery became known, there was a sudden spontaneous
burst of cheers and applause. Toward the end of his life, when
Eakins was asked what honors he had received for his art, he
proudly replied that he had been given an ovation at Lancaster. Actually, he received a number of additional honors, but
he regarded none of them as of any importance. His awards

were too little and too late; his recognition was only partial.

In 1902, Eakins had painted a self-portrait. As might be expected, he saw himself with the same incorruptible honesty with which he viewed any other sitter. In his fifty-eighth year he had grown heavy with age, his hair had become gray and sparse, his beard and mustache framed an infinitely tired face. Disillusionment, sadness, resignation are clearly written in the eyes. The picture is the portrait of a failure, but it contains no trace of self-pity. The eyes that fix the gaze of the beholder are the eyes of an intelligently courageous man.

In his sixty-sixth year, Eakins' once-robust health began to decline. Despite failing eyesight, he made a last valiant effort to paint a friend's portrait, but even with Susan Eakins' help it was hopeless. In the early summer of 1916, after a long period of semi-invalidism, he became too ill to leave his bed. On the morning of June 25, exactly a month before his seventy-second birthday, he lapsed into a coma from which he never awoke. Simple funeral services were held in the house where he had lived his life, attended only by members of the family and his closest friends. In accordance with his wishes, there were no religious services, no eulogies, and no flowers. In death as in life, he held to his principles.

A little over a year later, the Metropolitan Museum of Art held a retrospective show of Eakins' work. The Pennsylvania Academy followed suit, paying him homage with a huge exhibition of his paintings. Tribute followed tribute. In the eyes of the critics he was no longer the "butcher," no longer "the brutal artist," but a painter of genius, "one of the . . . greatest artists this country has produced."

Thomas Eakins was at last redeemed.

GILBERT STUART

Commodore Isaac Hull

COURTESY OF THE METROPOLITAN MUSEUM OF ART,
BEQUEST OF CHARLES ALLEN MUNN, 1924.

WASHINGTON ALLSTON
The Flight of Florimell (detail)
COURTESY OF THE DETROIT INSTITUTE OF ARTS.

GEORGE CALEB BINGHAM

Fur Traders Descending the Missouri

COURTESY OF THE METROPOLITAN MUSEUM OF ART,
MORRIS K. JESUP FUND, 1933.

GEORGE INNESS

Autumn Oaks

WINSLOW HOMER

Eight Bells

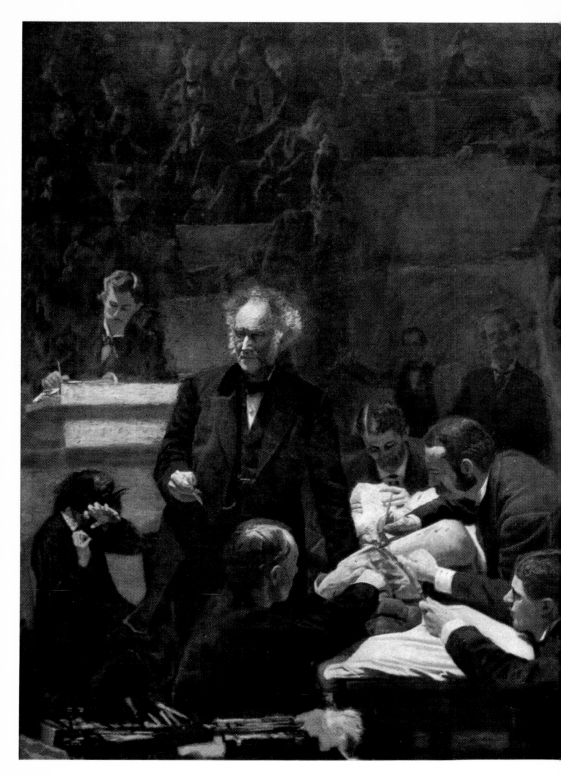

THOMAS EAKINS

The Gross Clinic

COURTESY OF THE JEFFERSON MEDICAL COLLEGE OF PHILADELPHIA.
COLOR PLATE: COURTESY OF GEORGE BRAZILLER, INC.

ALBERT PINKHAM RYDER

Toilers of the Sea

COURTESY OF THE METROPOLITAN MUSEUM OF ART,
GEORGE A. HEARN FUND, 1915.

JOHN SINGER SARGENT

Madame X

COURTESY OF THE METROPOLITAN MUSEUM OF ART,
ARTHUR H. HEARN FUND, 1916.

PHOTOGRAPHY BY SANDAK, INC.

JAMES ABBOTT McNEILL WHISTLER
Arrangement in Flesh Color and Black:
Portrait of Théodore Duret
COURTESY OF THE METROPOLITAN MUSEUM OF ART,
WOLFE FUND, 1913.

MARY CASSATT

Lady at the Tea Table

COURTESY OF THE METROPOLITAN MUSEUM OF ART,
GIFT OF THE ARTIST, 1923.

JOHN SLOAN

Sixth Avenue Elevated at Third Street

COLLECTION OF THE WHITNEY MUSEUM OF AMERICAN ART, NEW YORK.

JOHN MARIN

Sea Piece

COLLECTION OF THE WHITNEY MUSEUM OF AMERICAN ART, NEW YORK,
GIFT OF THE FRIENDS OF THE WHITNEY MUSEUM OF AMERICAN ART.

STUART DAVIS

The Paris Bit

COLLECTION OF THE WHITNEY MUSEUM OF AMERICAN ART, NEW YORK,
GIFT OF THE FRIENDS OF THE WHITNEY MUSEUM OF AMERICAN ART.

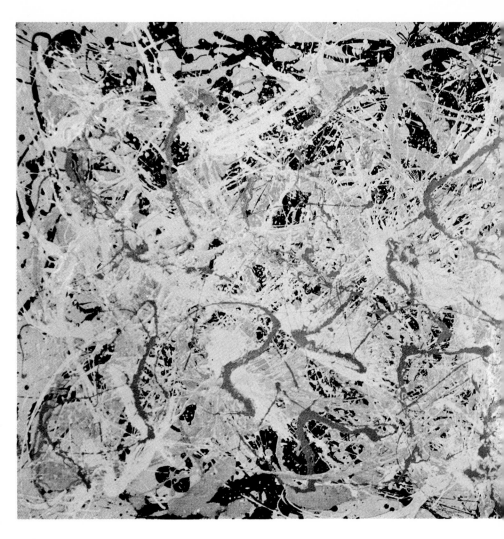

JACKSON POLLOCK
Number 27
COLLECTION OF THE WHITNEY MUSEUM OF AMERICAN ART, NEW YORK.

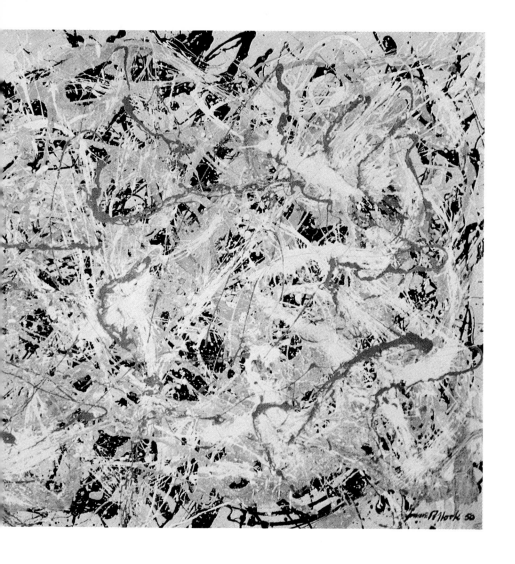

BEN SHAHN

Conversations

COLLECTION OF THE WHITNEY MUSEUM OF AMERICAN ART, NEW YORK,
GIFT OF THE FRIENDS OF THE WHITNEY MUSEUM OF AMERICAN ART.

7

The Hermit of
West Fifteenth Street

ALBERT PINKHAM RYDER

1847–1907

When Albert Pinkham Ryder was sixteen, his father presented him with a set of paints and brushes. Many years later Ryder described his reaction to the gift.

"When my father placed a box of colors and brushes in my hands, and I stood before my easel with its square of stretched canvas, I realized that I had in my possession the wherewith to create a masterpiece that would live throughout the coming ages. The great masters had no more."

Ryder was neither fool enough nor so naïve as to suppose that the old masters "had no more." He understood that they did indeed have more—creative genius. But he took their

95

genius for granted, as he took his own for granted. Thus, the missing ingredients for the creation of a masterpiece had been paints, brushes, and canvas; with those in his possession he had everything the old masters had.

It was not boastfulness but a quality of perfect innocence and candor that allowed him to express himself in this remarkable way. He had a devout trust in the absolute rightness of his artistic vision that never wavered for an instant in the long and frequently dismal years ahead. Recognition as America's greatest and most original romantic painter did not arrive until after he was dead. If it had come in his lifetime, Ryder would have been delighted, but neither surprised nor overwhelmed. This gentle, dreamy, and almost childlike man's belief in himself was sufficient unto his need.

"Pinkie," as he was called in his youth, was born on March 19, 1847, in a big old house in New Bedford, Massachusetts. He was the youngest of the four sons of Alexander Gage Ryder and Elizabeth Cobb Ryder, both descended of old Cape Cod families. The elder Ryders were members of a sect of the Methodist faith which held concepts much like those of the Quakers, the chief settlers of New Bedford. They were gentle, pious, tolerant folk, simple of manner and dress.

New Bedford was the great whaling capital of the United States. In 1850, when Albert Ryder was three years old, it had achieved the distinction of having become the richest city per capita in the world. The whaling industry thrived; oil, blubber, and bone were in constant demand; New Bedford was the most important port on the Atlantic seaboard.

Albert grew up with a fondness for the ever-present smell and sound and sight of the sea. His child's imagination fed on the haunting intensity of its moods; he learned not only to understand but to appreciate its many and varied aspects. Here he discovered the romantic beauty of moonlit waters that figured so largely in his paintings.

Albert's childhood and adolescence were serene and happy. Although he showed an early interest in drawing, it was color that truly fascinated him. Sometimes he would be so captivated by the colors in a picture book that he was totally unaware of the world around him. Even the insistent clang of the dinner bell could hardly rouse him from his trance.

Shortly after his graduation from the Middle Street Grammar School, Albert developed an infection resulting from a vaccine poisoning. The illness affected his vision. Reading became difficult, bright lights were painful, and, to the end of his life, he suffered from chronic inflammation of the eyes. Because of his disability, all thought of any further education had to be forgotten. It was not a major blow to Albert. As long as he could see color and form, he was content.

Alexander Ryder never quite understood his youngest child. Albert was so very different from his brothers. Edward N. and Preserved Milton had followed the normal New Bedford course and gone to sea. William Davis, the eldest, was in New York City, where he was married to a nice young woman, and, with his father-in-law, was running a successful restaurant. In time William would become a prosperous businessman and the owner of the Hotel Albert, a famous Manhattan landmark. They were steady, level-headed boys. It was only Albert whose head was filled with dreams of becoming, of all things, an artist. Yet Alexander Ryder, despite his bewilderment, was tolerant of, even sympathetic with, his youngest son's ambition. He bought him paints and brushes, and arranged to have him apprenticed to an artist who could teach him the rudiments of mixing and applying colors.

The apprenticeship was brief. Albert believed that he could learn more from the intensive study of paintings than from a teacher of limited knowledge. In the course of things, he came across the landscapes of Albert Bierstadt, who had once lived in New Bedford, and whose family still occupied the house opposite the Ryders'. Albert Bierstadt had become one of the most prosperous and popular painters in America. The grandiose, theatrical—but by no means inexpert—quality of Bierstadt's canvases inspired in Albert Ryder the desire to try his own hand at landscape painting. He took himself eagerly out into the fields. He was profoundly dissatisfied with his first attempts. It had occurred to him that, in attempting to paint realistically, he was waging a losing battle. How could he ever hope to surpass, or even equal, the perfection of nature?

Then, one memorable day, he made the discovery which laid the foundation for his future greatness. In describing the occasion, he declared that suddenly "the old scene presented itself . . . before my eyes framed in an opening between two trees. It stood out like a painted canvas . . . three solid masses of form and color—sky, foliage and earth—the whole bathed in an atmosphere of golden luminosity. I threw my brushes aside; they were too small . . . and taking my palette knife, I laid on blue, green, white and brown in great sweeping strokes. . . . I saw nature springing into life upon my dead canvas. . . . Exultantly I painted until the sun sank below the horizon. Then I raced around the fields like a colt let loose and literally bellowed for joy."

In a single, revelatory afternoon, Ryder's genius had opened the way to a completely new concept of painting. These three forms, "sky, foliage and earth—the whole bathed in . . . golden luminosity" were to be the unyielding basis for all his future paintings.

Although Ryder might have been content to spend the rest of his days in New Bedford, circumstances did not allow it. The whaling industry had received a grievous blow with the discovery of petroleum, and steel was also fast replacing the use of whalebone for corset stays. Along with many others,

Alexander Ryder lost his job in the stricken industry. There was no other means of making a living in New Bedford. In 1870 the Ryders moved to New York, relying on their successful son William for financial assistance.

Ryder was twenty-three years old, a tall, heavy-set young man with a full, reddish-brown beard, "very neat, with a New England regard for the proprieties." His shyness and his sweet nature were quietly engaging. He did not make many friends, but those he won remained staunch and loyal to the end. "He never talked much; he was an excellent listener, and his laugh was very infectious," an old friend said of him.

In a turnabout from his former attitude, Ryder now applied for admission to the National Academy of Design. He was turned down. The National Academy at that time was all-powerful. Its school was the largest and most influential in the country, and its exhibitions the most important. Although Ryder felt the rejection keenly, he was not discouraged. For a time, he studied with William E. Marshall, a portrait painter and engraver, and then resubmitted his application to the Academy. This time he was accepted.

His pleasure in the school was short-lived. The major portion of the Academy's teaching method involved drawing from plaster casts. Ryder derived little knowledge and less satisfaction from this kind of sterile teaching. He quickly abandoned the Academy and its casts, and resumed painting on his own.

During this period, Ryder painted a large number of landscapes, usually containing an animal or figure in the composition. The greater portion of these pictures were painted in the golden light of the late afternoon, or in the silvery glow of moonlight. They had about them a veiled, poetic quality as of a half-remembered dream. In contrast to the huge, sometimes wall-sized panoramas then so popular, his canvases were extremely small. One of his pictures—a self-portrait—was painted on the back of a cigar box to which he had glued a tiny piece of canvas.

At the age of twenty-six, Ryder exhibited one of his pictures for the first time in a show of the National Academy. A year or so later, when he sent another painting to the Academy, it was not accepted. Fortunately, Daniel Cottier, an Englishman who had just opened a branch of his London gallery in New York, had seen the rejected work. He invited Ryder and four other rejectees of the Academy to hang their work in his new showplace. The exhibition was moderately successful, and Cottier was able to persuade a few discerning clients to buy some of Ryder's paintings. Cottier became his dealer and the two men became lifelong friends.

For a number of years a growing rebellion against the outmoded views and autocratic behavior of the Academy had been gaining strength. In 1877 a group of insurgent painters, called "The New Movement," founded the Society of American Artists as a liberal-minded challenge to the Academy's prestige. The Society grew less democratic with the years, and was eventually reabsorbed into the framework of the National Academy. Ryder was one of the twenty-two original founders of the new group. He remained a member all his life, and frequently exhibited his work in the Society's shows. "Had it not been for the Society," a fellow member commented, "it is doubtful whether such an unmistakeably genuine painter . . . would ever have had his pictures hung where they could be seen."

What little attention Ryder received from the critics was usually unsympathetic. Most of them carped about his "bad drawing," a not unjustified criticism, but unimportant in view of his other qualities. One critic, blind to the beauty of the remarkable luminosity he achieved, challenged him to "show what you can do in the glare of day! See whether your poetry is strong enough . . . to stand the wear and tear of life!"

Ryder calmly continued to go his own way, immune to all disapproval. He devoutly believed that an artist "must live to paint and not paint to live." He worked very slowly, often taking years to complete a picture, painting and repainting it until it satisfied his almost fanatical standards. Occasionally his friend Cottier sold one of his canvases, but the proceeds were never sufficient to relieve Ryder's poverty. His needs were small; he asked no more than a roof overhead and some food, yet only too frequently he could afford neither colors nor canvas. For lack of money, he bought the cheapest colors available. When he had no canvas, he painted on flat bits of wood picked up at random. On one occasion, he is said to have torn the wooden slats out of his bed in order to have something to paint on!

It is possible that Ryder had less knowledge of the technique of painting than any other great artist who ever lived. He knew nothing of the properties of the materials he used and little more about using them. These matters were of no importance to him. What he didn't know he improvised, usually in ways that would have horrified any trained artist. So impatient was he to get on with his work that he rarely allowed the day's painting to dry properly. He would lay a coat of varnish over the picture in progress so that it would be dry enough to be worked on early the next morning. Once, after offering a painting to a friend, he submerged the entire canvas in water to wash it clean; and then proceeded to wipe it dry with an extremely dirty towel!

For this appalling ignorance of the basic principles of art, Ryder eventually paid very dearly. Today, his paintings are in a shocking state of preservation. Almost all are badly cracked or blistered, since the paint was never allowed to dry thoroughly. Most are discolored or blackened, some so drastically that the beauty of the original hues can only be appreciated from color photographs taken many years ago, before the pictures had begun to deteriorate.

None of this mattered to Ryder. He firmly believed that, just as the sculpture of ancient Greece had retained its beauty despite the ravages of time, so would his pictures.

Ryder was thirty-three years old before he had ever lived by himself. His brother William gave Ryder enough money so that he was able to rent his own studio in East Washington Square. Two years later, he made the first of four journeys abroad. He spent a month in London, at the Regent's Park house of his friend Daniel Cottier. In the summer of 1882, in the company of Cottier and Olin L. Warner, a sculptor, Ryder toured France, Holland, Italy, Spain, and Tangier. He was not the best of traveling companions, since he disliked hurry and moving about from one place to another. He expressed little interest in the art treasures of the European museums. The only paintings that mattered to him were his own. He went abroad again in 1887 and 1896, as a passenger aboard the ship of Captain John Robinson, a friend and an amateur painter. Both times his chief diversion consisted of spending hours up on the ship's deck, staring at the gleaming waters—"soaking in the moonlight," as he put it.

Soon after moving into his own studio, he began to broaden the scope of his subject matter. Scenes from mythology, the Bible, poems, even the operas of Richard Wagner found their way into his compositions. His paintings were superbly designed. The balance of the dark masses against the light, the sinuous rhythms, the jewel-like radiance of his color, all combined to produce works of rare beauty.

An incident which occurred during this time moved him to paint one of his most famous and haunting pictures. He had become friendly with a waiter at his brother William's hotel, the Albert. The waiter often discussed with him his hopes of making a killing at the race track. One morning the waiter told Ryder that he had a tip on a race that afternoon, and proposed to back a horse with his entire life's savings. Ryder tried to dissuade him, but to no avail. The waiter made his bet, his horse lost. Early the next morning Ryder appeared at the hotel filled with concern. His friend was dead. He had shot himself the night before. This suicide, and the circumstances that caused it, inspired what is perhaps Ryder's best-known picture, "The Race Track," which depicts Death on a horse, scythe in hand, slowly riding around an eerie, moonlit racecourse.

He now sold an occasional picture, and the critics had become somewhat more temperate in their reactions to his work, but never gave him any real recognition during his life. His simple soul delighted even in the small acclaim he won, and it spurred him on to greater achievement. In a letter to a friend, he told what it was like to yearn for perfection:

"Have you ever seen an inch worm crawl up a leaf or twig, and there clinging to the very end, revolve in the air, feeling for something to reach something? That's like me. I am trying to find something out there beyond the place on which I have a footing."

As he grew older, Ryder slowly retreated from the normal contacts of life. His whole universe was wrapped up in his painting, and nothing else concerned him. He almost never went to museums and galleries, rarely discussed art with other artists, and even seemed uninterested in exhibiting his work.

In 1902, he moved into two rooms on the upper floor at 318 West Fifteenth Street, his last home. Never much of a social creature, he now became a recluse and an eccentric. He lived in unbelievable squalor. His rooms were stacked high with packing cases, old trunks, and tottering heaps of magazines and newspapers. Dirty dishes lay everywhere; empty cereal boxes collected in a pile that rose to the ceiling. He slept on a pallet on the floor. His landlord was not allowed entry to paint or repair. His large frame had taken on weight with the years, and his once handsome red beard was now gray and matted with dirt. He dressed like a derelict, and was occasionally mistaken for one. He seemed completely unaware of his appearance or surroundings, and once said to a friend who made a tactful reference to the disorder of his rooms:

"I have two windows in my workshop that look out upon an old garden. . . . I would not exchange those two windows for a palace."

He began writing poetry as a "companion piece" to the pictures he painted, or to celebrate occasions in the lives of his friends. He could frequently be seen sitting on a park bench, scrawling endlessly on sheets of paper, some of which might be carried away by the wind. He spent many nights wandering aimlessly through the deserted city streets, no matter what the weather. Moonlit nights particularly suited his mood.

Ryder found new friends in the Fitzpatricks, the couple who rented the apartment below his. Mr. Fitzpatrick was a carpenter, and his wife an amateur painter. An intimacy soon developed that went deeper than all of Ryder's other friendships. When he became ill, Mrs. Fitzpatrick nursed him back to health. Against his fierce opposition, she even tried—in vain—to make order out of the impossible chaos of his apartment. Both Fitzpatricks voluntarily assumed the role of guardian angel to Ryder, and looked after him to the day of his death.

Notwithstanding the extreme modesty of his demands, Ryder was constantly beset by poverty. Only toward the end of his life, when his paintings had begun to command a fair price, did he become free of grinding want. His innocence in financial matters was legendary. One day a friend visited him. Concerned about Ryder's welfare, he asked him if he had any money. Ryder told him there was "some paper in the cupboard." There, among the empty boxes and soiled dishes, the friend found a check for a considerable amount of money. Ryder was completely ignorant of how one cashed it. He was so impressed by his friend's knowledge in the matter that he afterward always referred to him, sincerely, as a "financial wizard."

Despite his many eccentricities, Ryder's gentle nature remained unchanged. His dealings with people were marked by an old-world courtesy, and he was generous with what small goods he owned. At Christmas, he always sent a modest gift, letter, or poem to his friends.

He was passionately fond of music. On one occasion, he went to the opera to see Wagner's *Götterdämmerung*, and was so inspired by its splendors that, although it was after midnight when he returned home, he promptly shucked off his coat and began to paint. After forty-eight hours of feverish creation, uninterrupted by food or sleep, there emerged the painting of "Siegfried and the Rhine Maidens," one of his many lovely canvases.

The inspiration and creative genius which had produced such splendid work suddenly deserted Ryder when he was in his early fifties. For years it had been his custom to work endlessly on a new picture. Now he took to repainting the old ones. He hated to allow any of them out of his possession, even after they had been bought and paid for. Often he borrowed pictures back from their owners so that he could rework them. In one such case, he complained that he was "worried somewhat of his [the owner's] wanting to take his picture away before I had finished, but lately he has been very nice about it—only comes around once a year or so." Another purchaser jokingly said that he would have his funeral procession stop by to pick up his painting on the way to the cemetery. To which Ryder declared, "It couldn't go out even then unless 'twas done."

Although Ryder had long since severed his association with the National Academy, no longer caring about exhibiting his work, the Academy belatedly recognized his growing reputation, and voted him an associate member. Four years later he was elected a full Academician. His old friends still came to see him, as well as a few young artists who admired his work, most notably Marsden Hartley, later to become renowned in his own right.

It was a group of younger painters who persuaded Ryder in 1913 to hang six of his pictures in the Armory Show, a remarkable exhibition that introduced modern art to the United States. Many years after his death, Ryder was rediscovered by the most modern of the abstract painters, who felt that his powerful sense of design and bold handling of mass bore a prophetic kinship to their own work. In fact, one of Ryder's pronouncements could be carried as a banner by the very latest school of painting.

"Modern art," said Ryder, "must strike out from the old and assert its individual right to live. . . . The new is not revealed to those whose eyes are fastened in worship upon the old."

Natural shyness, and a reluctance to spare time away from

his work, led Ryder to eschew new acquaintances. He never minded when his old friends dropped in, but urged them to come alone. On the very rare occasions when he was compelled to visit a rich client or to "see the pictures," he would don a silk hat and the appropriate accompanying attire. His manners were impeccable and charmingly old-fashioned in a world which increasingly put small value on such refinements.

In 1915, Ryder fell gravely ill. The Fitzpatricks nursed him as well as they could, until it became evident that he was too sick for home treatment. He was taken to St. Vincent's Hospital, in Greenwich Village, and spent several months confined to bed. Upon his discharge from the hospital, the Fitzpatricks took him home with them to Elmhurst, Long Island, where they were now living. Here, in the bucolic atmosphere of a peaceful suburb, Ryder spent the remaining two years of his life. His death came nine days after his seventy-first birthday, on March 28, 1917.

The Metropolitan Museum paid full tribute to Ryder's genius with a memorial exhibition of his work in the same year that he died. When the Museum of Modern Art first opened in 1927, it granted to Ryder his due rank as one of the great artists of America in a joint exhibition with those other great men of art, Thomas Eakins and Winslow Homer.

Now that he was dead, the demand for Ryder's work became enormous. Prices skyrocketed to fabulous sums. During his entire lifetime he had painted only about 150 pictures. Now the market was glutted with a profusion of spurious Ryders. Museums, galleries, and private collectors were all deceived by the numerous forgeries. At one time there were in existence five times as many false as there were genuine Ryders. Even the forgers could not be absolutely sure that they were not copying other forgeries.

In time, painstaking investigation separated the fraudulent from the real. Ironically, it was Ryder's appalling carelessness and technical ignorance that provided the key. Unlike Ryder, the anonymous forgers were too soundly trained to have ever wiped a painting dry with a dirty towel.

8

The Virtuoso

JOHN SINGER SARGENT
1856–1925

Joseph Pulitzer, founder of the newspaper empire that bore his name, entered the studio of John Singer Sargent, settled comfortably in a chair, and made ready to talk about himself frankly as a prelude to having his portrait painted. But Sargent merely set the pose and then, dispensing with any further preliminaries, started working. Nonplused, Pulitzer expressed his surprise that Sargent had made no attempt to study him or engage him in a conversation, in order to draw out the subsurface qualities of his character.

With absolute candor, Sargent replied, "I paint what I see

. . . I don't dig beneath the surface for things that don't appear before my eyes."

The contrast between Sargent and his contemporary, Thomas Eakins, is a striking one. While Sargent, painting his elegant surface visions, lived in the lap of luxury, acclaimed by royalty, the art world and the public, Eakins painfully dug "beneath the surface" and struggled in almost complete obscurity. While Sargent was unable to cope with the hordes clamoring at his studio door, Eakins was reduced to begging the subjects for his portraits from among his family and friends. While Sargent could command any fee he cared to name for a portrait, Eakins sold scarcely a single canvas.

Eakins was armored against adversity by his total belief in the rightness of what he was doing; Sargent, at the height of his career, began to entertain serious doubts. He realized, a little too late, that he had in large part dissipated and misused his prodigious talent. Desperately he tried to channel his efforts into more creative directions, but his prosaic eye and aloof mind could not hurdle the barrier that now stood between him and genuinely creative artistry. He had lived too long with his credo of "I do not judge, only chronicle."

Nevertheless, although Sargent never reached the sublime pinnacle his extraordinary talent might have led him to, many of his works—particularly his early oils and the preponderance of his watercolors—stand without apology as works of great stature. As for the bulk of his vivid, technically exquisite portraits, they remain for the world to wonder at and to regard with unabashed admiration.

Mary Newbold Singer, the daughter of a prosperous Philadelphia leather merchant, fell incurably in love with Italy during a youthful visit to Europe. After her marriage to Dr. Fitzwilliam Sargent, an eminent Philadelphia surgeon, she harped constantly on the subject, striving to imbue her more sedate husband with the same sense of excitement that possessed her. But it was not until her father died that this willful, impulsive young woman achieved her ambition. She succeeded in convincing her husband that her inheritance at last permitted them to live abroad. Although it meant giving up a lucrative practice, Dr. Sargent nevertheless resigned his post and with his wife sailed for Italy, the land of her dreams.

The Sargents settled in Florence, where there was a sizable American colony. The beautiful city, for centuries an international gathering place of artists, writers, and intellectuals, appealed to Mrs. Sargent's cultural aspirations. Two years later their first child arrived. John Singer Sargent was born on January 12, 1856, in the Casa Arretini, overlooking the Arno River near the ancient Ponte Vecchio. In all, six children were eventually born to the Sargents, only three of whom survived, John and his two younger sisters, Emily and Violet.

Mrs. Sargent's restless nature drove the family to wandering around Europe like a tribe of Bedouins. The children were born in various parts of the Continent, depending on where the family chanced to be at that particular moment. John, American by virtue of citizenship, born in Italy, at home in any country of the world, truly cosmopolitan, nevertheless throughout his life felt strong ties to his American heritage.

The major portion of his early years was spent in Florence, where his father undertook the task of giving him an education. John was an active, normal youngster who was, according to his father, "quite a close observer of animated nature." During the almost continuous travels of his early years, he learned to speak fluent Italian, French, and German in addition to English. Mrs. Sargent attended to the cultural side of her son's education. She exercised her flair for music and watercolor painting by giving John instruction in both these

arts. His unusual ability to paint and draw made itself immediately evident, as did his interest in art. When he was not
out sketching with his mother, he was making drawings in the
notebook which he carried everywhere. The paintings of the
masters, to which he was exposed at an early age, fascinated
him, and he undoubtedly absorbed much from them.

At twelve, John was an unusually tall, slim boy. The ruddy
complexion, dark hair, and brisk step of his adult years were
already present. His gay nature and gentle disposition were
punctuated by occasional bursts of temper when he felt un-
justly used. A boyhood friend described him as a "big-eyed,
sentimental, charming boy, playing the mandolin very pleas-
antly."

The question of John's future developed into a determined
tug-of-war between his parents. It was Dr. Sargent's supreme
desire to see his son become a career officer in the United
States Navy. To encourage this ambition, he never missed an
opportunity to take John aboard American warships whenever they dropped anchor in European waters. But neither
John nor—more importantly at this stage—his mother was
interested. Mrs. Sargent was determined that John must become an artist. In Carl Welsch, a German-American artist
on a visit to Rome, she found professional support for her belief in the boy's talent. Welsch, impressed by the ability displayed in John's drawings, offered to teach him the fundamentals of painting. This was John's first formal instruction
in art.

Although he disapproved of an artistic career, Dr. Sargent,
as usual, bowed to the wishes of his strong-willed wife. In
the fall of 1870, John was enrolled in the Accademia delle
Belle Arti. At the same time, he attended a school run by a
French political refugee, where he was given a general education. At the end of his first year at the Accademia, he won

the annual prize awarded to the best student. It surprised no one, in view of his amazing natural gifts, but confirmed even more strongly his mother's belief in her son's talent.

For the next few years, sandwiched between the constant wanderings of the family, John pushed on with his studies. Before long, John was bored with the Accademia, terming it the "most unsatisfactory institution imaginable." But he conceded that, despite the monotonous drawing from casts, he was learning the important fundamentals of drawing. Even at this age, when the imaginative spark of youth normally glows so brightly, his work was literal. He drew only what he saw, neither plumbing for hidden depths nor indulging in flights of creative fancy.

In the early spring of 1874, the Sargents went to Venice. Here, several years later, they met the famous American artist Whistler, who had arrived to do a series of etchings. Mrs. Sargent seized the opportunity to trot out her son's watercolors and drawings. Whistler admired the work, and was generous with words of encouragement. Later on, Whistler was to change his tune, marking Sargent down as a mere fashionable painter. Despite this, Sargent remained a loyal enthusiast of the older artist. At a time when Whistler was in grave financial difficulty, Sargent invited him to help with murals he had been commissioned to paint for the Boston Library. Whistler refused the offer but, in one of his highly infrequent complimentary moods, called it an act of "rare and noble camaraderie."

The problem of where to send John to continue his studies was given prolonged thought by the elder Sargents. The choice narrowed down to England and France. On the one hand, the English schools were inferior to the French; on the other hand, the French painter was an artistic "radical" and Paris held many moral pitfalls for a young man. In the end, art triumphed over caution, and in May, 1874, the family moved to Paris.

Sargent was eighteen years old when he took the examinations required for entrance into the Ecole des Beaux-Arts. Each aspirant for admission had to pass rigorous tests in anatomy, perspective, ornamental design, and figure drawing. Sargent complained about the "unreasonably long, difficult and terrible" examinations, but in October he was among the successful students admitted to the studio of Carolus-Duran, one of the leading portrait painters of Paris. Although he declared that young Sargent had "much to unlearn," Carolus-Duran was quick to recognize his pupil's talent as "promise above the ordinary."

Sargent applied himself with great seriousness to learning his craft. He attended classes both morning and afternoon. When no model was present, he induced a friend to pose for him. From five o'clock in the afternoon until seven in the evening, he did additional work at the Beaux-Arts. After dinner he attended an evening class under the guidance of Léon Bonnat. On Sundays he painted at home.

Sargent very rapidly became the outstanding member of his class. In fact, his glittering virtuosity, technical facility and fluent brushwork soon threatened to outstrip the master's. Yet Sargent was modest about his gifts, and freely acknowledged the debt he owed to Carolus-Duran. He was totally without conceit. His attitude was reserved, his manners were impeccable. He was intelligent, somewhat shy, and affable without being overfriendly. He had grown into a tall, slim, handsome young man, with a habit of stooping to minimize his height. A rather full dark beard framed a well-set head, whose dominant features were a large nose and alert gray-blue eyes. He seldom participated in the gay student life. He preferred to spend his free time with his family and a few

close friends, among whom he often indulged his love of
music by playing the piano.

Early in 1877, Sargent took the first step toward an independent career. He sent a portrait to the annual exhibition of
the Salon. Its acceptance signified the end of his student
days. He could now consider himself a professional. In the
same year, Carolus-Duran invited Sargent and another American art student to help him with murals for the Luxembourg
Palace. The master also consented to sit for Sargent. The result was a beautifully finished portrait, marked by the elegance
and flair that were before long to become famous. Sargent
sent the picture to the Salon, where it created an immediate
stir. When one of the leading French art periodicals reproduced the portrait on its front cover, Carolus-Duran became
inflamed with jealousy. The pupil had outstripped the master,
and the master knew it. Sargent's remarkable talent had already carried him so far in so short a time.

This small flurry of success brought Sargent a number of
commissions, some sales, and a few prizes. His prestige as a
portrait painter slowly began to rise. But Sargent, still eager
to learn, left for Spain to study the old masters in the Prado
Museum, and thence to Holland to see the work of Franz
Hals. He was most moved by the genius of the Spaniard
Velázquez. For a month he devoted himself to seeking the
answer to the secret of Velázquez' greatness by making copies
of his work, and poring over his technique and use of color.
In his spare time, he occupied himself by making sketches
of the Spanish people.

Upon his return to Paris, Sargent embarked on several
paintings. One of them, "El Jaleo," was evolved from the
sketches he had made in Spain. This work revealed a new
maturity and an increased elegance in style, a dramatic awareness of the play of light and shade, and a masterful use of

color. The brushwork, always adept, was now bold and sure, each stroke important and telling. When "El Jaleo" was shown in the Salon in 1882, it was received with loud acclaim. Sargent had caught perfectly the explosive movement of the Spanish dancer and the undercurrent of emotion that swayed the guitarists and the audience to her rhythms. Soon after, another painting, "Portraits d'Enfants" (a picture of the four daughters of Edward D. Boit) was almost as much praised. It was strikingly daring in composition, with its four figures emerging from various sections of the canvas, and brilliantly handled in the counterplay of large masses of light against dark. One of its few detractors called it "four corners and a void." But most of the critics agreed with Henry James' enthusiastic admiration. It remains one of Sargent's finest works, a masterpiece of arrangement.

At twenty-six, Sargent was the author of the two most important paintings in the Salon, and he stood on the threshold of fame. Henry James declared that Sargent offered "the slightly uncanny spectacle of a talent which on the very threshold of its career has nothing more to learn." Another critic respectfully suggested that "one does not know which to admire most, the simplicity of the means which the artist has employed, or the brilliance of the result which he has achieved." The success and the reputation he had so swiftly won soon brought Sargent more commissions than he could comfortably handle.

At a fashionable gathering, Sargent met Madame Gautreau, the wife of a French banker, and a belle of the gay social world of Paris. A stunning beauty and a daring dresser, Madame Gautreau habitually dusted her pale white skin with lavender-tinted powder. Sargent was inflamed by an inordinate desire to paint her. Not only was he much taken by her unusual good looks, but he realized that executing a successful portrait of her would open up the doors to the fashionable and moneyed world of Paris.

In 1883, Madame Gautreau yielded to Sargent's pleas, and allowed him to begin a full-length portrait. Sargent did not have an easy time of it. His subject, bored by the demands he was making on her time, found constant excuses to free herself from the imprisonment of a frozen position. It was almost impossible for Sargent to pin her down to sitting for any useful length of time. He complained, in his turn, about her "unpaintable beauty and hopeless laziness." He characterized her skin tones unflatteringly as a "uniform lavender of blotting-paper colour."

The picture was finally completed. Although he was not entirely satisfied with it, Sargent sent it to the Salon exhibit in 1884. In anticipation of a rush of commissions, he moved to larger and more fashionable quarters, and even engaged several servants for his new studio.

The opening of the exhibition was traditionally a great social event, attended by the *haute monde* of Paris. The portrait of Madame Gautreau was prominently displayed. Sargent had painted her in a low-cut black evening dress, her head turned in cameo profile. The simplicity of the work gave the painting a statuesque elegance rarely seen. The pale skin with its lavender overtones glowed with an unearthly radiance.

The portrait was greeted with a furor of indignation and disapproval. Except for a very few who hailed it as a masterful and beautiful painting, condemnation was universal. The public was shocked by the immodesty of the costume and aghast at the color of the skin tones—despite the fact that Sargent had painted the dress and the skin exactly as they were.

Madame Gautreau retreated in horror at all this notoriety;

Sargent skulked through the corridors to avoid being seen. Newspapers featured the event in headlines, magazines printed articles, humorous poems, and even imaginary interviews with the unfortunate Madame Gautreau. One critic derided the "ugliness of the profile . . . the pearl blue on the skin, at once cadaverous and clownlike." Another said that the subject looked "decomposed." Madame Gautreau and her mother invaded Sargent's studio in hysterical tears, pleading with him to remove the offending picture from the walls of the Salon. All this furor unnerved Sargent. Indeed, when the Metropolitan Museum purchased the canvas in 1916 he had still not entirely gotten over the affair, and insisted that the name of the picture be changed because "of the row I had with the lady years ago. . . ." The Museum complied—the picture is now known as "Portrait of Mme. X."

The neat plans that Sargent had so hopefully made for his future were destroyed. The fuss created by his portrait frightened away potential customers. His work, so recently admired, was now the object of derision. The blow to his pride was severe. He packed and left for London, hoping that in his absence the storm would abate and eventually be forgotten.

His entrance into the world of British art received something less than a warm welcome. An American with a French training in art was a person to be regarded with suspicion and mistrust by the academic-minded artists and critics who dominated the scene. His first exhibited picture, a portrait of the wife of the First Secretary to the American Embassy, was promptly disparaged by a leading critic as "hard, metallic, raw in colour, and without taste. . . ." Fortunately, the lady's friends thought it "chic personified in paint," and several portrait commissions were forthcoming. One of them,

"The Misses Vickers" was rejected by the Royal Academy, but eventually hung at the insistence of a few members of the Academy who threatened to resign if it was not. In a poll taken by a newspaper, it won the dubious honor of being named the worst picture of the year.

The most interesting of Sargent's commissions was one to paint the portrait of Robert Louis Stevenson. The poet and novelist, then near the end of his short life, found Sargent a "charming, simple, clever, honest young man." Of the portrait, Stevenson wrote amusingly that "he represents me as a wierd [sic], very pretty large eyed, chicken-boned, slightly contorted poet." Sargent, dissatisfied with his work, insisted on painting a second portrait, and this Stevenson found to be "touched in lovely, with that witty touch of Sargent's: but of course it looks damned queer as a whole." The second painting was unusual in composition, showing Stevenson striding around his parlor twirling his mustaches. His wife, covered by a shawl, sat in a chair more out of the picture than in. Sargent was still using the unusual point of view for his paintings.

By the early part of 1885, Sargent was obtaining enough commissions to warrant renting a studio on Tite Street, where many well-known artists lived and worked. But it was not until the following year that he finally relinquished all thought of returning to Paris. The Gautreau scandal had damaged his reputation beyond all hope of repair. He resigned himself, not too reluctantly, to remaining in England.

Henry James, by now a close friend of Sargent's, introduced him into London's society circles, loyally proclaiming his talents. But the critics remained cool in their reception of his work. He was too French in his style and too "radical" for their somewhat stodgy tastes.

But the tide turned when, in 1887, Sargent sent a painting titled "Carnation, Lily, Lily, Rose" (named for a popular song) to the Royal Academy exhibition. Influenced somewhat by his friend Claude Monet, the French Impressionist painter, Sargent experimented with an involved use of color and light. The scene of two young girls holding illuminated lanterns in a garden was begun out-of-doors during the brief twilight hour. Each evening, for the twenty-minute period when the light was exactly right, Sargent had painted a little more of the picture until, long after the start, it was finally finished.

The reception of "Carnation, Lily, Lily, Rose" surprised and delighted him. The critics hailed it as a triumph, and the Academy selected it for purchase, paying him seven hundred pounds. That same year, Henry G. Marquand, a wealthy American financier, invited Sargent to name his price for a portrait. Since he did not care to leave England at this point, Sargent asked for $3,000, a price he thought would discourage Marquand. It was roughly three times the sum he could command in Britain. Marquand agreed to the fee without a murmur, leaving Sargent without any alternative but to sail for America. His only previous trip to the land to which he gave his allegiance had been at the age of twenty, for a brief visit to relatives.

The notoriety of the Gautreau portrait, which had wrecked his career in Paris and aroused suspicion in England, brought him fame in America, to his astonishment. Through Marquand, he met and was entertained by many of the richest and most influential citizens of the time. A laudatory article by Henry James appeared in *Harper's Magazine*. The first exhibition of his paintings, held at the St. Botolph Club in Boston in January, 1887, was thronged by the cream of Boston society. Six portraits, several Venetian scenes, a number of landscapes, and "El Jaleo" were shown. The painting of the Spanish dancer was bought by an ardent American admirer, and the National Academy acclaimed it the "most important work by an American artist abroad that has yet been brought to this country." The critics and public were lavish in their praise, and soon the elite were flocking to his studio, clamoring for his services.

Overnight, Sargent had become America's foremost portrait painter. The demand for his elegant, chic, brilliantly painted portraits was almost more than he could handle. When he returned to London, he found that the reverberations of his American success had preceded him. Not only was he now fully accepted in England, but in France as well. Six of his portraits, hanging in the Paris International Exhibition in 1890, won for him the medal of honor and brought him the signal distinction of being made a Chevalier of the Legion of Honor.

By the time he was thirty-five, Sargent was heralded as the finest living portrait painter in England. Duchesses and the lesser nobility, famed actors and actresses, the wealthy—all demanded, begged, pleaded to be painted by him. Popular periodicals published caricatures of long lines of nobility and prominent society personages camped on Sargent's doorstep. The name of John Singer Sargent had become a byword for fashionable elegance, and his portraits hung in the homes of anyone who mattered. In 1894 he was elected to the National Academy in America, and made an associate of the Royal Academy. Three years later he was accorded full membership in the latter institution. His commissions were so numerous that he was forced to take more spacious quarters on Fulham Road. Occasionally the painting room was so crowded that he barely had room to move. He was, as one critic put it, "the most conspicuous of living portrait painters." Many years later, attempting to explain Sargent's fantastic popularity, the noted English author Sir Osbert Sitwell said, "They [the rich] loved him because . . . he showed them to be rich: looking at his portraits, they understood at last *how* rich they really were."

Sargent's immense popularity soon began to have an adverse effect on the quality of his work, thus bearing out the prophetic words of Henry James, who had once asked, "May not this [Sargent's popular appeal] breed an irresponsibility . . . on the part of the . . . genius who has . . . all his fortune in his pocket?" For now, wearied and bored by the overwhelming demands on his services, Sargent began to let down the bars of his artistic conscience. Where before he had lavished on each portrait the full measure of his gifts, now he painted by rote, substituting facility for effort, appearance for substance.

If none of this seemed to matter to his clients, it was of great importance to Sargent. He became progressively less happy with his profession until, before long, he became mortally sick of it. At the high point when his name was synonymous with fame and success, he declared that he wanted "no more paughtraits," as he disgustedly referred to them. "I abhor and abjure them," he wrote, "and hope never to do another. . . ." The man whom Rodin, the great French sculptor, called "the Van Dyke of our times," vainly pleaded, "Ask me to paint your gates, your fences, your barns . . . but *not the human face.*"

Periodically, over the years, Sargent had escaped the demands of portraiture by traveling to the Continent to paint watercolors. Not by nature a man to search out picturesque or quaint areas, he settled his easel wherever he happened to be, and painted what was directly in front of him. But what was in front of him—the corner of a building, a fountain, a view of the mountains—he painted boldly, brilliantly, impressionistically. He found a second refuge from "paughtraits" when he was commissioned to do a set of mural decorations for the Boston Public Library. Turning to the project with joy and relief, Sargent threw himself into this creative effort as if it marked his rebirth as a serious artist. In an effort to discourage clients, he had increased the prices of his portraits until they were all but prohibitive. Yet the cries for his work continued undiminished. He locked his door, deafened his ear, refused more commissions than he accepted— to no avail. If he would not do an oil portrait, then his public would accept a charcoal sketch, no matter how outrageous the fee. Each barrier he erected merely served to make a work by his hand more desirable. It was impossible for him to make the complete break he so ardently professed to want.

The theme Sargent chose for his murals was based on the history of religion. Because of the pressure of his other work, it was a good deal more than a decade before the murals were completely finished. Sargent was forty-seven years old when he arrived in the United States in 1903 to supervise the installation of a section of his mural. The reception then given to the mural was overwhelmingly favorable. With the passage of time, it has come to be recognized that his wall decorations rank well below his best work, and are markedly inferior to many of the portraits he despised doing.

For the next few years, Sargent spent the major portion of his time working on mural decorations and watercolors. The demand for his work had not decreased, but he had learned how to make his refusals stick. He kept the number of his commissions down to a bearable minimum. Nevertheless, his reputation as the most important living portraitist in England

and America showed no sign of waning. In 1907, he was recommended for a knighthood, but politely declined with the explanation that he was not "one of His Majesty's subjects but an American citizen." His friends, his fellow artists, and his public all held him in awed respect. Sargent, however, referred to himself as a "profoundly unsociable crank." When he was painting the portrait of Lady Sassoon, her relatives complained that there was something wrong about the mouth. In a towering rage, Sargent screamed at them, "Of course there is something wrong with the mouth! A portrait is a painting with a little something wrong about the mouth."

When World War I broke out in 1914, Sargent scarcely seemed aware of it. It might have been taking place on a distant planet for all the interest he showed. It wasn't until 1916, after he had returned to Boston to put the finishing touches to the Library murals, that he acknowledged the existence of the conflict. Having reluctantly accepted a commission to paint John D. Rockefeller's portrait, he turned his entire fee over to the Red Cross. His aroused conscience would not allow him, as he put it, any more "fiddling and doing watercolours while Rome is burning." The British government asked him to return to England to do additional portraits for the benefit of the Red Cross, and he was also invited to go to France to do commemorative war paintings.

In June, 1918, Sargent left for the front to gather material for his reflections of the war. He was sixty-two years old, grown from youthful slimness to middle-aged corpulence—"carved out of beef," as a friend said. In the battle area, he calmly sat in the shade of a huge white umbrella with a green lining, and, while shells burst overhead, painted sketches of the conflict. His work beneath the umbrella (which the General Staff soon ordered to be camouflaged) resulted in the production of numerous watercolors and several oil paintings. Among them were "The Arrival of American Troops at the Front, France, 1918," and a picture bluntly called "Gassed." The latter was an actual representation of a gas barrage, a "harrowing sight [of] a field full of gassed and blindfolded men," as Sargent described it.

When the government returned him to London in October, he was besieged by the members of the Royal Academy, imploring him to accept the presidency of that august body. "I would do *anything* for the Royal Academy but that," he wrote, declining the honor, "and if you press me any more, I shall flee the country. . . ." He was still, as he had been for many years, the most sought-after, the most consistently admired American painter of the century.

Sargent's attitude toward his work was now hypercritical. Of his beautiful painting of the Boit children he declared that it was "merely an amateurish sort of arrangement that could find its rebuke in any good Japanese print." He contemplated adding another figure to the magnificent "El Jaleo" to improve the composition. His portrait of Marquand reminded him of a "plucked fowl." When his watercolors were exhibited with those of Winslow Homer in Paris in 1923, he refused to look at them. At the retrospective show of his work held in 1924 at the opening of the Grand Central Art Galleries in New York, he was conspicuous by his absence. The critics sang paeans of praise, but Sargent, who remained in England, did not care. He was convinced that he had squandered his prodigious gifts by painting pictures that gave him little or no joy.

The exhibition at the Grand Central Galleries once more unleashed a flood of demands for his portraits. Desperately, Sargent pleaded with gallery officials to "say that I am a physical wreck and unable to answer letters." He turned down one offer of $25,000, and refused to paint Calvin Coolidge and the Queen of Romania at any price.

Sargent arranged passage to the United States for the middle of April, 1925. The last of his Boston Museum decorations, which he had started upon the completion of the Library murals, were now done and he said, regretfully and with a hint of bitterness, "I suppose, I may die when I like." He felt he had come to the end of his line. Several days before his departure, he attended a farewell party given by his sister Emily. A few close friends of the family were present, including the Barnard girls who had many years before posed for "Carnation, Lily, Lily, Rose." The party broke up at about ten-thirty. Sargent rode home in a taxi with a friend. When they parted, he called out a goodbye and a promise to see him in six months. Early in the morning of the next day, April 15, 1925, the maid who attended Sargent found him in his bed, his eyeglasses pushed back on his forehead, his copy of Voltaire's *Dictionnaire Philosophique* at his side. He had died in his sleep.

During his lifetime Sargent had never wanted for money or fame. He had been awarded honorary degrees by many of the major universities of America and England. His work had been bought by most of the great museums. His watercolors were sought after as works of glittering beauty. But with his death, his reputation suffered a severe decline, contrary to the fortunes of so many artists who achieved posthumously the rewards they were denied in their lifetime. The younger artists, washed by the waves of the modern French school of painting, scornfully dismissed Sargent as a fashionable relic of an outdated century. For them Sargent's flaws overwhelmed his virtues; they dwelt on his shallowness and overlooked his genuinely artistic virtuosity. But with the passage

of time, and of movements, Sargent's reputation has been re-
stored, the extraordinary quality of his brush given sober
recognition.

With more bitter truth than perhaps he realized, Sargent
had once proposed the following epitaph for his tombstone:
"Here lies John Singer Sargent; there is something wrong
with the mouth."

9

The Performer

JAMES ABBOTT MC NEILL WHISTLER

1834–1903

For more than forty years James Abbott McNeill Whistler made London his stage, performing under the iridescent spotlight of his personality, entertaining a hugely amused, sometimes contemptuous audience. An eccentric, a dandy, a clown, a wit, Whistler was the most flamboyant public figure of his time. He flouted the prim morality of the era; he attacked mediocrity with savage scorn; flying the banner of "art for art's sake," he slashed into the stuffy, outdated academic banalities of the reigning art world.

Yet no matter how outrageous his behavior, Whistler's devotion to his profession was utterly serious. As an artist, he was completely dedicated, a revolutionary whose cause was the liberation of art from the dungeon of stale tradition. American by birth, trained in France, by choice a resident of England, Whistler's art belongs to no country and no school. It is as uniquely his own as was his riotously individual personality.

With typical impudence, Whistler once declared, "I shall be born when and where I choose." He was, in sober fact, born in Lowell, Massachusetts, on July 10, 1834. His father, Major George Washington Whistler, a military engineer, was a West Point graduate, a man of lively and charming disposition. Several years after his first wife, Mary Swift, died, Major Whistler married her closest friend, Anna Mathilda McNeill. The new Mrs. Whistler took over the management of the household and the rearing of his three children, George, Deborah, and Joseph, who was to die in childhood. A small woman, gentle and devout, Anna Whistler was a fine mother to her new family.

The first son to be born of this second marriage was christened James Abbott Whistler. When he was older, he dropped the name of Abbott and substituted his mother's Scottish maiden name. Mother and father were enchanted by their new offspring. The Major, boasting of the child's good looks, declared, "It was enough to make Sir Joshua Reynolds come out of his grave and paint Jemmie asleep." James— Jimmie or Jemmie, as he was called—was a delicate child, subject to bronchial ailments. His doting mother carefully guarded his health, and kept him close to her side.

When James was three years old, the family moved to Stonington, Connecticut. Major Whistler, who had earlier resigned his commission, became consulting engineer, and later chief engineer, for the Western Railroad of Massachusetts. Three more sons were born to the Whistlers during this period, but only one, William, survived.

In 1841, Tsar Nicholas I of Russia sent his emissaries to the United States to hire an engineer to supervise the building of a railroad from St. Petersburg to Moscow. The position, carrying the then munificent salary of $12,000 a year, was offered to Major Whistler. He accepted, and in the autumn of 1842 departed for Russia with the family to follow later.

After an arduous journey by ship, railroad, steamer, and stagecoach, Mrs. Whistler and her children arrived in St. Petersburg and took up residence in large and gracious quarters with windows overlooking the Tsar's Winter Palace. Alert and inquisitive nine-year-old James was fascinated by his new life. The Tsar's soldiers in their resplendent uniforms, the fur-clad crowds speaking their strange tongue, the exotic beauty of the sparkling snow-swept city with its strangely ornamented buildings, the displays of fireworks that painted the nights with bright colors—all of this stirred his youthful imagination and stimulated his already keen visual sense. He drew at every opportunity, displaying, in these impressions of the life around him, a precocious but very real talent. Soon he was enrolled in the Imperial Academy of Fine Arts, where he spent four years. In his final examination he stood at the head of his class. Meanwhile, he was tutored in French, the language of the Imperial Court, as well as in other academic subjects.

In the summer of 1848, Mrs. Whistler and the children went to England for a visit. Deborah, now a young woman, met and married Seymour Haden, a young surgeon and an etcher of some repute. At the wedding, James, as his mother wrote, was "the only groomsman, and very proud of the honour." During their stay in England, Major Whistler, who had arrived for the wedding, commissioned Sir William Boxall to paint his young son's portrait. The picture shows a smiling, dark-haired, intelligent-looking boy who hints only faintly at the mercurial individual that would emerge later.

An outbreak of cholera in Russia kept Mrs. Whistler and her children in England while her husband returned alone to complete his almost finished task. Shortly after being decorated by the Tsar with the Order of St. Anna, Major Whistler contracted cholera. His wife hurried to join him, and she was at his bedside when, in April, 1849, he passed away. Shortly after the funeral, Mrs. Whistler began the long, bleak journey back to Stonington with her fatherless sons.

Another and less glamorous existence began for the family upon their arrival in the United States. An annuity of fifteen hundred dollars a year left no leeway for luxury. The family moved to Pomfret, Connecticut, living in several rooms of a farmhouse, while the boys attended school at Christ Church Hall. The complete change of atmosphere and the narrow Puritanism of his surroundings were unsettling to James. He sorely missed the excitement, the comforts, and the glamour of his recent life. He was an uninterested student, bored with his work, chafed by confinement. His high spirits, his growing exhibitionism, and his delight in poking fun at authority soon led his headmaster to recommend his removal. Mrs. Whistler, blind to the possibility of any fault in her favorite child, reasoned that "Jimmie's eagerness to attain all his desires for information and his fearlessness often make him offend and it makes him appear less amiable than he really is." For her, "Jimmie" could do no wrong.

Acting on his mother's wish that he follow in his father's footsteps, young Whistler, in July of 1851, was enrolled as a cadet in the United States Military Academy. He was seventeen years old. His scholarly aptitudes did not improve at West Point. The only subject in which he excelled was drawing. But, despite his poor standing as a student, he established a reputation based on his quick wit and ready reply, easy charm, and blithe disregard for regulations. "Curls," as he was nicknamed, acted with the casual air of a paying guest enjoying a pleasant holiday. It was hardly surprising that, at the end of three years, he was dismissed from the Academy—specifically, for deficiency in chemistry. Although he treated his expulsion lightly, his ego was sorely bruised. He could not bear failure, even though in this case he had brought it on almost deliberately. In later years, discussing his expulsion, he would remark flippantly, "Had silicon been a gas, I would have been a major-general." But he never lost his affection for the military institution. Years later he sent the Academy library a copy of a book he had written, bearing the inscription: "From an old cadet whose pride it is to remember his West Point days." And West Point returned the compliment by dedicating a plaque in his memory.

To appease his mother's disappointment in her favorite son, Whistler reluctantly went to Baltimore to see if his brother George would give him a job. To his relief, George turned him down. Whistler went on to Washington, where he petitioned Jefferson Davis, then Secretary of War, to reconsider his dismissal from West Point. However, Secretary Davis sent Whistler to see Captain Benham, chief of the drawing division of the United States Coast and Geodetic Survey. The Captain was much impressed by the young man's ability to draw, and, in November, 1854, hired him as an engraver at a salary of $1.50 per day.

Whistler quickly mastered the essentials of the engraver's art—so quickly, in fact, that he soon became bored. Etching pictures of the coastline fell somewhat short of inflaming his vivid imagination. To amuse himself, he took to drawing fanciful heads and figures in the blank areas of the plates. In his off hours, he cultivated the more sophisticated members of the diplomatic corps. His fluent knowledge of French, his unusual background and his acid wit gave him easy access to these circles. Soon he was spending more time socializing than working at his job. In the first two months of 1855 he worked a grand total of twelve and one quarter hours!

It was at this time that his unusual attire first began to attract widespread attention and draw comment. Parading down the streets of Washington, he would appear at one time in a Scotch plaid hat and shawl, at another in a large slouch hat and flowing coat worn over an unbuttoned waistcoat. He arrived at a formal party with his frock coat pinned up to simulate a dinner jacket. He delighted in shocking public opinion, and was amusedly aware that he was creating a legend. At twenty-one, he was designing the pattern of unconventionality which he followed for the rest of his life.

Whistler's enchantment with the gay artist's life in Paris, as described in several books he had read, inspired him with the idea of studying painting in the French capital. He resigned from his job in February, 1855, and as a memento, he engraved a small devil on the lens of a magnifying glass used by the staff. In the summer of that year he sailed for France, having received his mother's blessing and the promise of a yearly income of $350 to be supplied by his brother George. He was never to set foot again in the land of his birth.

In Paris, Whistler enrolled in the studio of Marc Gabriel Charles Gleyre, an academic painter and teacher. Gleyre's belief that all color was based on black made a lasting impression on Whistler. Little else did. The daily round of studio routine bored him to tears. The "idle apprentice," as he came to be known, was more absent from class than present. A small, dapper figure, with a mysterious foreign air, he could usually be seen wandering the boulevards of Paris, or seated in a café, sketching the passing show. In the words of a friend, he was a "most amusing and eccentric fellow . . . with his long, black, thick curly hair, and large felt hat with a broad black ribbon."

He spent many hours in the Louvre copying the old masters, and sometimes selling his copies for twenty-five dollars to visiting American tourists. His evenings were passed in conversation with friends, or dancing at gay student balls until the early hours; his "morning" waking hour was noon. The money sent by his brother was inadequate for the style of living he insisted upon following, and his extravagances kept him in continual debt. He borrowed where he could, existed on credit, and, when he came by a few dollars, scattered them recklessly.

In the summer of 1858, Whistler made a tour of the French countryside, bringing back with him a series of etchings which were published in a folio known as "the French set." His skillful handling of the tonal variations of light and shade and the delicacy of his line established at once his reputation as a master etcher. Ever after, no matter how his reputation as a painter fluctuated, his position as one of the finest practitioners of this difficult art remained unchallenged.

In the fall, Whistler and a French fellow student, Henri Fantin-Latour, joined a small group of young men working in the studio of François Bonvin under the guidance of Gustave Courbet, the great nineteenth-century French realist. Courbet's scenes of everyday life, painted with a heavily loaded brush and somberly colored, were in radical contrast to the French Academy's classical approach. One of the finest of Whistler's early canvases, "At the Piano," was directly influenced by Courbet's mannerisms. In the picture, the monumental form of a black-gowned woman seated at a grand piano (his sister Deborah) is beautifully balanced by the figure of a child (his niece Annie), dressed in white and leaning against the instrument. It was a sensitive, masterful work, foreshadowing his later distinctive decorative style.

"At the Piano" marked the end of Whistler's student days and his debut as a professional artist. Along with two of his etchings, it was sent to the Salon exhibition of 1859. The Academicians in control of the Salon accepted the etchings but rejected the now-famous painting, along with the works of several other nonconformists. Bonvin, irate at the rejection of what he considered the best talents of the day, organized his own show of the refused works. "At the Piano" was singled out for much praise by the younger painters, and by Courbet himself.

Whistler had heard that the market for painters was prospering in England, and so made plans to go to London. His sister Deborah extended the hospitality of her house to him. He accepted, taking it upon himself also to include Fantin-Latour and another French artist-friend, Alphonse Legros. Deborah's husband, Dr. Haden, was the soul of generosity. Not only did he house and feed the three indigent artists, but he even bought some of their work. In return for this magnanimity, Whistler and the two Frenchmen scoffed at Haden's quite respectable etchings, and treated his artistic opinions with fine scorn. This situation could not last long, nor did it. Legros and Fantin-Latour returned to France, and Whistler moved to a studio in Lindsey Row, Chelsea, a district favored by artists and writers.

In 1860, "At the Piano" was accepted in the Royal Academy Exhibition, where, to Whistler's delight, it found a purchaser. Two years later he sent another canvas, "The Woman in White," to the Academy; it was rejected as "too odd." Undaunted, Whistler shipped it to the new Berner Street Gallery, where it was hung, but was poorly received.

"The Woman in White" traveled to the Salon exhibition of 1863 in Paris. It was rejected, but shown at the Salon des Refusés—a show consisting of the works of artists who had been refused entry by the Academy—in the company of such now-famous men as Monet, Degas, Pissarro, and Manet. French opinion of "The Woman in White" was divided between scorn and admiration. In any case, it was one of the most talked about paintings in that unusual exhibition. One French critic thought it a "most remarkable picture, at once simple and fantastic." Another called it "oddly ugly"; still another felt it was the most important painting in the room.

Later, in London, after Whistler had changed the title of the picture to "The White Girl: Symphony in White No. 1," a critic took exception to the variety of colors he found in this "white" painting. Whistler unsheathed his sting. "Bon Dieu," he wrote in one of the first of his long series of letters to newspapers, "did this wise person expect white hair and chalked faces? And does he then . . . believe that a symphony in F contains no other note, but shall be a continued repetition of F, F, F? . . . Fool!"

The word symphony was the signpost to the new direction Whistler's painting was taking. Leaving Courbet's realism behind, he was turning toward a more abstract style, and he emphasized this quality by deriving his titles from the field of music, the most abstract of all the arts. Hence his "symphonies," "nocturnes," and "notes." Although basing his pictures on reality, his subject became of less importance to him than composition, line, and color. It was his stated belief that "art should be independent of all clap-trap, should . . . appeal to the artistic sense of eye . . . without confounding this with emotions entirely foreign to it. . . ."

He responded almost instantaneously to the discovery of Japanese art as a synthesis of all he had been trying to say.

He adapted the structural simplicity, the sensitive line and the delicate tonality of the Japanese print to suit his own needs. Subtle color harmonies, painted in thin—sometimes transparent—washes, and formal "arrangements" were now the essentials upon which he based his painting.

The years beginning with 1870 were Whistler's finest and most productive period. With the exception of a short time in 1865 when, quixotically, he went to South America to help Chile and Peru in their war against the Spaniards (an entirely unsolicited help), Whistler made London his permanent home. Notwithstanding the indifference of the Royal Academy, he had gained a reputation as an artist of considerable merit, and was getting a number of fashionable clients and important commissions. Some of his best canvases were painted during these years, among them the famous "Portrait of the Artist's Mother; Arrangement in Grey and Black"; the handsome and sympathetic portrait of Thomas Carlyle; "Miss Cicely Alexander; Harmony in Grey and Green"; full-length portraits of Sir Henry Irving and Ellen Terry, the two most outstanding actors of the day; Pablo Sarasate, the violinist and composer, as well as many of his loveliest "Nocturnes," "Harmonies," and the "Thames set" of etchings. A butterfly, originally suggested by a fellow artist as an interesting approximation of his initials, Whistler now worked into the integral design of each canvas, using it in place of a signature.

Whistler's eccentricity increased in direct ratio to his popularity. He became known throughout London for the bizarre extravagance of his personality. He took to designing his own clothes, and chose the color of his socks and even his shoelaces to harmonize with his outfit. He carried a long bamboo cane (he owned two: a pale one for the day and a dark one for the evening), which he flourished with abandon. A military mustache and goatee, eyes that sparkled brightly from under heavy brows, and a monocle screwed into his right eye all accentuated his Satanic appearance. A lock of white hair like a feather, described by him as having been touched by the Devil, added a final flamboyant touch. The butterfly monogram was embroidered on all his handkerchiefs, and inlaid in his palette. His biting wit and sharp tongue—and the American pancakes he served!—made his Sunday breakfasts a must for the *haute monde* and the literati. His table setting and the food on it were carefully selected so that they would not clash with the color harmony of the room. His home was decorated with Japanese simplicity, and painted in pastel colors to simulate the effect of sunlight. A bare minimum of furnishings gave his guests no choice but to stand or sit on the floor.

Although he occasionally trained his sharp tongue on his clients, he left all his eccentricities outside his studio door. When he painted he was a sober, dedicated artist. He labored fiercely and tirelessly to produce the unlabored aspect of his canvases. Sitters were sometimes reduced to tears of exhaustion by the long hours he insisted on spending at the easel. If he was dissatisfied with any portion of a picture, he rubbed out the whole thing and started over again. For his "nocturnes," he spent innumerable hours memorizing the scene he would later paint in the studio. No matter how many hours, days, even months went by, a picture was never finished until he was absolutely satisfied with the results.

In 1872, he was commissioned to paint portraits of the family of Frederick Leyland, a wealthy Liverpool shipowner who had some time before purchased Whistler's "Princess of the Land of Porcelain." When the portraits were completed, Whistler prevailed upon Leyland to allow him to redecorate the dining room of a palatial new home Leyland was building. Whistler's concept was to paint the room, known as "The Peacock Room," in simulation of the brilliantly colored feathers of that bird. Occupying the place of honor over the mantelpiece would hang the "Princess of the Land of Porcelain."

Whistler moved himself, his equipment, and several assistants into Prince's Hall, as Leyland's house was called. He printed cards inviting the public to watch the performance. At teatime he entertained guests with monologues about his work, Leyland, or any other subject that caught his fancy. The work progressed slowly. The project, begun in the spring of 1876, was still uncompleted almost two years later. The original payment of five hundred guineas had been doubled, and now Whistler demanded an increase of yet another thousand guineas. Leyland's irritation at this high-handedness turned to anger. In high dudgeon, he dismissed Whistler, sending him a check for two thousand pounds. This constituted an insult, since artists were paid in guineas and tradespeople in pounds. Whistler was furious. By way of a spiteful parting shot he painted one entire wall of the dining room with an allegorical picture showing a battle between a rich and a poor peacock. Not content with this display of bad temper, he later vented his anger in three more pictures, peopled with odd and unpleasant creatures, directly insulting Leyland. A critic called them a malicious joke from which "beauty exudes like the scent of a poisonous flower."

News of the affair flashed through fashionable London with incredible speed, and now the word *notorious* became attached to Whistler's reputation. His every word, his every action was food for gossip. And his prestige, never high in the esteem of the powerful Academicians, was further lowered. Still, those people who dared ignore public opinion sought his services, flocked to listen with their own ears as his sharp tongue flayed his enemies. On the strength of the money he expected to make from this new-found popularity, Whistler engaged E. W. Godwin, an architect, to build him a house on Tite Street, in the smart quarter of Chelsea. To help pay for the "White House," as he called it, Whistler pawned the picture of his mother, but later redeemed it.

When the new Grosvenor Gallery opened in London in 1875, as a rival to the Royal Academy, Whistler was one of the painters invited to exhibit. Everyone from the Prince of Wales down to the least important art critic attended the grand opening. Two famous lecturers from Oxford University —Oscar Wilde, the poet, and John Ruskin, the dean of critics—were among the crowd. Whistler's canvases were summarily dismissed by the majority of the savants, and scathingly denounced by Ruskin, who was particularly outraged by "The Falling Rocket: Nocturne in Black and Gold," a painting of the fireworks display over the Cremorne Gardens. Ruskin fulminated in print against "the ill-educated conceit" and "willful imposture" of Whistler's work; and concluded his diatribe by storming, "I have seen, and heard, much of cockney impudence before now; but never expected to hear a coxcomb ask two hundred guineas for flinging a pot of paint in the public's face."

Whistler sued for libel.

The trial opened on November 26, 1878, and drew a crowd of spectators surpassing in glitter a smart opening night in the theatre. The press gallery was jammed with correspondents. The trial gave promise of being the best entertainment of the century. When Whistler took the stand, Ruskin's attorney brought in "The Falling Rocket" for identification. Asked if it was indeed a view of Cremorne, Whistler replied that it was not an exact reproduction, but an "artistic arrangement," marked "two hundred guineas." Leading Whistler on, question by question, the attorney established that it had taken the artist only two days to "knock off" the picture. Do you then—the lawyer demanded—ask the exorbitant fee of two hundred guineas for forty-eight hours' work? "No," replied Whistler, his monocle gleaming with disdain, "I ask it for the knowledge of a lifetime."

Whistler's reply brought the house down.

When he was asked if he disapproved of criticism, he responded that he respected it only when it came from one who had spent a lifetime in the practice of art. "For the opinion of a man whose life is not so passed I would have as little regard as you would, if he expresssed an opinion on law." Could Whistler make the attorney see the beauty of "The Falling Rocket"? Whistler paused for effect, then said scornfully, "I fear it would be as hopeless as for a musician to pour his notes into the ear of a deaf man." The audience rocked with laughter; the courtroom was rapidly taking on the mood of a music hall. After Whistler's testimony was ended, only a few minor artists came to his defense. On the other hand, many of England's most prominent painters confirmed Ruskin's opinion, stating that Whistler's paintings were "unfinished," overpriced, or both.

The court found Ruskin guilty of libel, and granted Whistler one farthing for damages, with court costs to be shared equally by both parties to the suit. The jury thus indicated its contempt for Whistler's art. The populace had been amused. They enjoyed him as a spectacle, but refused to take him seriously as an artist or a man.

Ruskin had been dealt a severe blow, but Whistler himself —the nominal victor—had been bankrupted by expenses incurred by the trial and his career almost completely wrecked. Creditors repossessed his house and his furnishings. To keep canvases from falling into unscrupulous hands, he burnt, slashed and defaced them. A few he hid in a friend's home. People still came to watch him perform, but none were brave enough to give him a commission. As his anger grew, so did his defiance of public opinion. His many eccentricities became even more pronounced. His humor turned bitter, his laugh high-pitched and shrill, his pranks more carefully calculated to outrage.

The Fine Arts Society, which had exhibited his etchings, came to Whistler's rescue. They commissioned him to execute a series of twelve etchings of the Venetian scene, and advanced a sum of money against future sales. In the late fall of 1879, Whistler departed for Italy, where he soon became the hub of a group of young foreign artists. He could be found almost daily in St. Mark's Square, surrounded by his followers, and as one friend said, "praising France, abusing England, and thoroughly enjoying Italy." He hired a barge and a band one night and rode the Grand Canal to the strains of "Yankee Doodle" while displaying his paintings. To the coattails of an academic artist sitting close to St. Mark's Church to sketch detail, he pinned a sign saying, "I am totally blind." He showed his contempt for the world that had refused him recognition.

Whistler, who loved the half light and the mists of London, complained that the Italian sun was too brilliant, the streets too picturesque. Nevertheless, when he returned to London in November of the following year, he brought back with him forty etchings, a number of watercolors and pastels, and a few oils.

Ironically, in his absence there had been a subtle turn in his favor. Victorian morality was giving way to a new freedom of thought and action. The older members of the Academy were being replaced by a new group of more "modern" artists. The younger painters now started gathering around Whistler, acknowledging him as their master. Simultaneously, he began to acquire a reputable following in America, where museums were exhibiting his pictures, and collectors buying them. Nevertheless, his notoriety still worked against him, and new commissions were rare. "In the seventies," according to his friend and biographer, Joseph Pennell, "it needed courage to be painted by Whistler; now it was to risk notoriety and ridicule."

The first show of Whistler's Venetian etchings—despite the crisp brilliance of his work—did not fare well. But it brought the Fine Arts Society publicity, and they followed it with a fairly successful exhibition of his pastels. With the proceeds from this show, Whistler moved from his boarding-house back to Tite Street, a few doors away from his former home. A second show of the etchings in 1883 was noteworthy mainly for its startling decor and bitter humor. Whistler's "theme" for the exhibition was yellow and white. Walls were painted white; chairs, floor, and flowers were yellow. Assistants wore yellow ties; Whistler wore yellow socks. Yellow and white paper butterflies were passed out to the visitors. The catalogue contained the biblical phrase, "Out of their own mouths shall ye judge them," on the title page. Following the title of each picture was a quotation from a critic attacking the work. Whistler's audience was hugely entertained, but the pictures won scant praise.

Whistler's heretical views on art and his astute showmanship caught the eye of Mrs. Richard D'Oyly Carte, the wife of the well-known theatrical entrepreneur, and producer of the Gilbert and Sullivan operettas. She conceived the idea of presenting him in a lecture at Prince's Hall, London, on the evening of February 20, 1885. It was called the "Ten O'Clock" lecture, after the hour at which it was held. As was customary in any event involving Whistler, the hall was jammed to capacity. The elite, the press, anyone who could purchase a hard-to-get ticket was present.

Whistler, dressed in evening clothes, stepped out on the platform. In the words of one observer, he seemed "a jaunty, unabashed, composed, and self-satisfied gentleman armed with an opera hat and an eyeglass." "Listen!" he began, "There never was an artistic period. There never was an art-loving nation." He proceeded to establish his contention that it was the right of the artist to determine what was art, and the right of nobody else. The audience that had come expecting some amusing demonstration was doomed to disappointment. Whistler was utterly serious.

The younger painters were enthusiastically in agreement with Whistler's credo; almost everyone else opposed. The poet Swinburne called him "an impenetrable blockhead," and his lecture "thick-witted, tasteless, senseless." Oscar Wilde, himself a poet, declared that only the poet was "the supreme Artist." Whistler wasted no time in striking back. He spoke slightingly of Swinburne and said of Wilde, "Oscar has the courage of the opinions . . . of others."

Whistler was fifty years old. Fate, which had not previously used him kindly, now allowed him some measure of acceptance. His "The Yellow Buskin" won a second prize at the International Exhibition in Munich. In accepting the award, Whistler could not resist the opportunity to call the medal a "second-hand compliment." He was made a Chevalier of the Legion of Honor of France, given a first-class medal at the Paris Universal Exhibition, and a gold medal at the Amsterdam Exhibition.

Coincident with this spurt of good fortune, Whistler, the lifelong bachelor, married Beatrix Godwin, the widow of the architect who had built the "White House," Whistler's former home. It was a happy relationship. Mrs. Whistler, a tall, plump woman who towered over her husband, devoted her energies to keeping "James" contented. Under her gentle but firm guidance, he began to quarrel less, and scarcely made any new enemies.

In the spring of 1890, the Whistlers moved to Cheyne Walk, a short distance from his former quarters. In the summer of that year a collection of Whistler's letters, his personal account of the Ruskin trial, various pamphlets he had written, his lectures, and other material, was published in book form, under the title, *The Gentle Art of Making Enemies*. It was dedicated to "the rare Few, who, early in Life have rid Themselves of the Friendship of the Many. . . ." Throughout the pages of the book, the butterfly, now wearing a forked devil's tail, flitted in a variety of attitudes ranging from joy to hatred.

In the years that followed, Whistler's reputation grew steadily. His paintings were exhibited widely in Europe and the United States. In 1891 his portrait of Carlyle was purchased by the Glasgow Corporation. That same year the French government bought the portrait of his mother for the Luxembourg. This "Arrangement in Grey and Black," as Whistler preferred to call it, has become almost universally accepted as the symbol of motherhood. It was later reproduced on a postage stamp "in memory and honor of the mothers of America." A large retrospective show of forty-three pictures at the Goupil Galleries in London won unanimous praise. The paintings he sent to the Columbian Exposition in Chicago won a medal, the first such honor ever given to him by his own country.

In 1892 the Whistlers moved to Paris, settling in the Rue du Bac in Montparnasse. Whistler wanted to be in the city where the "new" art was developing. On the whole, he was ignored by the leading French painters; he was too much of an exhibitionist for their tastes. Edgar Degas once said to him reprovingly, "My dear Whistler, you have too much talent to behave the way you do."

For several years Mrs. Whistler had been ailing. By the end of 1894 her condition was diagnosed as cancer. The Whistlers returned to London to seek medical help, but it was in vain. On May 10, 1896, Whistler's beloved "Trixie" passed away.

In the next few years, Whistler shuttled between his home in Paris and the London home of his friend, the publisher William Heinemann. He was past sixty, and aging rapidly. A bronchial condition which had plagued him throughout his life now attacked him with increasing severity. It was during this period that Charles Lang Freer and Henry C. Frick—wealthy American industrialists and art patrons—introduced his work into many important American collections, including their own. In 1898, he was elected first president of the newly formed International Society of Sculptors, Painters and Gravers. For a brief period he taught in an atelier in Paris, but was too impatient and intolerant to make a good teacher.

In 1902 he bought a new house in Cheyne Walk. He wandered through the rooms, ill and weak, dressed in an old, worn, fur-lined overcoat that substituted for a dressing gown. When he felt well enough to work, he sat at his easel. When a friend came to see him, they would play dominos, at which he cheated outrageously. He rarely went out and slept fitfully both day and night in an easy chair. A friend, who visited him on one of his better days, described him as "feverishly alive . . . with his bright withered cheeks, over which the skin was drawn tightly, his darting eyes . . . his exquisite hands, never at rest. And his voice, with its strange accent, part American, part deliberately French, part tuned to the key of his wit. . . ."

In the early months of 1903, Whistler's heart grew weaker. His physician ordered him to bed, but he refused to obey. His cough had grown so bad that he was frequently forced to write to save his voice. On the morning of July 17, he wandered into his studio to see some of his work, and it was there, later in the day, that he was found dead.

Whistler's funeral was held five days later, on one of London's hot, gray summer days. Extra police, called out to control the huge crowds that were expected, lined the area around Old Chelsea Church. But the total attendance at the services consisted of the few remaining members of his family and a meager scattering of friends.

James Abbott McNeill Whistler was no longer news.

10

The Old Maid

MARY CASSATT

1844–1926

"I would almost rather see you dead," Robert S. Cassatt thundered when his twenty-year-old daughter Mary announced her intention of becoming an artist. In that nineteenth-century era of seemly behavior and rigid convention, dabbling in watercolor or painting on china was permissible for a young lady, but a serious career in art was not. And when the young lady's family ranked among the elite of Philadelphia's social families, her ambition was downright outrageous.

Mary Cassatt did not quail or retreat an inch in the face of her father's wrath. Instead, she fought his decision with

148

stubborn, dogged, iron-willed resolution, until at last he relented. In the pursuit of her goal, Mary Cassatt defied tradition, violated public opinion, renounced her social position, and gave up all thought of marriage and a family. Her sacrifices were many and great, but, together with talent and a single-minded determination, they led her on to become America's most important woman artist and the leading woman painter in all art.

Mary Stevenson Cassatt, oldest daughter of Robert S. Cassatt, a wealthy banker, and Katherine Kelso Johnston, was born on May 22, 1844, in Allegheny City, Pennsylvania, where her father was then mayor. The Cassatts had three other children, Alexander J., Gardner, and Lydia. Wealthy and socially prominent, the Cassatt family lived in an atmosphere of ease and refinement. Both Robert and Katherine Cassatt shared a profound admiration for the culture of France. Katherine was the daughter of a wealthy Pittsburgh family. In her childhood she had learned to read, write, and speak French to perfection. She encouraged her children to do the same. Robert's French heritage predisposed him to a deep respect for the land of his ancestors. "He did not have the soul of a business man," Mary once said. "He was imbued with many French ideas, and devoted himself to our education." When Mary was about seven years old, the Cassatts moved to France, ostensibly to consult a physician about the health of one of their children. But it was of greater importance to Robert to give his children a European education against a background that would instill in them his own appreciation of French culture.

The family settled in the Hotel Continental on the Rue de Rivoli in Paris. It was an exciting era in the history of France. From the balcony of her room overlooking the Seine, Mary was able to witness the coronation of Napoleon III as

Emperor of France. In her walks with her nurse she observed the colorful sights and sounds of Paris, from the haughty elegance of the Champs Elysées to the roistering student life of the Latin Quarter. Despite her youth, Paris left an imprint on her sensitive mind that lasted all of her long life.

After five years of absorbing the customs, the language, and the art treasures of France, the Cassatts returned to the United States. They moved to Philadelphia, which was then the home of some of America's most prominent families. Mary returned to school to continue her education. It soon became evident that she had little desire to join the social whirl that engulfed her contemporaries. Instead, she showed great interest in the creative arts, and spent much of her leisure time drawing.

At twenty, an age when most of her friends were busily preparing themselves for their debut in society, Mary Cassatt began a determined campaign to be allowed to study art. Tall, slim, dark-haired, plain-looking, she carried herself with a dignity and assurance that bespoke the security of a wealthy background. She possessed a quick, intelligent mind, a sharp tongue, and, above all, an unswerving, indefatigable will. All of this she put to work in the service of her ambition, until at last her father surrendered and permitted her to attend classes at the Pennsylvania Academy of Fine Arts. After a period of drawing from casts, Mary became convinced that the Academy was an inadequate teacher. Now she besieged her father with demands that she be allowed to pursue her art education abroad, and once again, astonishingly, she triumphed. Without a backward glance she abandoned a life of ease, wealth, and social prestige, and embarked on a career that was difficult enough for most men, and almost impossible for a woman.

In 1866, at the age of twenty-two, Mary Cassatt sailed for

Europe, accompanied by her mother. Instead of enrolling
in the Ecole des Beaux-Arts in Paris, as did most young art
students, she went to Italy to begin her own study of the
paintings of old masters. Mary settled in Parma, and began
an intensive analysis of the work of Correggio—"going to
school to Correggio," as she called it. From Parma she went
to Spain, and in the Prado Museum in Madrid studied Velázquez and Rubens. The latter "so transported" her "with admiration," that she devoted the entire summer to studying his
paintings.

After several years of relentless, untiring work, Mary felt
that she was ready to exhibit her first painting. To the Paris
Salon exhibition of 1872 she sent "On the Balcony," a picture much influenced by her idols, Velázquez and Rubens, yet
displaying her own rare gift. To avoid any undue embarrassment to her family, she listed her name as Mary Stevenson.
Her painting was accepted, a rare honor for so young a
woman. In the next two years her canvases were again hung
at the Salon exhibition. Each of them bore the individuality
of expression and draftsmanship that would later develop
more fully into her own distinctive style.

Finally, after years of dedicated work, capped by the success of her first efforts, Mary felt herself ready for Paris. She
arrived there in 1873, and rented a large studio apartment.
Under pressure from her family—one of the few times she
allowed them to call the turn—she enrolled in the studio of
Charles Chaplin, a fashionable academic painter. Although
M. Chaplin was quick to appreciate her talent, she left him
after a few sessions, believing that he had little to offer her.
She resisted all efforts to get her to enter the Beaux-Arts or
one of the other famous ateliers, feeling that they lacked the
vitality and direction she sought. She was extremely modest
in her appraisal of her gifts and sensitive to her weaknesses

as a painter, and returned to the museums for her source of knowledge. Here she found a hint of her future course in the honest realism of the French painters Courbet and Manet.

Remarkably enough, in "naughty Paris" Mary lived the same genteel, decorous existence that she would have followed back home in Philadelphia. She was a gentlewoman and an artist and "she drew," as a friend said, "that almost impossible line between her social life and her art. . . ." Neither was allowed to impinge on the other. In 1877, when her father and sister Lydia came to Paris to stay, the family rented a large, gracious apartment on the Avenue Trudaine. Ten years later Mary moved to the Rue Marignan, close to the fashionable Champs Elysées. For the remainder of her life this was her winter residence. Summers were spent in the coolness of a villa in the nearby countryside. The apartment was furnished with a refined elegance commensurate with the Cassatts' wealth and social position, and staffed with competent, uniformed servants. Tea was poured each afternoon from the old silver service into delicate china, to the accompaniment of polite, mildly intellectual discussion. The family's interests were broad and diversified, and they spoke knowledgeably on politics, travel, and the arts. It was only when a discussion on art was in progress that Mary's voice could be heard above the others.

In 1874, a year after Mary came to Paris, an exhibition was held of the work of a group of independent painters whose principles would before long revolutionize the art of the entire world. Edgar Degas, a French painter, had organized this first public showing of the French Impressionists. Its members—soon to become famous—included Degas, Monet, Pissarro, Renoir, Sisley, Cézanne, and Morisot. They adhered to a revolutionary technique of applying pigment in small dabs of pure color in order to achieve the illusion of light, and to express a spontaneous vision of what they observed. The academicians were outraged. Instead of the dark, polished, detailed paintings that were in favor, these rebels sought to bring to their work the emotional impact of a momentary glimpse, a highly personalized "impression." The brilliant palette, the soft focus, and the deliberate lack of finished realistic detail were an affront to the reigning principles of art.

The new movement was to carry Mary along in its wake.

One day, wandering through Paris, she came upon some paintings in the window of a picture dealer. Pausing, she saw, for the first time, the work of Edgar Degas. It was a revelation to her. She returned time and again. "I used to go and flatten my nose against that window," she said, "and absorb all I could of his art. It changed my life. I saw art then as I wanted to see it." At length, she entered the store, and bought a number of Degas' pastels to hang on her walls. She had been quick to recognize in Degas, as her biographer, Achille Segard said, "the continuation of the great masters."

Inspired, she set to work in a new style on a portrait of her sister Lydia. Discarding the dark hues of the old masters, she brightened her palette and adopted the bold manner of Degas and the Impressionists. As she had fully expected, the finished painting was rejected by the Salon exhibition of 1876. To prove to herself that the Académie prized conformity above all else, she repainted the background and subdued the color of the rejected canvas, and the following year, when she resubmitted it, it was accepted. It was the last time she offered a picture to the Salon. She was finished with conventional art. "I had . . . recognized who were my true masters," she said.

Mary Cassatt was thirty-three years old when she first met Edgar Degas. Her joy knew no bounds when he invited her to join and exhibit with the Impressionist group. "At last," she said, "I could work with absolute independence without considering the opinion of a jury." With one exception, in 1882, Mary Cassatt exhibited with the Impressionists until their last show in 1886.

It was a crucial point of her life. At the very onset of her career, when she could have assured herself of an easy future in academic circles, she had chosen instead to align herself with the Impressionists, the outcasts of the art world. As she had done before, she defied public opinion to follow her own lead.

The first time Edgar Degas saw one of Mary Cassatt's paintings, he declared, "There is one who feels as I do." He went further, stating that she was possessed of "infinite talent." He so admired her painting, "The Blue Sofa," that he offered to exchange one of his own for it—a remarkable gesture for a man who otherwise had little use for women.

So began the long, devoted association of Mary Cassatt and Edgar Degas. It was based completely on a mutual love of art and a profound respect for the other's talent. It made for a loyal friendship in which there was no hint of any romantic attachment. Bound by common interest, ideals, and aspirations, they were simply fellow artists. Together, they attended exhibitions, dined, and painted. Degas' young nieces accompanied Mary and Lydia on their walks and their rides in the Bois de Boulogne. When Mary Cassatt went to buy a hat, Degas went along—and sketched her. He painted her portrait several times and used her as a model on occasion. His friendship for the American girl was all the more remarkable for his being a notorious and avowed misanthrope.

The course of this curious relationship was not always smooth. Degas' sardonic manner and acid tongue were responsible for frequent ruptures. Quarrels were frequently so bitter that reconciliations could be effected only through the determined efforts of friends. Once, after seeing one of Mary's prints, Degas said he refused to admit that a woman could draw so well. To Mary, who believed in judging a work on its own merit, regardless of sex, this remark was like waving a red flag. Degas could devastate her by calling one of her drawings "sweet," a term repugnant to both.

Although she generally restrained herself, despite extreme provocation, there were times when her own sharp tongue and independence of spirit would add fuel to the flames. She became violently upset by one of the portraits Degas painted of her. It showed her sitting in a garden, her elbows on her knees, with some playing cards in her hand. Her sense of dignity was deeply offended. She later sent it to her dealer, Durand-Ruel, with specific instructions to sell it to anyone but an American. She did not want her countrymen to see her in such an unladylike attitude. "This portrait . . . has artistic qualities," she granted, "but it is painful to me and represents me as a person so repugnant that I do not want anyone to know that I posed for it." Yet, despite their battles, Mary remained unshakably loyal to her mentor. She believed devoutly in his genius, and forgave him his faults as a man for his greater virtues as a painter.

In 1879, when Mary exhibited with the Impressionist group for the first time, she hung two paintings—"The Cup of Tea," a portrait of her sister Lydia, and "La Loge," a portrait of a young woman seated in a box of a theatre. "La Loge" was one of the finest works of her Impressionist period, fresh and alive. In reviewing the exhibition, the great French novelist, Emile Zola, then an art critic, said, "Mlle. Cassatt, an American, I believe, recently made her debut with some remarkable works of unusual originality." It was a rarely sympathetic viewpoint. Few other critics found anything to like in the work of the Impressionists. The outlook of these new painters was still too daring, their ideas too radical. Mary cared little for the opinion of hostile critics. She respected only the men of vision whose ranks she had joined. And, in turn, she was accepted as an equal by Cézanne, Monet, Renoir, and the other giants of the new art movement. In time, she became so completely identified with the French Impressionist painters that it was not until a number of years after her death that it became generally known that she was an American.

Mary Cassatt was now painting the pictures for which she would in time become famous—portrayals of women engaged in the many attitudes of the life she knew so well: attending the theatre, serving tea, having a fitting at the dressmaker's or trying on a hat. She also began the first of many canvases and pastel drawings on the theme of mother and child. Although she painted endless variations of this time-honored subject, each new picture held a fresh insight, a new revelation of the tender relationship of parent and child. Her keen eye sought out the character, the nuance of emotion, the subtle gesture that gave depth and meaning to motherhood. She never overstepped the bounds of truth, never descended to cheap sentimentality. Like Degas, she saw the loveliness of each commonplace attitude with a sympathetic eye. Her palette, influenced by the Impressionists, retained its own vivid individuality; the color of her skin tones glowed with life; the natural gesture of a young child was caught with unaffected honesty and rendered with truth and beauty.

She began to experiment in etching not only because she enjoyed the medium, but as a form of self-discipline. "That is what teaches one to draw," she said. Working on copper plate directly from the live model, she set herself the highest and most difficult standards of perfection in drawing. According to Segard, her biographer, she "chose to use metal and a steel point, so that the plate would hold every trace of her mistakes or corrections." As usual, she chose the most difficult path for herself. Before long, she was producing etchings of astonishing quality. Attracted to Japanese prints, she set out with typical determination to learn everything from them that could be learned. Adapting the off-center composition, the sinuous line and the use of color to describe depth, she began to turn out color prints of remarkable beauty. Her reputation as a master of both black-and-white and color etching ranks today among the highest in the world.

The death of her younger sister Lydia in 1883 was a severe blow to Mary. When her father died seven years later, and her mother four years after him, she began to feel increasingly the loneliness of an alien. She was more than overjoyed whenever one of her remaining relatives chanced to come abroad. In 1893 she bought a country house, a château at Mesnil-Beaufresne, not far from Paris. Here she spent the majority of her summers each year for the remainder of her life.

"There are two ways for a painter," Mary Cassatt once said, "the broad and easy one or the narrow and hard one." For herself, there was only the latter way. She followed a rigorous routine that would have daunted many a man. She rose early, and was already at her easel by eight o'clock in the morning, hard at work; usually, she continued painting until it grew dark. Then, after dinner, her nights were given over to working on her etchings. Marriage and motherhood, if they entered her thoughts, could not stand up against her complete absorption in art. Her social life was restricted equally by her work habits and her natural reserve. Yet her intelligence, her broad interest in all facets of life, attracted the

friendship of such distinguished men as the statesman Clemenceau, the poet Mallarmé, the writer George Moore, and
many other intellectuals of the time. Her generosity to her
friends, particularly the artists among them, was free of any
trace of patronage. She bought their work simply because she
believed in their genius, and urged her rich friends to do the
same. She even paid some of the expenses so that her dealer
could send to the United States the first exhibit of Impressionist art.

Not until she was forty did Mary Cassatt judge herself to
be ready for a first comprehensive exhibition of her work. In
1891 she showed four oils and ten color etchings of women
and children at the gallery of Durand-Ruel in Paris. Her art
revealed a new maturity, a fresh, original outlook no longer
dependent on Degas' influence. Her drawing was superb, her
line delicate and tender, her form and color handled with
masterful sureness. The exhibition was favorably received,
particularly among the moderns. Her friend Pissarro, who
shared this exhibition with her, spoke of her "rare and exquisite works." Degas and all the Impressionist painters were
lavish with their praise. She was recognized as one of the
leading woman artists in France. The public, however, remained cool. The theme of mother and child was treated
with too little sentimentality, too realistically to win great
popular esteem.

Her reputation in America had not kept pace. By virtue
of her close association with Degas and the Impressionists,
she was classed as a French artist, and was virtually unknown
in her own country.

In 1879 she had sent two canvases to the exhibition of the
Society of American Artists in New York, but the response
was unfavorable. It was probably the first time an Impressionist painting had been seen in the United States. Mem-

bers of the Cassatt family were shocked by the daring realism of her work. They hid her paintings in rarely used rooms or concealed them in attics. Her painting of the "Lady at the Tea Table" had been exiled to the darkness of a closet. Many years later, the French government offered to purchase it for the Luxembourg, but Mary declined. She wished to donate it to an American museum. It was another eight years, however, before she felt that her name had enough significance to make the gift to the Metropolitan Museum worthwhile.

In 1892, one of her wealthy friends secured for her a commission to paint a mural for the Women's Building at the Columbian Exposition in Chicago. The work was hardly noticed. In 1900, on her first trip home to the United States since her departure some thirty years before, the Philadelphia *Public Ledger* announced her arrival with the following news item: "Mary Cassatt, sister of Mr. Cassatt, President of the Pennsylvania Railroad, returned from Europe yesterday. She has been studying painting in France and owns the smallest Pekingese dog in the world." She was then at the height of her career in France.

Mary remained in America for approximately a year. She had been troubled by failing vision, and hoped that a long absence from her easel might be beneficial. During her stay she went the rounds of the museums, and was appalled by the poverty of the art collections. She vowed to remedy this situation. Upon her return to Paris, she immediately descended on her wealthy American friends, calling upon them to buy European masterworks for the enrichment of their native land. To expedite the accumulation of great paintings, she generously offered her services as an expert.

In 1901 Henry O. Havemeyer, a millionaire sugar magnate, and his wife Louisine asked her to help them gather a collection of the finest paintings money could buy. They traveled to many countries, and with the help of Mary's considerable knowledge, were able to amass a magnificent collection. Their selection included the old masters, as well as such moderns as Degas, Renoir, Cézanne, Courbet, and Manet at a time when they were virtually unknown outside of France, and poorly esteemed even in their own country. Mrs. Havemeyer, a prominent member of Philadelphia society, had known Mary for many years, and, long ago, had bought her first Degas under Mary's promptings. Louisine found her an ideal companion. The "evenings were devoted to art talks," Mrs. Havemeyer recalled, "for Miss Cassatt was the most brilliant talker I ever listened to." For the next decade, Mary generously divided her time between painting and collecting art. Many of the great paintings which today hang in American museums—donated by their wealthy owners—were bought at Mary's insistence.

By the turn of the century, Mary Cassatt had won widespread recognition in France. She was made a Chevalier of the Legion of Honor in 1904, and her paintings were hanging in numerous European museums and distinguished private collections. But her identification with French artists was so close that America still remained slow to claim her as its own. A small beginning was made in 1904 when the Art Institute of Chicago invited her, while she was on a visit to the United States, to be guest of honor at their annual American Exhibition. Five years later the National Academy grudgingly granted her a mere associate membership, an honor she declined. In 1914, in her seventieth year, the Pennsylvania Academy of Fine Arts awarded her their gold medal. For the first time in her career she consented to accept a prize, possibly because it was a token of recognition by her home town. Despite these honors, it was not until many years later that the name of Mary Cassatt became famous in the land of her birth.

In her mid-sixties, her impaired vision compelled her to give up her etching. Reflections from the shiny metal plate became so painful that she could no longer discern the infinitely delicate lines she once scratched so confidently. Even with her now faltering vision, she continued to produce many paintings and pastel drawings of women and children. She stopped only when she became totally blind. Coincident with the outbreak of World War I, she had made plans to visit the United States in search of a doctor who might be able to restore her sight. But because of the hostilities, she decided to remain where she was. After so many years, she felt her first loyalty belonged to France. There were, she said, so many "duties to fulfill." Her gesture was more gallant than practical. She was in no condition to perform any helpful "duties."

The château where she summered each year lay close to the front, and had been commandeered by the army. Her old and devoted servant, Mathilde, had been forcibly returned to her home in the German part of Alsace. Alone, almost completely blind, Mary Cassatt departed for Grasse in the south of France. Desperately in need of treatment, she sought medical attention, but "where am I to find an oculist when every doctor is at the front," she wrote a friend. The one ruling passion of her life, her art, was no longer possible. Whatever art she saw now could only be seen in her mind's sight.

Her plight turned her bitter, a mood that was further accentuated by the news that her old friend Degas, who had also been blind for many years, had died in 1917. Although they had seen little of each other in recent years, Mary was deeply pained by his death. Her youth, her vision, her art, her old friend—all were gone. At the end of the war she returned to her home in Mesnil-Beaufresne. Although she used a cane to help her "see" her way around, her constitution was still vigorous, her mind as keen and active as always. But sightlessness was an intolerable burden to anyone who still longed passionately to paint.

Sometimes her days were relieved by a visit from an old friend or an occasional American artist abroad. They saw a still erect, slim old woman, dressed in a white jacket and lace cap, a shawl spread over her knees, carefully pouring tea without spilling it. But the effect of a fragile old lady was instantly dispelled the moment she spoke. She was acid-tongued, contentious, a "vinegary old maid," as someone called her. Her bitterness found its target in widely assorted areas. She believed herself a failure as a woman, so said a friend, since she had never married nor borne children. She was opposed to the Versailles Treaty, and vehemently denounced the principles of Woodrow Wilson and her old friend Clemenceau. She ridiculed Degas' peculiar custom of following funerals in his late years, declared that Monet lacked intelligence, and characterized Renoir's painting as too "animal." She had known both her compatriots, Sargent and Whistler, but disliked the former for a "dreadful" portrait he had done of her brother, and was shocked by the latter's unconventionality. Despite her own rich experience, she was convinced that American students no longer needed European art training, but must develop a wholly American outlook. The only people who now held her sympathy were the Socialists. "If I weren't a weak old woman," she told the art critic Forbes Watson, "I would throw away my limousine, give up the apartment and live without luxury." She looked, Watson said, like "a lean, bent, over-worked Puritan house-

keeper gone blind in her old age after incessant drudgery."
The indomitable spirit that had so long sustained her was
still there, only now it had no direction.

On June 14, 1926, at the age of 81, Mary Cassatt died at
her home in Mesnil-Beaufresne. She was at last released from
the excruciating pain of being unable to do the only thing she
ever wanted to do—paint.

It was not until 1947 that Mary Cassatt was given a large
retrospective show in the United States, and finally recognized by her own country as their "most eminent woman
artist, in both reputation and accomplishment." "There is
an inner conviction about her work," stated Frederick A.
Sweet, the curator of American art at the Art Institute of
Chicago, "which asserts itself over and above any specific
limitation of time and place."

Mary Cassatt may possibly have "failed as a woman," but
she triumphed as an artist.

11

Apostle of Ugliness

JOHN SLOAN

1871–1951

In 1933, sixty of the most important museums in the United States received this most unusual letter:

ANNOUNCEMENT TO DIRECTORS OF ART MUSEUMS: *John Sloan, the well-known artist, will die some time in the next few years (he is now sixty-two). In the event of his passing, is it likely that the trustees of your museum would consider it desireable to acquire one of his pictures? . . . After a painter of repute dies, the prices of his works are at once more than doubled. John Sloan is alive and hereby offers these*

164

*works at one-half the prices asked during the last five years.
. . . Yours, full of life—and a modicum of hope, John Sloan.*

Sloan sold exactly one picture through this startling method.

Ironically, although he was then near the height of his reputation, fully 90 percent of John Sloan's paintings were unsold, even though, as he put it, he now had "a much surer hand than I had in my younger period." In a rare newspaper interview he stated with some bitterness, "I would be willing to give up all my works here and my complete output during the rest of my life for a steady income of one hundred dollars a week."

Ever since he had begun painting seriously, almost half a century before, it had been John Sloan's hope to realize sufficient money from the sale of his work to allow him to devote full time to his easel. But this modest ambition was to be thwarted nearly all of his long career. It was only in the last years of his life that his pictures sold well enough to enable him to throw away the "crutches"—commercial illustration and teaching—that had forced him to become a "part-time" painter.

The man who was reduced to begging for a pittance deserved better. He was a gifted creative artist of powerful and independent vision. As Everett Shinn, a fellow painter, said, without him "art in America would have slept on, hobbled on, sinking lower and lower into cosmetic displays." A sharp-eyed yet compassionate observer of the contemporary scene, Sloan has been accepted as the dominant figure of the American school of Realism.

John French Sloan was born on August 2, 1871, in the small lumber town of Lock Haven, Pennsylvania. The only son and the oldest of three children born to James Dixon

Sloan and his wife Henrietta Ireland Sloan, John was, as he himself put it, an "indignant baby." His father, a cabinet-maker whose handicraft was rapidly being taken over by machines, was a gentle, kindly man with an aptitude for copying pictures and painting china, but none for business or earning a decent livelihood. When John was six years old, the family moved to Philadelphia in an attempt to improve their lot. His wife's family gave the elder Sloan a job as a traveling salesman for the Marcus Ward Company, British manufacturers of writing paper, and publishers of illustrated children's books.

The family was never far from want, although John's childhood was, as he said, "poor but not underprivileged." Because his father's work took him frequently from home, the job of raising the children fell into his mother's capable hands. Mrs. Sloan, a former schoolteacher and a woman of strong character and warm humor, taught her children to read and write, and imbued them with a strong moral conscience. By his seventh year, John was an adept and eager reader; at twelve, he was enjoying the plays of Shakespeare and the novels of Dickens. He sang in the church choir, invented puzzles, and entertained his friends with feats of magic. He loved drawing, and did a series of pictures for his favorite book, *Treasure Island,* inscribing "with illustrations by JFS" on the title page. His great ambition, however, was far removed from the world of art. He wanted, of all things, to be a dentist!

During the two years he attended Central High School, in Philadelphia, John met William J. Glackens, later a close friend and fellow artist, and Albert C. Barnes. In time, Barnes became a millionaire through his invention of Argyrol, a noted art collector, and the first purchaser of Sloan's paintings. John's education was abruptly ended by the failure of

his father's latest business venture. At sixteen, he left school
to help support his sisters and parents.

As a young man, John was tall and sturdily built, with a
shock of dark, neatly groomed hair framing a strong head.
Alert gray eyes glinted from behind the eyeglasses which he
wore all his life. His gentle, serious, even scholarly aspect
tended to make him appear older than he was. His first job
was that of assistant cashier in the firm of Porter and Coates,
booksellers and print dealers, at a salary of six dollars per
week. The job was eminently suited to his disposition. He
read in his spare moments and studied the available reproductions of the works of Rubens and Rembrandt. He taught
himself how to etch from a book and was soon making his
own prints. To augment his income he made pen and ink
copies of well-known pictures, and sold them for five dollars
each.

When A. Edward Newton, a clerk at Porter and Coates,
opened his own business he invited the talented young Sloan
to work for him. For about two years the eighteen-year-old
youth—the only male among twenty-eight girls—painted
matchboxes and decorated calendars, bookmarks, and other
sundry items. All thoughts of dentistry had abruptly vanished,
replaced by the more exciting vision of becoming an illustrator. To improve his knowledge and his technique, he attended night drawing classes at the Spring Garden Institute.

Eventually, bored with what was an ill-paying and future-
less job, he departed from Newton's to start his own career
as a free-lance illustrator. Sloan continued to live with and
support his family, but he rented a small studio of his own.
A few odd jobs came his way, but the only steady assignment
he received was from a coal company, for whom he designed
an advertising card once a month. His payment consisted of

four dollars in cash and a supply of free coal for his studio. His career was getting nowhere, and he could not exist much longer on his meager diet.

In February of 1892, Sloan gathered his work together, screwed up his courage, and boldly walked into the offices of the Philadelphia *Inquirer* to ask for a job. Since the reproduction of photographs was unknown at that time, newspapers employed a large staff of artists to cover news events as they happened, and to handle a variety of other types of art work. Sloan was hired to cover news assignments, but, disliking this kind of work, he asked to be transferred to the regular art department. For three years he drew decorative headings, portraits, and illustrations for the women's page and the weekly Sunday edition.

It was in the offices of the *Inquirer* that Sloan first met several fellow artists who were later to play an important role in his life. His old friend William Glackens was already a member of the staff when Sloan was hired. Soon after, Everett Shinn joined them and the three young men would go out on Sunday painting expeditions. Sloan had no desire to be a painter. He wanted only to become a fine illustrator.

The necessity of learning how to draw the human figure better sent Sloan to the night classes at the Pennsylvania Academy of Art. No models were used, and no instruction in painting was given. One night, bored by drawing the dusty gray casts, Sloan turned to sketch one of the students. Called to task for this breach of discipline, he rose angrily from his seat and stormed out, never to return. With forty other rebellious artists, he helped organize the Charcoal Club where, twice weekly, the members drew from live models and had their work criticized by Robert Henri, a professional recently returned from the Beaux-Arts in Paris.

In 1895 Sloan left the *Inquirer* to work for the *Press*, a rival morning newspaper. The *Press* art department was under the direction of Edward Davis, father of the now famous artist Stuart Davis. Sloan's fellow artists on the paper, George Luks, Everett Shinn, and Glackens—who had preceded him —were all eager young men with a burning ambition to paint. Sloan soon became a member in good standing of the group. The change of jobs proved a good thing in all ways. The *Press* gave Sloan an increase in salary, more interesting work, greater space for his drawings, and increased freedom. His career as an illustrator progressed most satisfactorily. He was soon the most valuable artist on the paper.

During the brief life of the Charcoal Club (it had expired after four months) Robert Henri had become Sloan's "father in art," and his closest friend. The two men shared the same studio, a room in downtown Philadelphia that became the gathering place for young independent-minded artists. Each Tuesday evening, a special group consisting of Shinn, Luks, Glackens, Sloan, and Henri met at the studio, where they drew, painted, talked about art and politics, and held gay parties. These were the men who formed the nucleus of the group that would soon change the face of American art.

Henri's intense excitement and his passionate belief in art infected the entire group. Although he had been trained in the art schools of Paris, Henri was not in sympathy with the radical ideas of the French artists Cézanne, Matisse, and Picasso. Rather, he was enamored of the freedom and vitality of the Dutch master Frans Hals, and the dynamic realism of the Frenchman Edouard Manet. It was Henri's passionate belief that an artist must participate in living intensely if he were to be a great artist. "All art that is worth while," he said, "is a record of intense life." To him, "pictures from life" were the only true expression of art. Henri inspired his students to live outside the artistic "ivory tower," to be independent in thought, to create emotion spontaneously by the use of bold, rapid brushwork. He insisted upon truth, no matter how ugly; upon reality rather than romanticism, in defiance of every standard of current thought and practice. "Do not be afraid of new prophets or prophets that may be false," he exhorted. "Go in and find out."

It was not until his twenty-sixth year that Sloan, under Henri's constant prodding, began to think seriously of becoming a painter. Not until he had completed a series of fine etchings for a set of novels did he start working on his first oils, mostly portraits. These were bold in character and technique, rapidly executed, and strongly influenced by Henri's theory that brush strokes must be visible. He painted only part time, refusing to give up the security of his job for the precarious income of the artist.

Shortly after his thirtieth birthday, on August 5, 1901, Sloan and Anna M. Wall, whom he had met at one of the studio parties, were married. "Dolly," as Sloan called her, was five years his junior, an auditor in Gimbel's department store. A tiny girl, Dolly was intelligent, friendly, vivacious, full of Irish charm, and given to bursts of inexplicable temper. For the more than forty-one years of their marriage the Sloans remained childless.

The invention of the halftone process of reproduction, which made it possible to reproduce photographs inexpensively, meant the end of large art staffs on newspapers. In November, 1903, Sloan was told that the *Press* could no longer use his services. His friends Henri, Luks, Glackens, and Shinn had moved to New York, where they were struggling to establish themselves as painters. They urged Sloan to join them, but he felt that first he had to set up some means of earning his living. A nagging sense of responsibility would not allow him to act otherwise. He was horrified at the thought of subjecting his wife to poverty, to the shame of unpaid bills, to dodging the landlord when he came around to collect the rent each month. His dignity demanded that he earn his own way. When that was done, and only then, would he indulge his passion for painting.

Several months later—having arranged a more or less secure income as a free-lance illustrator for several magazines—he and Dolly moved from Philadelphia to New York. They settled in an old building on West Twenty-third Street, near the Henris, eager for the great adventure of life in the teeming metropolis.

New York City thrilled Sloan. He loved it with the same intensity a landscape painter does the countryside. The bustle, the vitality, the excitement, the crowds, the color held an irresistible appeal to his heart and his eye. Greenwich Village, Fourteenth Street, Sixth Avenue, Fifth Avenue, Broadway, wherever he roamed, Sloan loved to watch the "drab, shabby, happy, sad and human" mass as they went about their daily lives. Each of his paintings, each etching was based on an actual incident. A crowd gathered in front of a small building watching a hairdresser at work became "Hairdresser's Window." Two young women, glimpsed through his window, became the unwitting subjects for "Three A.M." The inspiration for "Wake of the Ferry," one of his most famous pictures, was an actual ride on the ferry. Painted in a fluid and easy technique, his canvases were distinguished by bold brushwork and a rather dark palette. They were alive with the humor, drama, pain, and pleasure of daily existence. Keenly observed, they bore out Sloan's declaration that he "enjoyed" through his eyes.

The friendship between Sloan and Henri grew even closer than before. The old Philadelphia group dropped in regularly, to laugh together, argue about Socialism, or wax indignant over the high-handed rule of the National Academy. If Sloan had a commercial job to finish, he would work while his friends visited. Frequently, as in an etching called "Memory," he drew himself and his friends as they sat around the table talking. The entire group had grown accustomed to the odd hours of newspapermen, and, although no longer in the profession, they kept to old habits. The extra bed in Sloan's studio was put to frequent use, harboring one friend or another.

More and more frequently now, Sloan's work was being rejected at exhibits for "vulgarity." A realistic portrayal of common life in art was contrary to the Academy's ideal of smooth and polished "beauty." In 1904, Sloan, Henri, Luks, Glackens, and two newcomers to the group—Arthur B. Davis and Maurice Prendergast—exhibited their paintings at the National Arts Club. The show was greeted with loud shouts of outrage and horror by the critics and academicians. "Startling Works by Red-Hot American Painters" was the scornful heading for one review. Another called it "a most lugubrious show." Life, unless it was pretty, was not considered a fit subject for art.

The battle against the domination of conservatism in American art had begun. Henri, a most aggressive fighter, crossed swords with the National Academy. In 1907, angered by the rejection of his friends' work, he withdrew his own paintings, and urged his colleagues—now augmented to eight by the inclusion of Robert Lawson—to organize another exhibition of independent art. The Macbeth Gallery agreed to house the exhibition, to which each member contributed fifty dollars to defray expenses. Each was invited to send from four to ten paintings. Sloan showed seven.

The exhibition of "Eight Independent Painters" or the "Eight," as they were immediately termed by the critics, opened on February 3, 1908. As with the earlier show at the National Gallery, but more so, the reaction was swift and violent. Cries of "Apostles of Ugliness," "the revolutionary gang," and "the black gang"—referring to their somber palettes—rent the air. The *Globe* called Glackens' work "anemic," Prendergast's "an explosion in a paint factory" and Sloan's "neither good taste nor originality." Another critic fulminated: "Vulgarity smites one in the face at this exhibition. . . . Is it fine art to exhibit our sores?—Bah!" Only a few scattered notices were favorable.

But the publicity resulting from the attacks made the exhibition a huge success. The public flocked to the gallery in droves to see these "sensational" pictures. Sales amounted to four thousand dollars. "I feel," said Sloan, "almost as glad as though I had sold some myself." Because they were interested in seeing the work that had created such a stir, the Pennsylvania Academy and museums in eight other cities in the United States invited the group to show their paintings. Although they never again exhibited jointly, and although their work was extremely individual, the term the "Eight" became synonymous with the members of the group. Later, the name "Ashcan School," applied derisively at first, came to mean their particular brand of realism. The concerted action of The Eight had established a foothold for the independent artist and had given America its first honest look at itself.

A growing concern for the "underdog" led Sloan to seek an outlet in Socialism. A humanitarian rather than a political radical, Sloan objected to the exploitation of human beings by large corporations or "superior classes," to the grinding poverty of the many as opposed to the untold wealth of a few. In 1909, he began to contribute free drawings to *The Call*, the official Socialist newspaper, and a year later both he and

Dolly became active members of the Socialist party. Sloan helped organize meetings and hand out literature, and tried —unsuccessfully—to convert his many friends to his views. Twice he ran for the state Assembly, and twice failed to be elected. In the summer of 1912, he joined the staff of *The Masses*, a radical literary magazine, and some of his best satirical drawings were done for this periodical. But disillusionment with the aims of the magazine, which kept growing more militantly radical, impelled him to resign two years later. He also resigned from the Socialist party, thus ending his active participation in politics, although he remained a Socialist at heart all his life.

After the unexpected success of the 1908 exhibition, both Sloan and Henri felt that another and stronger attempt should be made in behalf of the nonacademic artist. Their first notion—to rent a permanent showroom to display the work of fifteen independent artists—was soon replaced by a more ambitious undertaking. Large quarters were rented on West Thirty-fifth Street for a nonjuried "Exhibition of Independent Artists." Anyone who paid an admission fee of ten dollars for one work, or thirty dollars for four, was welcome to hang his picture. On April 1, 1910, the show opened its doors to huge crowds. Two hundred and sixty paintings, 23 pieces of sculpture and 344 prints and drawings were displayed. "We are showing the New York public such an exhibition of American art," Sloan said with pride, "as has never been seen before." Another step toward altering the face of American art had been taken.

The hold of the Academy was completely broken with the organization of the now-famous International Exhibition of Modern Art, much better known as the Armory Show, because it was held in the 69th Regiment Armory in New York. It opened on February 17, 1913. Originally conceived as a strictly American exhibit, it was augmented to include a large section of the modern art of Europe. Henri disliked the work of the French modernists, objected strenuously, and, in fact, withdrew. Because of his friendship with Henri, Sloan did not actively participate in organizing the show. However, he helped hang it and also exhibited several of his own canvases.

For the first time the work of the modern European artists —Cézanne, Matisse, Picasso, Duchamp, and many others— received wide attention in the United States. Alfred Stieglitz, the noted photographer, had introduced a few of their works in his gallery, but the Armory Show was the first full-scale invasion of modern art. The attendance was enormous, the reaction horrified, angry, contemptuous, or—in a few instances—delighted. The public, the critics, the educated, the ignorant—all flocked to see, to laugh at, or to admire the work of these "madmen." Artists were divided into two violently opposed camps. But there was no denying that a new concept of art had come to stay. The exhibit turned into a triumph. When it was dismantled, a month later, all barriers against freedom in art had been completely demolished.

Henri's disassociation from the Armory Show removed him from leadership of the progressive movement in American art with one stroke. Friendship or no, the new European concept of painting made a profound impression on Sloan. He was thoroughly convinced of its validity as a "medicine" which would cure art of "the disease of imitating." "The blinders fell from my eyes," he said, and discarded the vigorous brush stroke advocated by Henri for a surer, more finished technique; a dark palette for a brighter one; a surface approach for a deeper, more thoughtful one. He turned back to the old masters for intensive study, saying ruefully, "I never learned my trade." Although his canvases were now less concerned with the life of the common man, and more with the effect of light on color and form, he did not by any means abandon realism. The city was still his inspiration.

In 1914 the Sloans left New York City to spend the first of five summers at Gloucester. Here he began to paint landscapes, which, however, lacked the character and vital mood of his cityscapes. He never felt the emotional tie to the open country that he had for the frenzied activity of the concrete city.

By now he had begun to win some fame. His work was on exhibition in many of the leading annuals. In 1913, Dr. Barnes had bought a painting for his collection. It was Sloan's first sale—and it came when he was over forty years old. Three years later he was given his first one-man show, at the Whitney Studio Club, the forerunner of the Whitney Museum. This was followed by a second and larger show at the Hudson Guild. Nevertheless, sales remained few and far between. Despite all that had happened in the art field, Sloan was still considered too realistic and common for American taste. Not many buyers wanted "ugly" pictures.

In 1916, Sloan was offered a teaching post at the Art Students League in New York on a schedule that enabled him to devote more of his time to his own work than had been possible before. Beginning at the age of forty-five, he continued to teach for almost a quarter of a century. He was an inspiring teacher whose students worshiped him.

When he was in his late fifties, Sloan's work underwent a sudden startling transformation. At an age when most artists are content to consolidate their knowledge, he discarded all he had ever learned and began experimenting with a new style, a new technique, and a new subject. "Teaching," he explained, "began to stir my interest in painting the figure." Except for an occasional city picture, he devoted himself exclusively to painting the nude in an infinite variety of poses.

He worked in luminous flesh tones, overlaying the whole canvas with a series of small strokes in pure color to emphasize the direction and solidity of his form. These new canvases were not received with much enthusiasm. Intense devotion to technique and form had robbed them of the vitality of his former work.

Upset by the cold reception given to his new work, he was further depressed by the death of Henri, who had remained his closest friend despite their artistic falling-out. He was still badgered by the everlasting need to make a living. His teaching assured him only of a regular, but small income.

In 1935, Sloan and his wife moved to the Hotel Chelsea on West Twenty-third Street, where he wintered for the remainder of his life. His health had been steadily deteriorating, and this was climaxed by a series of major operations. After a protracted period of convalescence, he returned to his work with great eagernesss. He was still experimenting with his new technique, and only rarely returned to his former style. When the critics gave scant praise to his new work he consoled himself by saying that they "didn't like my earlier paintings either." In defiance of the popular taste, he continued to work as he pleased, "not for the future, or history" but just for himself.

The recognition that had so long eluded him was at last granted to Sloan when he was over seventy years old. After nearly a whole lifetime of dividing his time between earning a living and painting, he realized enough money from the sale of his pictures to be able to give up his commercial work completely. Yet even now he didn't achieve genuine financial success. He merely earned enough to live on comfortably. But by his own terms this was enough.

Sloan was now regarded as the "dean" of the school of American realists, and the outstanding member of the famous

Eight. His earlier work, which had been too "ugly" for its time, was now the basis for his recognition. Ironically, his more recent paintings were not considered "modern" enough or even "ugly" enough for the present.

In May of 1943, Dolly, his wife of over forty-one years, died of a heart attack. Her later years had been troubled by a mental breakdown, and her death was a release from agony. A year later, at the age of seventy-three, Sloan married Helen Farr, a former student who had worked with him for several years, helping him revise and edit a book of his principles on art and life. The *Gist of Art*, as it was titled, was published in 1938. Sloan and his new wife enjoyed a happy companionship based on mutual understanding and respect. He painted affectionate portraits of her in "The Necklace" and "Tea for One."

Despite the fact that his health was no longer robust, Sloan remained alert and active. His large frame was now thinner, his hair completely white. He painted with his usual slow deliberation, laying down his brush only when the light became too dim to work by. He seemed indefatigable and declared that he felt indestructible. But his physician, more aware of his age and health, forbade Sloan to visit Sante Fe—where he had spent several summers—because of the strain the altitude would put on his heart. Instead, Sloan allowed himself to be taken to Hanover, New Hampshire. The landscape appeared to him like "a green salad" after the brilliance of the Southwest, but before long he was painting it with obvious enjoyment. His lodgings were not far from Hanover, where a collection of his canvases was owned by Dartmouth College, of which his cousin John Sloan Dickey was president. The year before, 1950, the National Institute of Arts and Letters had awarded him its gold medal, and the Whitney Museum was planning a large retrospective exhibition of his work for the winter of 1952. He celebrated his eightieth birthday in good spirits, making ambitious plans for a productive future.

Late in August he suffered a severe attack which was diagnosed as cancer. He was scheduled for an operation. On the day he was due to enter the hospital, he painted for several hours in the morning, ate his lunch, and then put himself in his surgeon's hands. Sloan was not to paint again. On September 7, 1951, a short time after the operation, he died.

The retrospective show at the Whitney Museum became a memorial exhibition, a tribute to the influence and the artistry of the "apostle of ugliness," the man who devoted his life to bringing truth to art.

12

The Failure Who Made Good

JOHN MARIN

1870–1953

At the age of thirty-seven, John Marin journeyed from Paris to Venice to ask his father for money. At this time of his life he was a man of medium height, slender, with a strikingly ascetic face that peered out from beneath a disorderly pile of brown hair resembling an inverted bird's nest.

The elder Marin's patience with his son was by now exhausted. "You're almost forty years old," he said. "What have you got to show for all these years?"

"Not very much," John Marin answered.

He had no money, no job, no family. He had never been able to hold a job for more than a few months, he had frittered his time away in a number of art schools, he had never settled down, or raised a family. By all conventional standards, he was a complete and abject failure. He understood all this.

But his own standards were a long way from the conventional. He was completely indifferent to money, to possessions, even to the simple creature comforts. Only one thing mattered to John Marin—his painting; and that, to him, was too important to be reckoned in such mundane terms as success or failure.

The major portion of his work was done in watercolor, an art form which, with only a few brilliant exceptions like Homer, Sargent, and the Englishman Joseph Turner, was considered in a category well below that of oil painting. Marin took this so-called inferior medium and equated its value with that of oils. He was judged not for what pigments he used, but for the vital contributions he made to art as one of the first great modernists in America.

John Chéri Marin III, the only son of John Chéri Marin II, a public accountant, and Louise Currey Marin, was born in Rutherford, New Jersey, on December 23, 1870. According to his biographer MacKinley Helm, Marin liked to say that his ancestors were "the best English ale, Dutch bitters, Irish gin, French vermouth, and plain Scotch." Actually, his immediate heritage was the French stock of his father and the English of his mother.

When John's mother died nine days after his birth, his father left him with his Grandmother Currey in Weehawken, New Jersey, where he was raised in an atmosphere "as thoroughly Yankee as apple pie and baked beans." Young John quickly became the center of attention for his grandmother, his Uncle Richard and his two maiden aunts, Jenny and Lelia. All of them pitched in to help rear the boy who, with his long nose and pale complexion, was so characteristically a Currey in appearance. John's father, traveling constantly on behalf of his prospering business, had only a small hand in the upbringing of his motherless child.

John attended the local schools in New Jersey. Aside from geometry, which briefly roused his interest, he was an indifferent student. School held no attractions for him; he much preferred to spend his time walking, fishing, or drawing. On warm summer days he particularly enjoyed tagging after his Uncle Richard. While Richard hunted, John filled the time by drawing sketches of animals in motion. A rabbit running, a bird in flight, a deer jumping a stream—these things delighted him. This instinctive feeling for the vitality of movement in nature was later reflected in his work. In fact, some of his theories of painting derived from these early observations, and he would frequently discuss them in terms of the small animals whose habits he knew so well.

"Take the idea of balance," he once said, in explaining a theoretical point. "Think of the wonderful balance of squirrels. They scratch themselves equally well with hind-paws or fore-paws without losing their balance. . . . I like my pictures to have that kind of balance. I stand them up on their end, turn them upside down, until I see that, like the squirrels, they have got balance in every direction."

When young John had finished a four-year high-school course at the Stevens Preparatory School, he enrolled in the Stevens Institute of Technology. He managed to struggle painfully through his first year, and then quit. Such matters as engineering were not for him.

In the respectable middle-class household which was run by his maiden aunts after Grandmother Currey's death, it was assumed that he would now earn his own living. Aunt Jenny and Aunt Lelia thought he ought to look for a position across the river in New York City. To their pleasure—and perhaps somewhat to their surprise—he returned one day to announce that he had been hired as a clerk in a wholesale notions firm on lower Broadway.

Their pleasure was short-lived. John had no more of a head for business than he had had for engineering. He mixed up orders, mailed packages to the wrong addresses, and managed to be confused by the simplest directions. He was soon fired.

In the next four years—capitalizing on his drawing ability —he worked in a number of architects' offices. Then, in 1893, he decided that he had learned enough to open his own office. He designed and built six houses, including one for his aunts in Union City, New Jersey, which he described as "plain, but they functioned for comfortable living." It could hardly be said that he was a conspicuous success as a builder. But at least, as his aunts told themselves, he was trying to do something.

Then one night he casually informed his aunts that he was giving up his business. Jenny and Lelia attempted to dissuade him. But their extreme fondness for their nephew outweighed their better judgment, and they allowed him to have his way.

During the whole of this period Marin continued to paint. Whenever he had time, usually on Sundays and on the long summer evenings, he went out-of-doors and made countless sketches from nature.

With the entire day now at his disposal, he spent his time in equal proportion between painting and loafing. He drove his poor aunts out of their wits. Dinners grew cold waiting for his return from a stroll or a painting trip. His clothes were unkempt, his unruly hair in constant need of cutting. Once Jenny and Lelia gave him thirty dollars to buy a much-needed suit. He returned with a magnificent illustrated volume of Shakespeare. He had been unable to resist such a bargain at only thirty dollars!

But while his aunts despaired over his "idling," he began to develop a personal style in his art, an interesting "short-hand" way of putting his visions down on paper, and so distinctive that a Marin is easily recognizable even at a distance.

When Marin was twenty-eight, his aunts—more from concern about his continued idleness than from any strong belief in his talent—prevailed upon his father to send him to an art school. The elder Marin had recently remarried and had a new wife to support. Grumbling that his son was quite old enough to take care of himself, he agreed to pay for John's schooling at the Pennsylvania Academy of Art, albeit reluctantly.

From the very first day of his enrollment Marin began to complain. He complained about the quality of the instruction, about his fellow students, about the distasteful practice of dissecting cadavers in order to study anatomy, and drawing from the same old casts. The school had resumed this practice upon Eakins' dismissal. In his two years at the Academy, Marin painted only twice from a model. Years later, explaining his dissatisfaction with the Academy's teaching methods, he cited a boy in one of his classes who could "transfer a Greek torso to paper and make it look nice and real—real as the plaster cast that he had copied!"

For Marin the faithful rendition of a stationary object had no meaning, it was not art. "Art," he said, "must show what goes on in the world."

Once again, with his genius for abandoning what he didn't like or believe in, Marin quit the Academy and returned home. At his aunts' urging, he spent a few months at the Art Students League. But he could no more conform with the League's insistence on drawing the plaster casts than he could the Pennsylvania Academy's. What he was interested in was "the world," and he "wanted to put it down in paint, all of it."

He turned back to the outdoors in search of subject matter. Furiously, he painted landscapes no matter what the weather, splashing colors with an excitement that reflected the inner fire so seldom visible on the surface even to the people who knew and loved him best. He worked at top speed, as if intent on recording the message of his eyes before it vanished from sight. On some of these expeditions he took along a dark-haired girl named Marie Jane Hughes, the older sister of a seamstress who occasionally did work for his aunts. They had met at a party and were immediately attracted to each other. Marie Jane was a gentle, quiet creature, warmly affectionate with people whom she liked, but wary of those she considered affected or hypocritical. Between her and Marin there sprang up a deep and gratifying understanding.

Aunt Jenny and Aunt Lelia were still wringing their hands over their nephew's apparent lack of aim in life. They mentioned his devotion to painting to Charles Bittinger, the senior Marin's new stepson. Bittinger, who was about to embark for Europe on his honeymoon, generously suggested to his stepfather that Marin might profit by studying art in Europe. When Bittinger's mother (the elder Marin's new wife) and Jenny and Lelia also added their pleas, Marin senior bowed to the majority will, and, with some misgivings, agreed to underwrite his son for a period of study in Paris "with the rest of the idlers."

Marin sailed for Paris in the summer of 1905. Once there, his stepbrother immediately took charge of him, installing him in a room on the Rue Campagne Première, two blocks from the famous Luxembourg, in the heart of the artistic Left Bank. He introduced Marin to life in the Bohemian quarter of Paris, and arranged for his enrollment in an atelier. Everything thus taken care of for him—as usual—Marin was all set to learn painting in the city of painters.

But it was not long before the old story repeated itself. Unmoved by his teachers and their teaching methods alike, he plodded from atelier to atelier. Whatever he hoped to find in this restless series of changes, the search was a failure, and he finally abandoned it completely. So far as he was concerned, Paris was no different from Philadelphia and New York.

The one significant event of this period was his discovery of the graphic arts. Plunging in with enthusiasm, he turned out a series of crisp, sharp-lined etchings which he tried to sell. But the current rage in prints was for the soft, moody effects of Whistler. Discouraged, he took to spending most of his days playing billiards, although he continued to etch from time to time, and occasionally painted a watercolor.

However indifferent his success as an artist, he did manage to become a fairly accomplished billiards player!

In 1907, after some two years in Paris spent mainly in loafing "with the rest of the idlers," Marin entrained for Venice and the encounter there with his father. The elder Marin at first turned a deaf ear to his son's request for additional funds to continue working in France, making a sardonic—and not wholly unjustified—reference to John's skill at billiards. It was Mrs. Marin who stepped into the breach. Not only did she persuade her husband that his son's talent was worthy of support no matter what appearances might be, but she also convinced John that, if he modified his etching style and concentrated on the more picturesque sights in Europe, perhaps the dealers might then be willing to handle his work.

Without any evident enthusiasm, but because he admired and respected his stepmother, Marin began turning out etchings of scenic places in Venice, Rome, and Florence, softening his crisp line to emulate Whistler's modulated tones. On his return to Paris he sold a few of these prints and temporarily eased the financial strain.

Marin remained in Paris for five years. These were the years of one of the most fertile and exciting periods in the history of modern art. Paris was in the midst of an artistic upheaval. In the great French capital, where art is traditionally the affair not only of the artists but of the populace as well, there were public pronouncements, manifestoes, arguments, even riots between the adherents of one or another school of art. Yet Marin, incredibly, living in the very center of the uproar, seemed quite unaware of anything going on. He went his way calmly, painting his unsalable pictures, relaxing with billiards and with friends.

The American photographer Edward Steichen, then in Europe, saw some of Marin's watercolors at the American Club and was much taken by them. He asked Marin to send some of his pictures to the United States for exhibition in a New York gallery called "291," which he ran with his partner Alfred Stieglitz. Steichen and Stieglitz, both of whom were destined to become the most famous photographers of their time, were eager to make their little gallery a showcase for the paintings of unknown American and European artists of promise. This meeting with Steichen proved to be the turning point of Marin's career. It led to a lifelong artistic association and personal friendship with Alfred Stieglitz, whom one critic called "the most important single figure in the development of modernism in America." He provided the impetus from which Marin was eventually to emerge as one of the most important American painters of his time.

Beset by homesickness and an ardent desire to see his devoted maiden aunts—and especially Marie Jane Hughes, for whom his feelings had ripened in his long absence—Marin sailed for home in the spring of 1910. Shortly after his return, he met Stieglitz for the first time. The paintings he saw hanging at "291" awakened an exciting response in him. They were new and daring; each was an attempt to break the old stale molds. Among the painters represented were Arthur Dove, Alfred Maurer, Marsden Hartley, Max Weber—names which would soon be heard in the world of art. Stieglitz invited Marin to join his "stable" of new artists, and eagerly Marin accepted. The man who had been an idler now became a dedicated artist, devoting all his time and effort to work.

Stieglitz, a sincere believer in Marin's talent, helped the artist in many ways. Not only did he advance him a small sum of money to enable him to paint without having to work at an uncongenial job, but he also steered his interest toward Cubism and the other new techniques of French painting. Marin, who had blithely ignored all of this when it surrounded him in Paris, became enthusiastic under Stieglitz's direction.

A vital factor in his artistic development at this point was his "discovery" of New York as a vital force. The noise, the intensity, the hectic movement, the looming skyscrapers— he saw them all now as if for the first time. In a fever of excitement, he expressed his feelings about the metropolis in a series of brilliant, dynamic watercolors. One of these, a startling impression of the Woolworth Building, he sent to the famous Armory Show. A critic referred to it contemptuously as "a clam with a bent neck." Marin took no heed. He plunged ahead with his work, capturing on paper a city that fascinated him as "a battle of buildings, pushing and pulling at each other." He did not attempt to reproduce the look of the city, but with a minimum of bold strokes expressed the stimulation it waked in him.

Marin and Marie Jane Hughes were married in December of 1912. They spent their honeymoon in Washington, D.C., and on their return moved in temporarily with Marie's sister in the Flatbush section of Brooklyn. Marin resumed work with increasing intensity. The 1913 Armory Show had established Stieglitz, who had a hand in its organization, as a figure of major importance in the modern art movement. It also imbued Marin with a sense of purpose, of "belonging." He no longer felt isolated; there were others, many others, who were also straining toward new horizons in art.

As he had discovered New York, so, in the summer of 1914, Marin discovered Maine. His reaction to the windswept landscape and rocky coast was immediate and overpowering. Like Winslow Homer, he really felt himself a part of the elements, surrounded by the forces of nature at their most violent. For the rest of his life he spent all his summers there. He moved from place to place, always in a direction that would bring him closer to the sea, whose stormy restlessness mirrored the urges pent up under his gentle exterior.

In his desire to capture the essence of nature, Marin invented artistic "symbols" for the things he saw, a further development of his earlier "shorthand" technique. Round or triangular spots of green color were trees, tiny squares or oblongs windows and houses. Rocks were expressed by an arc, waves by a series of undulating or curvy lines. Movement, which was an integral part of his compositions, was stated by a series of diagonal and curved strokes ingeniously shifting the eye of the beholder from one plane to another. He patterned his line not on the shapes he saw, but rather on the rhythms they expressed. He moved further and further away from realism, yet, as he said, he would never "get fresh with nature."

In his early work such as "Lower Manhattan" he had already begun the use of a number of these symbols. The whole composition was treated from an unusual point of view—looking down from the top of the Woolworth Building. Buildings, streets, cars, humanity merge in an almost abstract explosion of movement, like the intensity of a volcanic eruption. To express the gold leaf of the dome, Marin painted a yellow circle with radiating fingers, cut it out and sewed it (with large stitches) to his picture.

As he grew older, Marin's line became more economical and even more expressive of his intention. In "Pertaining to Stonington, Maine," he dispensed with all perspective and relied on the juxtaposition of intense bands of flat color to give the illusion of depth. Movement is projected by slashing curves and diagonals, by the use of intense color and the white paper. The painting stands as a "balanced" unity, done with an economy of means that expresses the genuine mastery of John Marin's watercolors.

Through the exhibitions in Stieglitz's gallery, he had acquired a small coterie of admirers, but only few purchasers. Before long, Stieglitz was temporarily forced to close his little gallery for lack of funds and a dearth of clients for his artists. Even though the modern movement had made a lasting impression on painters, the majority of the public still considered it a product of maniacs. Without Stieglitz's financial help, the Marins (who now included a son, John Chéri Marin IV) were almost at a loss. To make each penny count, they rented a hunting lodge in Maine, where they stayed until the bitter cold forced them back to New York. Desperately in need of money to feed his family, Marin sold a group of his etchings to the Biltmore Hotel for one dollar per etching.

The following year saw no easing of the Marins' plight. Because of a lack of funds, they were forced to remain in a freezing cottage in Maine until Christmastime. When they returned, they gratefully accepted Aunt Lelia's offer to stay in her house. Aunt Jenny had died three years before, and Lelia in her loneliness welcomed them. Later, they all moved to a two-story stucco house in Cliffside, New Jersey, directly across the Hudson from Grant's Tomb, and here—except for his summers—Marin lived out the rest of his life.

Over the next four years, largely through the persistence of Stieglitz, whose faith in Marin's genius never wavered, Marin sold some thirty-two of his watercolors. The proceeds lifted the immediate burden, but hardly eased the strain of continuing poverty. Yet it did not affect either the constant production of his pictures or his love of art.

Shortly afterward Marin initiated the use of bold, dashing lines in his paintings as a "frame" to enclose his subject matter, to "nail it down." A device to "keep the picture from sliding off the edge," Marin's "frame" had the effect of unifying the whole picture in a remarkable way. Art dealers began to take an interest in these new works, and for the first time in his life he became comparatively free of financial strain.

Within the next few years, Marin lost his beloved Aunt Lelia and his father. Interestingly enough, in his later years Marin senior had begun to take a fierce pride in his son's work, and the two, at long last, established a warm relationship. Unfortunately, the elder Marin died before his son achieved fame. With his passing, his widow, always concerned for her stepson, intensified her interest in Marin and his family. On one occasion she nagged Marin into having his infected tonsils removed, soothing his fears of surgery. She even accompanied him to the doctor's office remaining by his side throughout the operation.

Marin chafed under infirmity or ill health. It interfered with his work. The "loafer" had become a man whose days were filled with work.

In 1925, Stieglitz opened a new gallery, and his first show was an exhibit of the recent works of John Marin. This time, the critics, perhaps because they had finally caught up with Marin's vision, were enthusiastic. They acknowledged his preeminence in the field of modern American painting. One of them, in fact, went so far as to speak of the artist as "one of the world's great painters." As a result of all this praise, sales of Marin's paintings soared, and so did the prices they commanded.

In the years that followed, and as Marin's reputation and acceptance grew, he knew only one setback. During the 1940's he turned to oil painting, attempting to apply the same principles to it that guided his watercolor technique, but in more abstract terms. The reception of his oils was a great disappointment to him. The critics were cool to them, and so was the public. Somewhere, in the shift to a new medium, the grace and sparkle that characterized his watercolors was lost.

Fame finally came to John Marin in his sixty-third year: an exhibition called "Twenty Five Years of Marin," comprising all his work from the early Paris watercolors to his most recent paintings, was an unqualified triumph. Three years later the Museum of Modern Art, in an even larger show, devoted two of its floors to a giant exhibit of all of Marin's works. This was a supreme tribute to a still-living artist.

In the catalogue of the museum show—which included over two hundred works—Marsden Hartley, himself a noted painter, wrote:

"You will never see watercolors like these of John Marin again, so take a good look and remember, and if you are a painter, don't try to cope with the style because the style in this case is several times the man, love of life, love of work, love of Nature."

Success and the weight of his years did not diminish Marin's fury for work. Nor did his style become more conservative. Rather, it leaned ever further in the direction of the abstract. Unlike many of the abstractionists, he always painted from a subject, preferably a subject in nature. "The sea I paint may not be *THE* sea," as he put it, "but it is A sea, not an abstraction."

Marie Marin died in 1945, on March 1, her birthday. Marin was at her bedside, grieved at her passing, sorrowing that their son could not be present. Young John was fighting somewhere in the South Pacific during the Second World War. Marie's death created a void that for Marin no one else could fill. She had shared his life completely, uncomplaining in the lean years, with rare good sense in the good; she had seen to it that he wore his scarf when he went outdoors to paint, she had cut his hair, she had criticized his paintings. Although she admitted that she didn't quite understand all he was trying to express in his work, she had an unfailing eye for balance. "The picture don't seem to me to weigh right, John," she would say, and invariably her instinct was correct.

A year later Alfred Stieglitz, Marin's friend, sponsor, and dedicated supporter died. Shortly thereafter Marin suffered a heart attack. His recovery was speeded by the return of his son from the war. In the remaining years Marin and young John enjoyed an unusually warm and happy friendship. Young Marin was so concerned about his father's failing health that he took the elder Marin along on his honeymoon when he married in the summer of 1948!

To the end, Marin continued to spend his winters in the house in Cliffside, his summers in Cape Split, Maine. Few of his neighbors in Maine were aware that the gentle, unassuming old man with whom they went fishing, and who painted pictures that were beyond their comprehension, was a world-famous artist, rich in honors. They knew him simply as a good companion, "a curious little man, wiry and frail . . . incredibly wrinkled . . . peering out brightly and mischievously under an outlandish bang . . . dressed with a quaint old-fashioned elegance. . . ."

Several years before his death on October 1, 1953, with the presentation of a major award by the American Institute of Architects for his contribution to art, Marin was epitomized as follows: "Your vision has created for us a right and unalterable image of our rocks and sea, our plains and mountains and the living pulse of our cities."

The inept student, the man who couldn't hold a job, the loafer, the billiard shark—the many men who made up the one complex man of genius—had at last come into his own. The failure had become a resounding success in the eyes of the whole world.

13

The Modernist

STUART DAVIS

1894–

Stuart Davis was nineteen years old when the Armory Show rampaged through New York art circles with the fury of a tornado, up-ending all existing standards of painting. "That cataclysm in the course of American art," as Davis called it, had split the art world in two. One was either for or against "modernism." There was no safety zone, no middle ground. Matisse, a leader of the advance guard, was burned in effigy; artist scorned artist.

For Davis the Armory Show was a total revelation. He became an immediate convert to the exciting experimental approach to composition, subject matter and color. This was it! He would "have to become a 'modern' artist." With single-minded purpose and a bulldog tenacity, he set his sights on his deliberately chosen goal, and never wavered until he had become the first purely abstract painter in America, "the ace of modernists," as a critic once called him.

Stuart Davis was born on December 7, 1894, in Philadelphia, into a home where art was part of daily life. His mother, Helen Stuart Foulke, had studied painting and sculpture at the Pennsylvania Academy of Fine Arts, and it was there that she had met her husband, a fellow student. At the time of Stuart's birth, Edward Wyatt Davis, his father, was art editor of the Philadelphia *Press*, the newspaper on which John Sloan, George Luks, William Glackens, and Everett Shinn—future members of the Eight—were staff artists. The elder Davis painted in his spare time, sharing a studio with Shinn and attending classes taught by Robert Henri, mentor of the Eight. In 1901 the family moved to East Orange, New Jersey, and Edward Davis became cartoonist of the Newark *Evening News* and, later, for *Judge* and *Leslie's Weekly* magazines.

By the time Stuart had completed his freshman year at the East Orange High School, he had made up his mind to become an artist. The parental objections that often plague would-be artists were no problem to Stuart. The elder Davises were delighted, and willingly gave their consent to his quitting high school. His father arranged to have him enrolled as a student with Robert Henri.

Henri's school, which had opened in 1909, was considered wildly revolutionary in its teaching methods. The normal academic routine of the art school of that day was scorned. Instead, Henri urged his students to develop their own individuality and work from the imagination. No rules or techniques were laid down; all that Henri asked of his students was that they seek their subject matter in everyday existence, rather than search for ideal beauty. They were sent out into the streets to make drawings from life. In the studio these sketches were transformed into paintings. Each Saturday morning Henri sat in criticism, and with characteristic fervor and animation discussed not only his students' work, but also literature, music, art, and, again, life. For young Davis these lectures were "a liberal education."

Although he was only sixteen, Davis' obvious talent and considerable knowledge of painting won him quick acceptance by the older members of the class. He himself jokingly attributed it to his ability to buy his fellow students large quantities of beer. Medium in height and pleasant-faced, his eyes reflected an alert, intelligent mind. His easy-going, direct manner won him a number of good friends, among them Glenn O. Coleman and Henry Glintenkamp, both of whom were later to become artists of repute. Coleman, five years Davis' senior, at once assumed the role of guide. "Enthusiasm for running around and drawing things in the raw ran high," Davis recalls. They explored the city, walking under and over the Brooklyn Bridge, wandering through the narrow byways of Chinatown, discovering the derelicts in the Bowery, frequenting the music halls, and riding the canal boats that plied the coastal waters of New Jersey. In the Negro saloons of Newark, Coleman and Davis discovered the new jazz, and developed a love for it that persists to this day with Davis, and that has figured measurably in his work. With the purchase of a five-cent glass of beer, both young men could sit for hours, entranced by the music of Negro musicians who played "for the love of art alone," as young Davis said. He felt it was the "only modern thing in American culture before 1913," the only experimentation that was in tune with its time.

The traditional struggle of young artists to find a place to show their work hardly existed for Davis. He exhibited his first painting in the same year that he had begun his art school training. To the show of the Independents, along with such men as Henri, Sloan, and other members of the Eight, he sent "The Music Hall," his first work of truly professional calibre. Notwithstanding a strong influence of the French artist Toulouse-Lautrec, and a still immature style, the painting was executed with sureness and skill. It was singled out for attention in a review in the New York *American*, written by the artist Guy Pène du Bois. For a sixteen-year-old to receive notice was indeed extraordinary.

For the next three years, Davis applied himself seriously to extending his knowledge of painting. In 1912, John Sloan, who was then art editor of *The Masses* magazine, asked Davis to join the staff. In his spare time, while still attending classes at Henri's, Davis contributed to the publication realistic satirical drawings that bore little resemblance to his impetuous manner of painting. One of his covers was termed the best of the year by the popular newspaper columnist Franklin P. Adams. Four years later he resigned with Sloan, because of a difference of opinion on editorial policy. Meanwhile, during this period he continued to exhibit his work, often in the company of such artists as Sloan, Luks, Glackens, and Bellows. In 1912 his work was shown at the New York Water Color Club, and in 1913 at the MacDowell Club in New York. Reviews of his work were mixed. One critic proclaimed him a "great" talent, while another declared that he thought of art only as "a monkey shine of technique."

Increasingly, Davis became aware that something was lacking in his work. The shortcomings of Henri's teaching methods had begun to trouble him. Heavy emphasis on "antiartistic" subject matter, on vitality and emotion did not seem to him to balance out insufficient work on color theory and composition. The fine line that marked the "difference between descriptive and illustrative painting," Davis realized, had never been clearly defined by Henri. The early stimulation of Henri's teaching and personality no longer satisfied him. He started to search for a fresh approach, a new vision.

It was at the Armory Show, where he was exhibiting five watercolors, that Davis found the image and the ideas he had been seeking. The radical outlook of the new European painters was more exciting and stimulating than anything he had ever before encountered. The work of Van Gogh, Gauguin, and Matisse, in particular, attracted him. Their innovations in the use of color and their radical treatment of subject matter and composition opened his eyes to infinite possibilities. The decision to become a "modern" artist almost made itself.

A commission from *Harper's* for a drawing a week provided Davis with the income he needed to devote himself to his new purpose. He left Henri's school and set off eagerly for Provincetown, Massachusetts. Here he found that the clear brilliance of the light was especially conducive to adopting a simpler and more direct approach to painting. Under the influence of Van Gogh's work his technique grew more heavily brushed and textured, his color more vivid. He discarded conventional use of perspective, and began to build his pictures in flat planes, relying on the use of color to suggest depth. He had set out with cool deliberation to think in a different fashion so that he "could paint a green tree red," as he put it, "without batting an eye."

Several summers later, on John Sloan's recommendation Davis went to Gloucester, Massachusetts. He made his entrance in a recently purchased secondhand car, roaring into the old fishing village at eighteen miles an hour, pursued by

a mounted policeman for exceeding the speed limit and disturbing the peace. Before long he had made the acquaintance
of the artists and writers who lived there, as well as the natives, with whom he would often play chess. Davis found
Gloucester highly stimulating to his imagination. He abandoned the process of painting directly from life, making only
sketches and color notations, returning to the studio to work
out his paintings. Although his paintings were still recog-
nizably drawn from nature, he had developed the use of abstract geometric form, and a radical theory of composition
which spread the traditional center of interest from edge to
edge—the "all-over" concept. He sought to "twist and shape"
subject matter to his own vision.

In the last few months of the First World War, Davis
served in a branch of Army Intelligence, where he drew maps
and charts. After the Armistice, he returned to New York
and with Coleman rented a studio on upper Broadway close
to Henri's old school.

During the war a large number of avant-garde European
artists had settled temporarily in New York, and their work
was winning a great deal of attention. These Post-Impression-
ists, Cubists, Fauvists, Synchromists—as they variously called
themselves—scoffed at all the traditional rules of art. Their
byword was complete freedom of expression for the artist.

Davis, fascinated as always by what was modern, began to
work in Cubist collage, a method whereby abstract shapes
were painted on a canvas in conjunction with odd bits of
material glued to it to form a composition. Deliberately un-
realistic, the Cubist painters used flat planes and multiple
simultaneous views, giving the impression that one was looking at all sides of an object at the same time. After seeing
the work of many of the French painters, Davis felt himself
liberated and free to experiment in any manner, "without any

sense of guilt." He painted a number of collages, using such actual objects as a package of Lucky Strike cigarettes, salt cellars, and bathroom fixtures. For the first time he used words and letters on his canvas, believing that signs were an integral part of the American scene. Although his approach was modern, Davis had not yet developed his own brand of modernism. He was still a long distance away from achieving his full ambition.

In 1927, after fourteen years, he complained that he "was still working on the little matter" of becoming a modern artist. His resolution, nevertheless, was still as firm as when he had originally made it. He felt that he had solved, at least to his own satisfaction, the use of color. There remained the serious problems of form and spatial relations. Modern art was intellectual in concept, and could only be successful if all these problems were clarified. Davis redoubled his efforts to find the formula.

One day he nailed an eggbeater to the surface of a table in his studio. For a full year it became his sole subject, the exclusive focus of all his painting. Viewing the eggbeater as a series of shapes rather than as an object, a thing, he began to invent geometrical forms that took impulse from his ideas rather than from the subject matter. He painted a series of "Eggbeater" pictures, identified only by numbers to show their progression. Bearing no resemblance to reality, they consisted of vibrant color integrated with abstract forms playing over the surface of the canvas. By the end of the year Davis felt that he had attained his goal. His concept was now truly abstract. He could call himself a "modern" artist. Notwithstanding the modernism of his theories, his paintings still had their roots in the forms of nature.

In May, 1928, Mrs. Juliana Force, director of the Whitney Studio Club, where Davis had exhibited several times, bought several of his pictures. With the proceeds—nine hundred dollars—Davis traveled to Paris, the mecca of modern painting. He packed one suitcase and two Eggbeater paintings. Upon his arrival in mid-June, the customs inspector refused to allow him to bring the canvases into France. They were, he insisted, messages in code. Haltingly, Davis, who could speak no French, tried to explain. It was not until he used the word *Cubist* that the inspector understood. The paintings were allowed to enter. Davis installed himself in a small studio on the Rue Vercingetorix, paying three months' rent —twenty dollars—in advance. The studio contained sleeping quarters, an alcohol stove for cooking, and a lamp that hung in the middle of the room. Water was available in the outside hall. The arrangement more than satisfied Davis' needs.

"I liked Paris the minute I got there," Davis said. He was delighted by the Frenchman's acceptance of an artist as a respected member of society. He enjoyed the city; the contrast of old and new pleased his eye. In the more leisurely tempo of living, so different from that of New York, there was time to meet friends, to sit and talk at the pleasant little outdoor cafés scattered throughout Paris. Davis fell in love with the city as so many other artists had before him. He expressed this affection by painting a series of Parisian street scenes of great warmth and charm.

After an interlude in which he "did nothing but paint and walk through the streets," Davis became homesick for the tempo and excitement of American life. He sailed for the United States on the maiden voyage of the liner *Bremen.* After Paris, the frenzy and "giantism" of New York overwhelmed him. It was a while before he could reaccustom himself to the pace of the city and resume his normal routine of work.

Less than two months after his return, the great Depression hit the country. Although he sold a few paintings, he was, like most Americans, hard up financially. In the late summer he left for Gloucester, where his father owned a small house. He continued to paint, turning out a series of pictures in the style of the Eggbeater. In 1931 he was hired as an instructor for the Art Students League in New York, a post he held until the following year. In 1932, when construction of the new Radio City Music Hall was completed, Davis was commissioned to paint a mural for the Men's Lounge. The eleven-by-seventeen-foot work, which he painted in Gloucester, was a lively montage of a variety of athletic and outdoor activities. The fee was sufficient to allow him to stay in Gloucester and paint for yet another year.

On Christmas Day, 1933, Davis returned to New York. "I scarcely had a cent in my pockets," he said, "and very slim prospects." The next morning he applied for a job on the Federal Works of Art Project and was hired. To augment his salary, he also started teaching a few pupils privately. He joined the Artist's Union, and worked on its magazine, *The Art Front*, dedicated to helping the artist in his struggle for economic security. Out of a deep belief that artists must participate in world affairs, he helped found the American Artists Congress, an organization of painters opposed to Fascism, and became its national chairman. He resigned in 1940, when he felt that the group no longer stood for the principles on which it had been established.

On October 12, 1936, Stuart Davis and Roselle Springer were married, as Davis rather vaguely puts it, "somewhere in Maryland." Roselle was a student of painting and sculpture, and she shared many of Davis' interests, including his love of jazz. Currently, the Davises make their home in midtown Manhattan not far from the little night clubs specializing in jazz. They have one son, Earl, born in 1952.

For much of the time during the thirties, Davis was too

involved with political activities to produce much of his own work. However, he waged a vehement campaign advocating the cause of modern art in newspapers and magazines. He attacked the American regionalism of such painters as Thomas Benton and Grant Wood as "painting that is a jolly lark for amateurs to be shown at country fairs." In the time that he was employed by the Federal government, he completed two murals—one for New York's municipal radio station, WNYC, on "electronic abstractions"; the other, "Swing Landscape," for a housing project that was never built. "Swing Landscape" advanced the idea that swing music, then sweeping the country, was a kind of American landscape. The work contained no literal musical symbols. The title took its name from the intense liveliness of the painting, from the jumping, jazzy arrangement of the intense color, and the flat abstract shapes. One critic complimented Davis when he called it a "non-objective inebriant. . . ."

Davis was commissioned in 1939 to execute a mural for the Communications Building at the New York World's Fair. Painted on an outside wall, 45 feet high by 132 feet wide, it traces the history of communications. The work was done in a linear design of white fluorescent paint on a black ground. Davis also did a two-page color drawing of the World's Fair for *Harper's Bazaar*. This same year he was dropped from the rolls of the Federal Arts Project, having finished the six-year maximum term allowed by the government.

Once again unemployed, Davis said he did "the conventional thing—hired a studio and devoted himself to painting." He received little or no recognition in the period that followed. There were no more mural commissions nor offers of exhibitions from the New York galleries. The public, he declared bitterly, was like "an omelet," incapable of stirring itself to understand new ideas. He sold his work on infrequent occasions, accepting whatever he could get for it.

His style, now completely mature, had become more complex and more abstract. Shapes and colors writhed and cavorted in joyous movement over the entire surface of the canvas, some of it still recognizable pieces of Americana. Letters of the alphabet, words, even complete phrases wound sinuously through his compositions. His titles, which were not always pertinent to the work, contained a strong element of playfulness. Not unlike Whistler, he liked to use musical terms, but in the idiom of contemporary jazz. Some of his titles based on "bop" music or Davis' own brand of humor are: "Owh! In San Pao," "Rapt at Rappaport's," "Something on the Eight Ball," "For Internal Use Only," and "Hot Still-Scape for Six Colors."

In the forties, recognition began to come to Davis. In 1940 he was named art instructor at the New School for Social Research, a position he held for a decade; and he was also made a visiting art critic at Yale University. In 1943 he was given a show at the Downtown Gallery in New York—his first one-man show in nine years. It was a lively show in more ways than one. Without Davis' knowledge two of his friends arranged for a pair of jazz pianists to play while the audience looked at the pictures. Mildred Bailey, a famous blues singer, obliged with several numbers. Duke Ellington, W. C. Handy, and other jazz notables, all friends of Davis', were also present. The exhibition was a rousing success both as entertainment and financially.

Quite suddenly he had come into his own. He was given a retrospective exhibition in 1941 at Indiana University, and another in 1945 at the Museum of Modern Art; a one-man show in the American section at the Venice Biennale in 1952; and one-man shows by the Walker Art Center in Minneapolis, the Des Moines Art Center, the San Francisco Museum of Art, and the Whitney Museum of New York—all in the same year, 1957. He won first prize in the Pepsi-Cola competition for a painting, and was awarded honors by the Carnegie Institute, the Art Institute of Chicago, and the Pennsylvania Academy. His design for a mural for United Nations Headquarters in New York took first prize. He was awarded a Guggenheim fellowship, and was elected a member of the National Institute of Arts and Letters.

Davis has grown more portly with age. He is a courteous, intelligent, and articulate man. His physical carriage and the alert, independent gleam in his eye belie his years. This "shy bulldog," as *Time* magazine once referred to him, works in a large studio, which, despite being full of painterly appurtenances, is neat and orderly. The long hours he spends at his easel are sometimes enlivened by a television program with the sound turned off. For Davis it is "like having a window into the street." More often he works to the accompaniment of jazz records. He is a devotee of the music of Earl Hines, Art Tatum, Oscar Peterson, and other notables in that field. When they are playing in any of the nearby clubs, Davis and his wife go to hear them. Davis has no "ivory tower." He lives in, paints, and belongs to the twentieth century.

The spontaneous effect his pictures give are achieved only by long hours of labor. He is, in his own words, a "murderously slow" worker. He produces at the most eight or ten pictures a year, and has been known to spend as much as six years working on a single painting. His canvases are vivid abstractions, masterful in their application of design, color, and form, jumping with the energy and freedom of jazz improvisation. Of an exhibition of his work held in 1962, *Time* magazine commented: "In all his notable career Davis has never seemed more vigorous." Long recognized as an "innovator and pioneer modernist," in the words of one critic, he is solidly entrenched as one of the ranking abstract artists of this century. He is highly respected by the younger generation of Abstract Expressionists, despite his slow, thoughtful manner of working—the direct antithesis of their rapid "spontaneous" attack.

Davis himself does not much care for the "dripping ritual" as he terms the style of painting of which Jackson Pollock was the foremost exponent. He holds that "abstract art is like all other art"—an expression of "a sense of meaning and unity in nature." He believes passionately that a man's art must be characteristic of the place and time he lives in. This conviction is of greater importance to him than the label of "modernist" he strove so long and diligently to acquire.

He sums it up by saying simply, "I paint what I see in America."

14

A People's Painter

BEN SHAHN

1898–

Young Ben refused to return to religious school. Nothing would change his mind. It had been bad enough, he resentfully informed his parents, when he had asked the rabbi who made God and had been slapped for impertinence. Now something different and even more unsettling had occurred. In discussing the history of the Jews, the rabbi had given the class an example of God's overwhelming wrath. The ancient Israelites had been warned that the Ark of the Covenant (containing the Hebraic Law) must never be touched by any man. One day, as the Ark was being carried into the Temple atop a pole, it began to waver. One most devout member of the congregation, fearful for its safety, leaped forward to prevent its falling. At the instant that his hand brushed the sacred vessel, he was struck dead.

Bewildered and indignant, young Ben revolted against what he considered a cruelly harsh judgment. It was a full week before his parents finally persuaded him to return to his studies. But he never forgot the story, never quite forgave a God who could punish the well-meaning with as much severity as those who were evil. Nor could he comprehend a society which accepted submissively a Deity who dealt out such stern justice. As he grew older, perhaps he became reconciled to the concept of an austere God; but he never became reconciled to injustice. Moral indignation at the misuse of power coupled with love for his fellow man—these were the dominant strains that molded the character and art of Ben Shahn. He never separated his art from his principle, painting what he felt most deeply and what he thought ought to be said. He is above all a painter of social themes, wielding a frequently savage, sometimes lyrical, yet always compassionate brush upon vital contemporary subjects.

Ben Shahn was born in Kaunas, Lithuania, then part of Tsarist Russia, on the morning of September 12, 1898. He was one of the five children of Hessel Shahn, a Jewish carpenter and wood carver, and Gittel Lieberman. For the first eight years of his life, Ben lived in the close-knit ghetto of the Jewish community, following the spiritual and religious traditions of his ancestors. The Sabbath was observed from sundown on Friday until sundown of the following evening. Candles were lit and blessed at the festive evening repast. The boys of the family accompanied their father to religious services on the Sabbath and the high holy days. Aunts, uncles, cousins, relatives of all degrees, lived in close association and were vitally involved in family problems, joys and blessings.

In the cold winter months when the river froze, Ben and his friends skated on the icy surface until their cheeks were red with frost and their toes numbed. In milder weather Mr. Shahn would sometimes hire a horse and carriage to transport his children to the neighboring village for a visit with their delighted grandparents. In the summer there were berries to pick and games to play. But if life held countless small pleasures for the young, it was for their elders a hard struggle.

In the fall of 1906 the Shahns joined the thousands of Jewish migrants fleeing the persecution of the Tsar and the poverty that hung over the ghetto like an evil spirit. The exodus to America held the promise of religious freedom and an end to the eternal battle of making ends meet. The exciting vista of New York City from the harbor gave the Shahns their first wide-eyed glimpse of the fabulous "promised land." Even the trolley ride across the Williamsburg Bridge, high over the East River, somehow seemed to offer assurance of the good life to come.

For Ben this new world held a few disagreeable surprises. He sat for the first time in a rocking chair, and clung for dear life to the arms of this odd contraption which seemed bent on unseating him. He grew violently ill at his first taste of tomato. People laughed at his ignorance, were amused by his bewilderment. It was not simple to master a new language or acclimate oneself to the clangorous rhythm of tenement living. But on the whole a sense of hope and glorious expectancy for the future pushed these difficulties into the background. He was going to an American public school, adopting the glamorous American customs, becoming an authentic "Yankee." He believed with all his soul in the "liberty and justice for all" contained in the allegiance he pledged to his new country.

After a brief stay with relatives, the Shahns moved to a

small cold-water flat of their own in the Williamsburg section of Brooklyn. Hessel Shahn had started his own business, a washing-soda factory, in the adjacent building. Life in America was off to a promising start.

One night, when Mrs. Shahn had left the children momentarily to run an errand, there was a sudden explosion and burst of flame from the building next door. The factory was on fire! Hessel Shahn's only thought was for the safety of his family. Without a moment's hesitation, as Ben Shahn recalls the incident, his father "clambered up a drainpipe and took each of my brothers and sisters and me out of the house, one by one. . . ." The tenement and the factory building were completely gutted. Hessel Shahn was painfully burned on his face and hands. The family was left with nothing but the clothes on their back. The security they had so ardently desired had vanished in the flames. It was a blow from which the elder Shahns never quite recovered.

It took Hessel Shahn several months to recuperate sufficiently to be able to look for a job. The family found another apartment on nearby Walton Street, where some of their neighbors kept milking cows in the rear yard. Later they moved once again, and in 1920 finally bought their own house, still on the same street, to have the room needed by their growing children. Hessel Shahn found employment making baker's troughs and shovels. Ill-paying though the job was, life had once again assumed its normal aspect.

The poverty from which the Shahns had vainly sought escape seemed destined to pursue them. Peaceful, gentle by nature, Hessel Shahn was not fortunate enough to provide for his family as well as he would have wished. His interests ran to philosophy and literature, and he attempted to pass on his love of these studies to his children. He was inordinately pleased by the signs of budding artistic talent displayed by

young Ben. Mrs. Shahn, grown bitter with a life of penury
and deprivation, yearned only for the security of a regular
income that would adequately provide for her growing family. With a persistence bred of necessity, she nagged at her
husband to seek steady employment. Disillusioned, quarrel-
some, she saw in young Ben's gifts a direct inheritance of his
father's insufficiencies. Artistic talents were completely alien
to her concept of the basis for a sound future, merely another
burden added to her already heavy load. She looked to her
other children for the business acumen she found so unhap-
pily lacking in both her husband and this son.

From as far back as he could remember, young Ben had
wanted to draw. When he was thirteen, he disproved, for the
first time, his mother's predictions of an indolent and un-
profitable future in his chosen career. He had become so
enamored of the thought of being able to earn money by
drawing that he had prevailed upon an uncle working in a
lithography plant to get him a job. He left school, where he
had been a good student, but continued his education at
night. In the next four years young Shahn's apprenticeship
taught him all the fundamentals of the lithography business.
Now, instead of having to learn drawing by copying the small
engravings that came with each pack of Sweet Caporal cigarettes, he was learning from professionals. At night school his
art teacher at once became aware of young Shahn's unusual
ability. He took the young man with him to an anatomy class
and on sketching trips through the Connecticut countryside,
guiding him meanwhile to a greater understanding of art.
Young Shahn felt the inadequacies of a curtailed education,
and eagerly sought to broaden his own cultural background.
To satisfy the demands of an omnivorous appetite for knowledge, he read with growing interest the literary and philo-
sophical masterpieces of the centuries.

Brown-haired, blue-eyed, at twenty-one Ben Shahn was a stocky, sturdy young man. He had not yet grown the walrus mustache he later wore. Characteristically gentle, with a great love for people, his temper was quick to flare at any type of injustice. With the intention of becoming a biologist, he pursued his education at New York University. He was dissatisfied by the instruction, and soon transferred to the College of the City of New York. Here he began contributing drawings to the campus literary magazine. Although he was pursuing his own inclinations, he was haunted by a sense of unhappy frustration. His salary, after paying his expenses at home, left him with little more than carfare. The job also deprived him of sufficient time to study. His early, immature conception of a future as a professional lithographer had been stripped of all glamour. The inadequate pay, the long hours of drudgery, and his own intense dislike of copying other men's work had made it highly unattractive. He was uncertain of his aspirations. He had realized that he was not a biologist, that his interest and his talent lay in the direction of art—but in what branch of art he did not know.

In September, 1922, shortly before his twenty-fourth birthday, Ben Shahn married Tillie Goldstein, the daughter of a prosperous merchant and Hebraic scholar. Tillie, like Ben, was an immigrant child of immigrant parents. They had grown up in the same neighborhood and had been courting for a number of years. She was an intelligent young woman with a mind of her own and a lively interest in art and literature. Despite her family's opposition—they regarded the Shahns as "lower class"—Tillie had been firm in her desire to become Ben's wife. The young couple moved to Columbia Heights, a much more genteel and fashionable section of Brooklyn. Ben left college and enrolled in the National Academy of Design—his first step toward a serious career in art.

He kept his job as a lithographer and studied at night. It was not until his thirty-second year that he was able to devote full time to painting.

After about three years of extra jobs and self-denial the Shahns had saved enough money to finance a trip abroad so that Ben could broaden his knowledge of art. They traveled from North Africa to Spain, Italy, and France. Shahn found the new European art fascinating. He was eager to learn from all the masters, both old and modern, and especially from the work of the contemporary French artists. Rouault and Dufy in particular were the men whose pictures bore meaning for him. After several months of absorbing whatever he could of technique and theory, the Shahns returned to Brooklyn. That same year he and Tillie bought a small, quite inexpensive cottage at Truro, Massachusetts, where Shahn could paint while on vacation.

In 1927 Shahn and his wife had saved enough money to go abroad once again. They settled in Paris, where the work of the men Shahn admired could best be studied. Meanwhile he worked on his own paintings. On July 14, 1929, Bastille Day, Tillie Shahn presented her husband with their first child, Judith. In the fall of the same year, the Shahn family left for home. Shahn now decided to risk earning his living through a full-time career as an artist. In 1930, Edith Halpert of the Downtown Gallery in New York offered him his first one-man show. The exhibition of oils and watercolors, markedly influenced by Rouault and Dufy, was well received. The work, which included landscapes and nudes, gave as yet little indication of his later distinctive style and perception.

Shahn was impelled by a need to find a much deeper meaning for his life and his work. He grew interested in the radical politics and art movements that had gained a following during the Depression years. His wife, now the mother of two children, was too deeply interested in raising a family and being a good housekeeper to share her husband's problems or enthusiasms. The ever-increasing diversity of interests nurtured a growing alienation between them. Before long the estrangement culminated in divorce.

Shahn, dissatisfied with his work, which he feared was immature and imitative, began probing for a more personal expression and more depth in his art. He felt his way in a series of watercolors of the Dreyfus case. The religious bigotry of the famous French treason trial had sparked both his imagination and indignation. He yearned to have been alive during the time when Christ was crucified, so that he could have been emotionally involved. Then, suddenly and with startling clarity, he realized, as he said, that he "was living during another crucifixion. Here was something to paint." The something was the Sacco-Vanzetti case, a striking example of injustice, bigotry, and ignorance.

On April 15, 1920, Nicola Sacco and Bartolomeo Vanzetti, two Italian-American anarchists, had been arrested and charged with the murder of a paymaster and guard at South Braintree, Massachusetts. They pleaded innocent, but, after a highly prejudicial trial, were found guilty and sentenced to die. Public opinion throughout the world erupted in a paroxysm of rage. Liberal citizens of every stripe, convinced that innocent men were being condemned to death because of their political beliefs, struggled furiously for more than six years in a vain attempt to free the two men. On August 26, 1927, Sacco and Vanzetti died in the electric chair.

Shahn had found his crucifixion. In seven months of intensive work he finished twenty-three gouache panels depicting the leading characters and events of the Sacco-Vanzetti case. In 1932 they were exhibited in the Downtown Gallery. The work, done in a flat linear style and muted color, was like a savage cartoon. The show was an instantaneous and overwhelming success. The critics were loud in their praises. *Hound and Horn*, an influential literary magazine, said that "with an appraising accuracy he [Shahn] installed the actors of that tragedy in their proper places in a frame, and their arrangement is an inscription more surgical than any partisan approach." The paintings, on sale for one hundred dollars each, found a quick market.

The Harvard Society for Contemporary Art asked permission to exhibit the pictures, and Shahn was also invited to participate in a show of mural paintings at the Museum of Modern Art. For the latter, he repainted three of the Sacco-Vanzetti panels—showing the committee of men who had reviewed the case wearing top hats, holding lilies in their hands, and standing in an attitude of mock sorrow over the coffined bodies. He submitted it to the Museum and it was indignantly rejected. When a powerful member of the board of trustees threatened to resign in protest, the mural was quickly reinstated. Most of the critics regarded the work as an effrontery. The *New York Times* was disgusted, calling it "a violation . . . of good taste." Interestingly enough, the *Wall Street Journal*, perhaps the most conservative of all New York papers, almost alone found merit in the mural. Shahn evaluated the entire incident as a victory in his personal battle against injustice.

It was at the Sacco-Vanzetti exhibition that Shahn first met Bernarda Bryson. Her background was as different from Shahn's as Tillie Goldstein's had been similar. Five years his junior, Bernarda was the descendant of Scotch pioneers, born and raised in Ohio. Her father, Charles Bryson, was the editor of the Athens (Ohio) *Gazette* and the Athens *Morning Journal*, and a man of liberal tendencies. In 1932, Bernarda had come to New York as an officer in the Artists Union, a left-wing organization designed to better the economic lot of artists. She persuaded Shahn, in whom she sensed a common viewpoint, to join the editorial board of the union's magazine, *The Art Front*. Shahn agreed, but soon resigned. He was too independent in his views to accept political dictation. Soon afterward, Shahn and Bernarda were married. She is a talented artist in her own right, and has worked with her husband on several murals. They have three children, Susan, Jon, and Abby.

Another visitor to the Museum of Modern Art had been Diego Rivera, the famous Mexican artist. An avowed radical, his reputation as an artist nevertheless superseded his political beliefs in the view of even the most conservative people, and he had been commissioned to paint a mural in the entrance of one of the newly-erected buildings in Rockefeller Center. Rivera was so impressed by Shahn's ability and independent viewpoint that he hired him as his assistant. Before long, a disagreement arose between the management and Rivera. Not unreasonably, the Rockefellers asked the Mexican painter to remove a head of Lenin, the first leader of the Soviet Republic, from the mural. When Rivera refused flatly, he and his staff were fired, and the mural scraped off the wall. But for Shahn it had been a valuable experience. He had learned from a master artist the technique of fresco painting, involving the organization of large masses of figures into a simplified structural composition.

In the next few years, Shahn, like many of his fellow artists, worked for various federal agencies. He was employed by the Federal Works of Art Project, a government-sponsored agency designed to help artists during the Depression years. From 1935 to 1938, he worked for the Farm Security Administration as an artist, designer, and photographer. During this period he did his first mural—for a federal housing project for garment workers at Roosevelt, New Jersey. A few years later, he moved to the project, where he still lives. In 1938, he and his wife won a competition to paint a large mural in the lobby of the Bronx Central Post Office, and in 1940 Shahn received a fee of twenty thousand dollars for a mural in the Social Security building in Washington. It was the first sizable amount of money he had ever earned as an artist. The mural is one of his finest works. Rivera's technique was supplanted by a personal style in which he treated the wall painting with the emotion and originality he invested in his paintings. James Thrall Soby, an eminent critic, said, "In an era when fresco painting has often assumed machinery's cold dryness, Shahn retains an almost romantic intensity of mood."

During these years of commissioned work, Shahn still found time to labor at his easel. Impatient with the slow-drying qualities of oil paint, he made use of the quicker mediums of gouache and tempera. On occasions he worked from photographs, which he rearranged and regrouped on the canvas to suit his composition. He is a master draftsman with a sharp eye and a great knowledge of the human form. His compassion and love for humanity are never absent. Reality of detail plays a vital part in each picture. "There's a difference in the way a twelve-dollar coat wrinkles from the way a seventy-five dollar coat wrinkles. . . ," Shahn says, in summing up his insistence on authenticity.

In 1940 Shahn exhibited the easel paintings he had finished in the past few years. They ranged in subject from biting social comment to memories of his childhood. In addition to a sharper and more forceful arrangement of line and composition, the new work was characterized by richer, more vibrant color. As time went on, his paintings became increasingly concerned with the individual and his loneliness and isolation in a world of conflict. In "Willis Avenue Bridge," several women sit sunning themselves on a bench, oblivious of each other. "Vacant Lot," "Handball," "Sunday Painting"—all are imbued with a tender love for city people.

When the United States entered the Second World War, Shahn joined the Office of War Information and began to paint posters connected with the war effort. His bold, incisive conception displeased his superiors. They felt that his work was too unpretty, too raw for public consumption. Shahn protested. War was an ugly business, and should not be prettified to suit the taste of displaced advertising men. Some time afterward, when the department was abolished, he at once embarked on a series of paintings which said about war what the bureaucrats had not allowed him to say.

Shahn's growing reputation as a painter brought him to the attention of the business world. In 1943, he received his first commission from an advertising agency. Ironically, his highly personal, "unpretty" style suddenly came into great demand —a demand that has increased steadily with the years. From the very beginning, he insisted on complete freedom in what he did, without interference from client or advertising executive. Then, as now, he accepted no work unless he approved of the idea or found it an artistic challenge. He declined an offer from the Chrysler Corporation because they wanted one of their cars included in the painting. He flatly refuses to alter a single detail of his work. On one occasion when he was asked to make some minor changes, he simply removed the painting to his gallery, where it was promptly sold to a prominent art critic. Shahn believes firmly that all art, whether fine or commercial, must have meaning. "For an artist to make a painting which is without significance to himself," he says, "is simply to commercialize his past achievement." Drug addiction, prenatal care, disease, mental illness, labor conditions in foreign lands—these are some of the meaningful subjects to which Shahn has been willing to lend his name and his talent.

At the same time that Shahn had begun to command large sums for his commercial work, he was all but donating his time and talents to labor. He worked as the head of the art department for the Political Action Committee of the CIO, one of the two largest labor groups in America. With three assistants, he designed posters, leaflets, brochures, or whatever was needed to publicize the PAC's various causes, which included support of Franklin D. Roosevelt's fourth term as President. Many of the posters which had been rejected by the Office of War Information were put to use at this time. Shahn was happy in this job. He felt that at last he was using his talent to promote the fight against ignorance, bigotry, oppression, and inequality. For the first time he could agree wholeheartedly with his employer's "morality."

In 1947 Shahn's artistic importance was given full recognition in a retrospective show at the Museum of Modern Art. The exhibition brought together most of his easel paintings, drawings, posters, illustrations, mural studies, and a collection of his photographs. It was an overwhelming success. Robert Coates of *The New Yorker* spoke of the "keen sense of social justice" that gave "added depth and passion to his work." Thomas Hess, an authority on modern painting, stated, "In this fusion of idea with matter, of emotion with form, lies the greatness of Shahn's painting and the awesome individuality of his technique." Another critic termed him "that rare synthesis, an artist's artist and a people's painter." Of the important critics only Clement Greenberg, a champion of abstract art, demurred. "There is a poverty of culture and resources," Greenberg wrote, "a pinchedness . . . a certain desire for quick acceptance." But the abstract school held no meaning for Shahn. Art had to communicate to be a living part of human existence. "I'm interested in life, and only in art in so far as it enables me to express what I feel about life."

In 1954, Shahn was selected by the Museum of Modern Art, along with Willem de Kooning, to represent American art at the Venice, Italy, Biennale Exhibition of International Art. De Kooning's abstract-expressionist creations were in direct contrast to Shahn's new realism. His most recent work was composed with delicate simplicity, more lyrical and reflective in feeling. Although it depended less and less on the "representational," it never departed from recognizable depiction of people and things. His color was scaled higher and had become more luminous, with the predominant use of a vivid red. As always, his pictures were concerned with the problems of humanity.

The response to Shahn's selection for the Biennale brought forth various reactions. His work, too individual to be strictly classified as belonging to any school, offended some and pleased others. *Time* magazine, in a review of the exhibition, said, "Shahn, whose work had its roots in proletarian fury, has now become fashionable. . . . At peace with the world in recent years, he has been overtaken . . . by his weakness for arty picture-making of an allegorical sort." *Life* magazine, on the other hand, commented that "instead of bitter protests against oppression, his colorful and strongly composed work is more characterized by bittersweet portrayals of men, women and children who stand alone and lost and sad." James Thrall Soby declared, "In recent years, Shahn has emerged as one of the most lyric of living American artists, his pictorial invention steadily more varied and rich, his technical fluency and warmth more and more impressive."

In 1956, Shahn was made Charles Eliot Norton professor at Harvard University, and his lectures on art and ideas were published in book form and illustrated with his own drawings.

Shahn's paintings today hang in many museums and form a part of the major collections of contemporary art all over the world. His purchasers come from all classes. Mrs. Halpert, his dealer, feels that "Shahn probably has the biggest audience of any American painter among discriminating young people."

In middle age, Shahn has become portly, his hair has thinned, and his mustache is gray, but his vitality has hardly dimmed. His manner is composed, his attitude relaxed, his bearing dignified, but he takes no less keen delight in living than ever. He takes an active part in the community life of Roosevelt, New Jersey, where he lives. For three years, from 1945 to 1948, he served as a member of the town council. For a time, he ran an art class for those of his neighbors who wanted to learn to paint. He was also instrumental in commissioning a bust of Franklin Delano Roosevelt which stands on the grounds of the town bearing his name.

Shahn's broad interests, his warmth and vitality have won him many friends. His associates are the carpenters, tailors, artists, and architects who are his immediate neighbors, as well as faculty members from nearby Princeton University. Shahn can frequently be found discussing labor matters with a tailor, building problems with a carpenter, or the question of realism versus abstract art with a fellow painter.

Shahn believes, perhaps more firmly than ever, that the function and responsibility of art are to express man "in his individualness and variety." He feels that abstract art, in cutting itself off from all outward meaning, has no real validity. For Shahn each painting, drawing, or print is a summation of his own credo. "A work of art in which powerful compassion is innate," he says, ". . . however difficult its language, will serve ultimately to dignify that society in which it exists."

15

The New Master

JACKSON POLLOCK

1912–1956

It is amusing to speculate on the reaction of Gilbert Stuart if by some trick of time he had been privileged to catch a glimpse of Jackson Pollock at work. With bewilderment—at the very least—he would have observed, first, that in the large barn Pollock called his studio there were no easels, no oil paints, no brushes except a few so worn out as to be useless. He would have seen lying on the floor a huge sheet of canvas out of which he could have fashioned three of his largest portraits, or more than a dozen of his smaller ones.

Where were the colors for grinding or even the tubes of oil paint which came into use after his day? Ranged in an untidy row stood large cans of ordinary commercial house paint, Duco enamels, aluminum paints, paints which Stuart would never have seen, but which are available in any modern hardware store. And what would Stuart have made of the pile of debris lying near the canvas—sticks of wood, trowels, knives, small mounds of sand, bits of broken glass, pieces of string, perhaps a few cigarette butts?

Surely, America's first great painter would have gasped in open astonishment at the sight of Pollock at work. He would have observed a tall, sturdy, partially bald man, dressed in blue jeans, neckerchief, and cowboy boots, spring into action and, with an almost mesmerized intensity, begin to weave his canvas into what a critic once called, with some justice, "a spectacular cat's cradle of interlaced color." Bounding around on all four sides of the canvas in a frenzied rhythm of dancelike movements, Pollock flicked his wrist, threw color with a darting movement, dripped and splattered paint off the edge of a stick, a worn-out brush, or a trowel, or simply lifted one of the large cans of paint and poured its contents from one edge of the canvas to the other. Then, he might embed into his picture old paint tubes, bits of colored glass, sprays of sand, a cigarette butt, or any other useful or useless object at hand.

Try as he could, Gilbert Stuart would have found in this canvas no figure, no landscape, no shape or form that he could recognize—nothing but an incredibly intricate structure of lines knitted together in a striking maze of color, like a delicately threaded, tangled web of richly dyed yarn. Stuart would doubtless have been at a complete loss to think of this man as an artist or his wild splatters as painting. Yet, if he had felt only outrage and shock and anger, he would have felt no different from many of Pollock's own contemporaries.

In the brief span of his lifetime, Pollock was probably the

most widely publicized, most universally known artist of his day. Scorned and derided, exalted and worshiped, he excited extremes of expression in both his admirers and detractors. There was no middle ground. He was regarded either as the ultimate symbol of the triviality and fakery of contemporary art, or the greatest American painter of his generation. By the time of his death he was firmly established as the dominant figure of the most thorough, the most savage rebellion in the history of American art. Even those who attacked him most blisteringly, who denounced him as the most arrant of impostors, could not deny his place as one of the most influential artists ever to have appeared on the American scene.

Paul Jackson Pollock, youngest of the five sons of Le Roy and Stella McClure Pollock, was born in Cody, Wyoming, on January 28, 1912. Both his parents were natives of Iowa, his father of Scotch-Irish and his mother of Irish descent. His father, whose original name was McCoy, had taken the name of Pollock from the family which had adopted him when his own parents had died. Following their marriage, Le Roy and Stella moved to a farm in Cody, where they remained for about three years. A quiet, gentle, and retiring man, Le Roy Pollock, helped by his five sons, spent long hours working a truck farm. Stella Pollock was the backbone of her family. She guided their affairs with a firm hand, saw to her children's education and religious training, encouraged their artistic inclinations, and managed the household. When the Wyoming venture failed, she prodded her husband to seek other, more fertile, and possibly more prosperous areas.

In the search for economic security, the Pollocks were in almost constant movement, migrating from one state to another. In 1915, they went from Wyoming to Arizona. Three years later, they were again on the move, this time to northern California. After five years of fruitless endeavor the

Pollocks pulled up stakes and moved to southern California, where Le Roy made one last desperate attempt at farming. Once more he was defeated. Beaten and hopeless, he abandoned the land and found menial employment with a group of land surveyors working on a government-sponsored project. A few years later, while his youngest son was still in his teens, Le Roy Pollock died as quietly and unobtrusively as he had lived.

Paul Jackson was thirteen years old when he entered the Manual Arts High School in Los Angeles. He was a tall, well-built young boy with a strong head framed by a shock of long brown hair, who spent his spare time riding, collecting flora and fauna, and modeling bits of clay into odd shapes reminiscent of pieces of driftwood. He loved to read, and fed his voracious appetite with all kinds of literature, including, oddly enough, the works of Indian philosophers. He was new to the area, friendless, and acutely lonely. Gawky, shy, inarticulate, he had difficulty reaching out for the camaraderie he yearned for; in turn, his contemporaries considered him a little odd and avoided him. He was an unhappy boy, who felt himself misunderstood and misjudged.

The first stirrings of artistic interest in him may have been prompted by a desire to prove to his classmates that he was someone of consequence. But, beyond this, he felt a need to create something, to channel his driving energy into making something with his own hands. He turned toward sculpture, aided and encouraged by his oldest brother, Charles, who had studied art. Before long, Paul Jackson expanded his new-found creative bent to include painting. Even at this age, he worked less often from nature than from the depths of his own imagination.

His native distaste for authority became manifest in his high school years. With one of his few friends, he helped edit a newspaper which denounced all forms of athletics, military training, and compulsory physical exercise. His resentment and defiance of both official power and conventional behavior soon exasperated the school authorities, and he was expelled. All through the brief span of his life he vacillated constantly between gentleness and violence. It was a struggle which finally ended in tragedy.

For the next two years Paul Jackson worked on various land-surveying projects. The work was arduous, the men he worked with were many years his senior, hardened, rough, and given to bouts of alcoholic excess. Paul Jackson refused to be intimidated by the harshness of his new existence. He was determined to prove his mettle and to hold his own, and he did.

The artistic interest first roused in high school had developed into a serious ambition. Charles, who had become an instructor of art at a Western college, sent his younger brother to New York to study with his own former teacher, Thomas Benton. Thomas Hart Benton, then at the height of his reputation, had studied in Paris in his youth. After a brief period under the influence of French modernism, Benton looked to the American Midwest for his subject, working in a flat, realistic manner, painting long, distorted figures, vaguely reminiscent of the Spanish master El Greco. Despite his earlier experiments in the modern style, he had developed a firm and outspoken opposition to European influence and avant-garde painting. Along with Grant Wood and John Steuart Curry—who also painted the same locale—Benton enjoyed an immense popularity with the public and the younger artists.

As soon as he arrived in New York in 1929, Pollock dropped his first name, and immediately enrolled in Benton's class at the Art Students League. For two years, under Benton's tutelage, he studied the old masters and learned to draw. Inevitably, he adopted some of his teacher's brushwork and rhythmic mannerisms. A mutual love of art plus a deep affection for the West sparked a friendship between teacher and student. Benton and his wife took Pollock under their wing, treating him with as much warmth and generosity as if he had been their own child.

Although Pollock revered Benton, he was too much of an insurgent to accept for long either the older man's authority or his anti-modern views. "He drove his kind of realism at me so hard I bounced right into non-objective painting," Pollock once said. In the work of the noted Mexican artists, Siqueiros and Orozco, he discovered an excitement and an intensity that seemed to suit his own vision. The harsh, brilliant palette and jarring rhythms of Orozco, particularly, appealed to the emotional turbulence of his own character. Slowly, steadily, during the next four years, Pollock moved away from realism to a form of semi-abstraction—dark, heavily brushed and textured canvases, full of tempestuous movement and half-recognizable imagery.

Between 1930 and 1935 Pollock made several journeys back to the West, riding freight trains, hitchhiking, and once driving an old Ford belonging to his brother Charles. He always returned to the East, the center of the nation's artistic activity. New York was for him a stimulating and compelling place to work. "Living is keener, more demanding, more intense and expansive in New York," he said. In 1935 he shared a Manhattan studio with his brothers, Charles and Sanford. Three years later, he set himself up in a studio on East Eighth Street, in Greenwich Village.

Like a hummingbird, Pollock flitted from one artistic influence to another, digesting what sustained him, rejecting what did not suit his needs. He was intrigued by the potentialities of Picasso's artistic radicalism. Taking up where Picasso left off, Pollock struck out in his own direction with a ferocity that brought startling results. He created paintings that were dark, crude, heavily textured semi-abstract fantasies, crawling with ambiguous, shattered, anatomical forms of birds, men, animals, and symbols—a disturbing display of nightmarish intensity.

Among the hordes of refugees fleeing Hitler's maniacal fury during the early days of the Second World War were a number of prominent European avant-garde painters. For the first time since the Armory Show, New York became the center of international artistic activity. The most important showcase for this new painting was Peggy Guggenheim's Art of This Century Gallery. Miss Guggenheim was particularly instrumental in introducing and fostering the work of the avant-garde and especially the Surrealist painters. The latter, attempting to capture on canvas the promptings of their subconscious minds and their "dream images," liberated the artist to a hitherto unheard-of degree from traditional subject matter and discipline. Their method permitted—in fact, encouraged—"accidental" effects and deliberately unfinished paintings. Their theories were just a step removed from the ultimate anarchy of Abstract Expressionism, in which the act of painting became more important than the idea or subject of the painting.

Pollock was inspired by the approach of the Surrealists to propel his art into total abstraction. He also came under the influence of the German modernist Hans Hofmann, one of the foremost proponents of Expressionism and "teacher" of many of today's leading abstract painters.

Although Pollock had exhibited occasionally in various group shows, it was not until 1942 that he had his first New York showing, in the company of such kindred spirits as John

Graham, Lee Krasner, and Willem de Kooning. Two years later, he married Miss Krasner. She was herself an avant-garde painter, who could understand and sympathize with Pollock's ideas and aspirations. A devoted wife, she provided loyal and steadfast support through the difficult later years of his life. Many of Pollock's finest works were painted during the years of their marriage. In 1946, the Pollocks moved to an old Victorian house in the village of Springs, near East Hampton, Long Island, where Pollock converted a barn on the property for use as his studio. Here he worked and spent most of his time.

Pollock was introduced to Peggy Guggenheim in 1942. Having completed his term on the Federal Arts Project, he was working at a part-time job as a carpenter. Miss Guggenheim was so impressed by the originality of his talent that she commissioned him to paint a mural for her New York apartment. Additionally, she gave him a contract which provided him with a regular income for the next few years. For the first time in his life, he enjoyed a measure of financial security.

In 1943, at the age of thirty-one, Pollock had his first one-man show, at the Art of This Century Gallery. Although most of the paintings in the exhibition still bore a trace of the figurative and were quite mild in approach compared to his later work, the show exploded in New York art circles with a loud detonation. The vast majority of informed opinion— critics, fellow artists, the art-conscious public—responded with contempt and derision. The comment of one critic, to the effect that Pollock's canvases looked "like a battlefield" strewn with pieces of Picasso, Surrealism, and Indian art, was gently chiding. For the rest, Pollock was roundly condemned as an untalented charlatan.

There were, however, a few voices of dissent crying in the

wilderness. Clement Greenberg, art critic of *The Nation*, declared enthusiastically that Pollock had created "a genuinely violent and extravagant art." The critic and connoisseur James Johnson Sweeney said that Pollock "offers unusual promise in his exuberance, independence, and native sensibility." And a number of the younger experimental artists rallied to his cause.

In the next twelve years, Pollock held eleven one-man shows. By 1946, he had broken completely away from any semblance of representationalism. His canvases quickly developed into powerful outpourings of emotion, full of writhing lines and furious blots of jarring color that departed from every known artistic tradition of the past. They were not born of long hours of meditation upon a subject or theme, nor drawn from observation; there were no preliminary sketches or working drawings. Entirely to the contrary, a painting was allowed to grow of itself—to grow from the very act of painting, from the spontaneous impulse of the emotions, from the depths of the subconscious.

As Pollock expounded, "The painting has a life of its own. I try to let it come through." In explaining why he worked with his canvas flat on the floor, why he moved all around it in his curious "dance," he said, "I can feel nearer, more a part of the painting. . . . I can work from the four sides and literally be *in* the painting."

His famous "dripping" technique might be traced back to his boyhood in the West. In studying the art of the American Indian, he had been particularly fascinated by the sand paintings of the Navajo tribe. These primitive art works, which were primarily invocations to the gods, were made by sifting colored sand through the fingers onto the ground in a brilliant pattern. The reaction to his new work, particularly to his "dripping" with house paint, was an outburst of fury.

The critics—almost to a man—were offended and outraged by his heresy, by his seeming scorn for painterly tradition. But again, to a very few, he was the hero of the new revolution in art. One of these admirers spoke of his canvases as an "energetic adventure for the eyes, a luna park full of fireworks, pitfalls, surprises and delights." "Seeing a Pollock," said another, "is entering it; one feels like the statuettes inside glass globes that, when shaken, are filled with snow flurries. The picture surrounds one, tumbling skeins of hue everywhere." Clement Greenberg, who was his earliest and staunchest defender, and whose interest left its mark on Pollock's work, hailed the paintings as "perfected works of art," comparing their radiance to the ancient Byzantine gold and glass mosaics.

The view that prevailed was the majority verdict: Pollock's works were "empty and pretentious wall decorations . . ." Not since the Armory Show had a movement in art so enraged the American populace. But where, in the earlier era, a whole school had been vilified, now although there were other practitioners of Abstract Expression, it was Pollock who became the arch villain of the lunacy of modern art, "the symbol of artistic anarchy." People either looked askance or were actually angered, in the conviction that the artist, tongue contemptuously in cheek, had deliberately set out to "take" them. Countless articles and photographs in leading magazines and newspapers brought Pollock fantastic notoriety; he became the most publicized figure in American art, the scapegoat of conservative artists and others who did not understand his work, misjudged his motives, or were revolted by his nihilistic approach to all the traditional concepts of art.

Even Pablo Picasso, perhaps the greatest artistic experimenter of all time, was scornful of Pollock's efforts. He is reported to have shown his contempt by waving in the air an ink-stained blotter and saying with disdain, "Jackson Pollock."

Phyllis McGinley, the talented writer of light verse, summed up the bewilderment of the public at large in her amusing poem, "Squeeze Play":

> *Jackson Pollock had a quaint*
> *Way of saying to his sibyl,*
> *"Shall I dribble?*
> *Should I paint?"*
> *And with never an instant's quibble*
> *Sibyl always answered,*
> *"Dribble."*

Pollock, serious and sincere in the pursuit of his vision, was embarrassed at his publicity when he was not embittered by the cheapness of the kind of fame it brought him. But for the most part he was indifferent to the public attitude. He continued to work like a man possessed, as if driven by a demon that foresaw what little time he had left on earth. The paintings grew colossal, nearly mural-sized, intricately patterned and laced with delicate interweavings of thin, many-colored, tortuous lines that covered the canvas from edge to edge. He no longer sought titles for them; he merely gave each a number as he finished it. His influence upon the new generation of artists became enormous. He was the uncontested hero of the avant-garde.

In 1948, Pollock made his European debut. The reaction, although considerably less violent, was a repetition of the American experience. The public and the older artists were shocked by his heretical approach; but the younger European painters were impressed. Not only did they appreciate his work, but many of them began to work in the same vein. The traditional tide had been turned. Now, at last, the new thought in art was moving into rather than out of Europe. Pollock had opened conceptual doors which, as one art historian says, "still pose a challenge to advanced styles of our day."

Respect for Pollock's art among persons of authority, however slow in starting, began to avalanche in the last decade of his life. In 1950, in recognition of his position as the leader of the avant-garde movement, the Museum of Modern Art organized a special show of his work for the exhibit of the Venice Biennale. Included were the paintings of Arshile Gorky and Willem de Kooning, two other Abstract Expressionist artists. Two years later Pollock held a large one-man show in Paris. Hans Namuth, a film producer, made a documentary movie on his art. Hardly an important American exhibition was held that did not include one or more Pollock paintings. In 1955, he was given a retrospective show at the Sidney Janis Gallery, which one critic hailed as "a tale of startling invention. . . ." His work was now being purchased for most of the major museums and private collections all over the world. He was at the height of his fame.

Suddenly, beginning in 1951, Pollock began a dramatic reversal. His new canvases were somber works in black and white. He began to discard his unorthodox tools, and increasingly made use of the time-honored oil paints and brushes, only rarely reverting to the drip method. Natural forms and figures became clearly identifiable; numbered titles vanished and were replaced by names relating to life. It was almost as if he were seeking absolution for his previous flight from reality.

The artistic and mental conflict that had plagued Pollock for many years, had by now reached a critical stage. Tortured by anxiety about his new work, the self-confidence that had sustained him through all sorts of adversity started to crumble; the wellsprings of his creative energy, which had seemed bottomless, began to run dry; the demon that had powered his work for so long turned malign. He drove himself desperately, mercilessly—and suddenly everything ended. He stopped painting completely. Except for a single picture, which he finished in 1955, he had ceased to be a painter.

In his agony, he found solace in heavy drinking. Although he had barely turned forty, he began to deteriorate rapidly. He grew bald, his figure became puffed and sagging, his bearded face haggard, lined, and worn. And his eyes, mirrors of the anguish of the struggle that was destroying him, were the eyes of a man who saw his own doom. He spent long preoccupied hours reading, or listening over and over again to the recorded voice of the Welsh poet Dylan Thomas—himself a damned soul doomed to an untimely death—reading his own poetry. He spent more hours staring at the sea near his home, perhaps because its breadth held the same sense of illimitable vastness as the Western landscape of his youth. Reserved, pleasant, and lucid in his sober moments—which were now less and less frequent—he became loudly belligerent and violent when he drank.

On the night of August 11, 1956, the expensive sports car Pollock was driving went out of control, smashing into a tree. He died instantly. In his forty-fourth year, he escaped from the agony of his insoluble problems. He was buried in the cemetery in Springs, Long Island, near the home he had lived and worked in. A huge fieldstone beside the grave is marked with the same distinctive signature Pollock affixed to his paintings.

A large retrospective show of his work, planned for 1956 by the Museum of Modern Art, became a memorial exhibition. Now that the products of his revolutionary vision had been stopped forever, the value of his paintings soared astronomically. One of his huge canvases sold for one hundred thousand dollars, and even a minor work could command a five-figure sum.

Interestingly enough, since his death Pollock has become an acknowledged "old master" of the Abstract Expressionist school—not only to those who first opposed him so savagely, but even in the eye of the public. He is now almost universally regarded as "the most original . . . among the painters of his generation." His profound effect on contemporary painting has been summed up by a European critic as "a magnificent achievement. . . . Its influence has not been limited to the United States alone, but has stimulated the artists of all countries. . . ."

In the future Pollock will perhaps be best known as the man who was the hero of the artistic revolution that at last freed American painting from its two hundred-year bondage to the European tradition, and established it as the dominant force in the world-wide republic of art.

Recommended Reading List

HISTORY OF AMERICAN ART

Painting in America by Edgar P. Richardson. Thomas Y. Crowell Company, New York, 1956.

Three Hundred Years of American Painting by Alexander Eliot. Time, Inc., New York, 1957.

Art in America by Suzanne La Follette. Harper & Brothers, New York, 1929.

The Light of Distant Skies by James Thomas Flexner. Harcourt, Brace and Co., New York, 1954. American art from 1760 to 1835.

American Painting from the Armory Show to the Depression by Milton W. Brown. Princeton University Press, N.J., 1955.

Romantic Painting in America by James Thrall Soby and Dorothy Miller. The Museum of Modern Art, New York, 1943.

BIOGRAPHY

Living Biographies of Great Painters by Henry and Dana Lee Thomas. Garden City Books, Garden City, New York, 1959.

Gilbert Stuart; A Great Life in Brief by James Thomas Flexner. Alfred A. Knopf, Inc., New York, 1955.

Bingham: Fighting Artist by Lew Larkin. State Publishing Co., St. Louis, Missouri, 1955.

The Life, Art and Letters of George Inness by George Inness, Jr. The Century Co., New York, 1917.

Winslow Homer—A Portrait by Jean Gould. Dodd, Mead & Co., New York, 1962.

Thomas Eakins by Roland Joseph McKinney. Crown Publishers, Inc., New York, 1942.

Thomas Eakins by James Thomas Flexner. The Metropolitan Museum of Art, New York, 1956.

Albert Pinkham Ryder by Lloyd Goodrich. George Braziller, Inc., New York, 1959.

The Man Whistler by Hesketh Pearson. Harper & Brothers, New York, 1952.

Mary Cassatt by Margaret Breuning. Hyperion Press, New York, 1944.

John Sloan: A Painter's Life by Van Wyck Brooks. E. P. Dutton & Co., Inc., New York, 1955.

William Glackens and the Ashcan Group by Ira Glackens. Crown Publishers, Inc., New York, 1957.

John Marin by MacKinley Helm. Pellegrini and Cudahy, New York, 1948.

Stuart Davis by James Johnson Sweeney. The Museum of Modern Art, New York, 1945.

Portrait of the Artist as an American: Ben Shahn by Selden Rodman. Harper & Brothers, New York, 1951.

OTHER BOOKS OF INTEREST

Mainstreams of Modern Art by John Canaday. Simon and Schuster, Inc., New York, 1959.

American Painters in Paris by Yvon Bizardel. The Macmillan Company, New York, 1960.

The Proud Possessors by Aline Saarinen. Random House, Inc., New York, 1958. Stories of famous collectors and their influence on art.

Bibliography

HISTORY OF ART

The Harper History of Painting by David M. Robb. Harper & Brothers, New York, 1951.

Fifty Centuries of Art by Francis Henry Taylor. Harper & Brothers, New York, 1954.

Men of Art by Thomas Craven. Simon and Schuster, Inc., New York, 1940.

AMERICAN ART

Early American Portrait Painters by Cuthbert Lee. Yale University Press, New Haven, Conn., 1929.

America's Old Masters by James Thomas Flexner. The Viking Press, Inc., New York, 1939.

First Flowers of Our Wilderness by James Thomas Flexner. Houghton Mifflin Co., Boston, 1947.

Highlights Among the Hudson River Artists by Clara Endicott Sears. Houghton Mifflin Company, Boston, 1947.

American Painting by Denys Sutton. Avalon Press and the Central Institute of Design, London, England, 1948.

American Painters of Yesterday and Today by Frederic Fairchild Sherman. Privately Printed, New York, 1919.

The History of American Painting by Samuel Isham and Royal Cortissoz. The Macmillan Company, New York, 1936.

A History of American Art by Daniel M. Mendelowitz. Holt, Rinehart & Winston, Inc., New York, 1960.

American Painting by Virgil Barker. The Macmillan Company, New York, 1950.

239

Art and Life in America by Oliver Larkin. Rinehart & Co., Inc., New York, 1949.

The History and Ideals of American Art by Eugen Neuhaus. Stanford University Press, Stanford, Cal., 1931.

The American Artist and His Times by Homer St. Gaudens. Dodd, Mead & Co., New York, 1941.

American Landscape Painting by Wolfgang Born. Yale University Press, New Haven, Conn., 1948.

MODERN ART

Art in America in Modern Times by Holger Cahill and Alfred H. Barr, Jr. Reynal and Hitchcock, New York, 1934.

American Painting Today by Nathaniel Pousette-Dart. Hastings House, Inc., New York, 1956.

Modern American Painting and Sculpture by Sam Hunter. Dell Publishing Co., Inc., New York, 1959.

New Art in America by John I. H. Baur. The New York Graphic Society, Greenwich, Conn., 1957.

From Realism to Reality in Recent American Painting by Virgil Barker. University of Nebraska Press, Lincoln, Neb., 1959.

The Story of Modern Art by Sheldon Cheney. The Viking Press, Inc., New York, 1958.

Revolution and Tradition in Modern American Art by John I. H. Baur. Harvard University Press, Cambridge, Mass., 1951.

Abstract Painting by Thomas B. Hess. The Viking Press, Inc., New York, 1951.

Paths of Abstract Art by Edward B. Henning. The Cleveland Museum of Art, Cleveland, Ohio, 1960.

Art in Our Time, edited by Alfred H. Barr, Jr. The Museum of Modern Art, New York, 1939.

New Images of Man by Peter Selz. The Museum of Modern Art, New York, 1959.

The Visual Arts Today, edited by Gyorgy Kepes. Wesleyan University Press, Middletown, Conn., 1960.

Art Since 1945, edited by Marcel Brion, Sam Hunter, *et al.* Harry N. Abrams, Inc., New York, 1958.

Modern Painting: Contemporary Trends by Nello Ponente. Skira International Corp., New York, 1960.

BIOGRAPHY

Washington Allston by Edgar P. Richardson. University of Chicago Press, Chicago, Ill., 1948.

George Caleb Bingham—River Portraitist by John Francis Mc-Dermott. University of Oklahoma Press, Norman, Okla., 1959.

George Caleb Bingham of Missouri by Albert Christ-Janer. Dodd, Mead & Co., New York, 1940.

Winslow Homer by Lloyd Goodrich. George Braziller, Inc., New York, 1959.

Winslow Homer, American Artist by Albert Ten Eyck Gardner. Clarkson N. Potter, Inc., New York, 1962.

Thomas Eakins by Fairfield Porter. George Braziller, Inc., New York, 1959.

John Sargent by Hon. Evan Charteris, K.C. Charles Scribner's Sons, New York, 1927.

John Singer Sargent by Charles Merrill Mount. W. W. Norton & Co., Inc., New York, 1955.

The World of James McNeill Whistler by Horace Gregory. Thomas Nelson & Sons, New York, 1959.

The Whistler Book by Sadakichi Hartmann. L. C. Page, Boston, Mass., 1910.

The Works of James McNeill Whistler by Elisabeth Luther Cary. Moffat, Yard and Co., New York, 1913.

The Life of James McNeill Whistler by E. R. and Joseph Pennell. J. B. Lippincott Co., Philadelphia, 1911.

The Graphic Work of Mary Cassatt by Adelyn D. Breeskin. H. Bittner & Co., New York, 1948.

Mary Cassatt by Achille Segard. Librairie Paul Ollendorf, Paris, 1913.

Mary Cassatt by Forbes Watson. The Whitney Museum of American Art, New York, 1932.

Mary Cassatt by Edith Valerio. Les Editions G. Gres et Cie., Paris, 1930.

John Sloan by Lloyd Goodrich. The Macmillan Company, New York, 1952.

John Marin, the Man and his Work by E. M. Benson. The Museum of Modern Art, New York, 1935.

Stuart Davis by E. C. Goossen. George Braziller, Inc., New York, 1959.

Stuart Davis by Rudi Blesh. Grove Press, New York, 1959.

Stuart Davis by Stuart Davis. American Artists Group, Inc., New York, 1945.

Ben Shahn by James Thrall Soby. The Museum of Modern Art, New York, 1947.

Jackson Pollock by Frank O'Hara. George Braziller, Inc., New York, 1959.

Jackson Pollock by Bryan Robertson. Harry N. Abrams, Inc., New York, 1960.

GENERAL

The Art Spirit by Robert Henri. J. B. Lippincott Co., Philadelphia, 1923.

The Shape of Content by Ben Shahn. Harvard University Press, Cambridge, Mass., 1957.

Art and Culture by Clement Greenberg. The Beacon Press, Boston, 1961.

Mississippi Panorama by Perry T. Rathbone. The City Art Museum of St. Louis, St. Louis, Missouri, 1950.

The Eye of Man by Selden Rodman. The Devin-Adair Co., New York, 1955.

Gist of Art by John Sloan. American Artists Group, Inc., New York, 1939.

Conversations with Artists by Selden Rodman. The Devin-Adair Co., New York, 1957.

Times Three by Phyllis McGinley. The Viking Press, Inc., New York, 1960.

MONOGRAPHS, CATALOGUES,
PERIODICALS, AND MAGAZINES

"George Inness—An American Landscape Painter" by Elizabeth Mc-Causland. The George Walter Smith Museum, Springfield, Mass., 1946.

"Fifty Paintings by George Inness" by Frederic Fairchild Sherman. Privately Printed, New York, 1913.

"George Inness and the American Landscape Painter" by Jacob Getlar Smith. *The American Artist*, April, 1956.

"Winslow Homer" by Kenyon Cox. Privately Printed, Frederic Fairchild Sherman, New York, 1914.

"Winslow Homer" The Walker Art Center, Minneapolis, Minn., 1944.

"The Watercolors of Winslow Homer" by Jacob Getlar Smith. *The American Artist*, February, 1955.

"Eakins as a Functionalist" by Lawrence E. Scanlon. *College Art Journal*, XIX, 4, Summer, 1960.

"Eakins in Washington" by John Walker. *Art in America*, 3, 1961.

"Thomas Eakins, a Retrospective Exhibition" by Lloyd Goodrich. National Gallery of Art, Wash., D.C.; Art Institute of Chicago; Philadelphia Museum of Art, 1961.

"Three American Watercolorists—Homer, Eakins, Sargent." *Metropolitan Museum Miniatures*.

"Albert Pinkham Ryder" by Frederic Fairchild Sherman. Privately Printed, New York, 1920.

"New Light in the Mystery of Ryder's Background" by Lloyd Goodrich. *Art News*, April, 1961.

"John Singer Sargent, a Retrospective Exhibition." Grand Central Art Galleries, New York, 1924.

"The Watercolors of Sargent" by Jacob Getlar Smith. *The American Artist*, March, 1955.

"Americans Abroad—Sargent's Scandal and Success" by Richard Gilman. *American Heritage*, Vol. XII, 6, October, 1961.

"Sargent, Whistler and Mary Cassatt" by Frederick A. Sweet. The Art Institute of Chicago, 1954.

"Manet, Degas, Berthe Morisot and Mary Cassatt." The Baltimore Museum of Art, 1962.

"Mary Cassatt—Loan Exhibition." Wildenstein Galleries, New York, 1948.

"Mary Cassatt—Peintre et Graveur." Centre Culturel Americain, Paris, 1959.

"Some Memories of Mary Cassatt" by George Biddle. *The Arts Magazine*, August, 1926.

"Reviving Mary Cassatt" by Robert M. Coates. *The New Yorker*, November 8, 1947.

"Mary Cassatt" *The Reader's Digest*, November, 1959.

"John Sloan—After Enough Years Have Passed" by Robert M. Coates. *The New Yorker*, May 7, 1949.

"John Sloan—His Art" by John D. Morse. *The American Artist*, January, 1952.

"John Marin" by MacKinley Helm. *Atlantic Monthly*, February, 1947.

"Profile of Stuart Davis" by Frederick S. Wight. *Art Digest*, May 15, 1953.

"Stuart Davis' Jive" by John Lucas. *The Arts Magazine*, September, 1957.

"Stuart Davis—True to Life" by Elaine de Kooning. *Art News*, April, 1957.

"The Art Galleries—Review of Davis Exhibition." *The New Yorker*, March 20, 1954.

"All American," a Review of Davis Exhibition. *Time*, March 15, 1954.

"Ben Shahn" by Selden Rodman. *Portfolio*, Zebra Press, Cincinnati, Ohio, 1951.

"Jackson Pollock" by Sam Hunter. The Museum of Modern Art, New York, Bulletin Vol. XXIV, 2, 1956–57.

"Hopper–Pollock" by Parker Tyler. *Art News Annual* XXVI, 1957.

"Profile of Jackson Pollock" by B. H. Friedman. *Art in America*, December, 1955.

"Jackson Pollock" *Life*, November 9, 1959.

"Pollock" *Arts & Architecture*, February, 1944.

"Jackson Pollock and Nicolas de Stael: Two Painters and Their Myths" by Hilton Kramer. *Arts Yearbook*, 3, 1959.

"Observations on a Few Celebrated Women Artists" by David Loeffler Smith. *The American Artist*, January, 1962.

"The Eight" *Life*, March 3, 1958.

"The World of the Eight" by Leslie Katz. *Arts Yearbook*, 1, 1957.

"From Pre-Raphaelitism to Bloomsbury" by Vernon Young. *Arts Yearbook*, 1, 1957.

"The Changing Landscape in American Art" by Vernon Young. *Arts Yearbook*, 2, 1958.

"The Art of Impressionism" by Joseph C. Sloane. *Arts Yearbook*, 2, 1958.

"Impressionists and Symbolists and Journalists" by Jacques Lethève. *Portfolio and Art News Annual*, 2, 1961.

"Art of the Americas" *Art News Annual*, XVIII, 1948.

"Realists and Magic Realists," edited by Dorothy C. Miller and Alfred H. Barr, Jr. The Museum of Modern Art, New York, 1943.

"Introduction to Abstract" by Thomas B. Hess. *Art News Annual*, XX, 1951.

"The New American Painting" The Museum of Modern Art, New York, 1959.

Index

246

About the Author

Mrs. Freedgood enjoys a varied career as a painter, a book and magazine illustrator, an art instructor, and a writer. Her paintings and prints have been exhibited at the Pennsylvania Academy, the Boston Museum of Fine Arts, the National Academy of Design, the Society of American Graphic Artists, and in the Overseas Exhibition of Contemporary Art sponsored by the United States Information Agency, among others. Her work has also been acquired by a number of private collectors. Mrs. Freedgood has illustrated several books as well as stories and articles in such national magazines as *Harper's, The Reporter,* and *Woman's Day.* She has taught painting to young people at the Silvermine School of Art in New Canaan, Connecticut, and has held private classes in drawing and painting for adults.

Mrs. Freedgood is a graduate of Pratt Institute, and has also studied at the Art Students League of New York, the Graphic Arts Center, and with Jean Charlot. She lives in Norwalk, Connecticut, with her husband, also a writer, and her daughter.